NEW BEGINNINGS

*The Skirball Museum
Collections and
Inaugural Exhibition*

Edited by Grace Cohen Grossman

Skirball Cultural Center
Los Angeles
An affiliate of Hebrew Union College

Dedicated to the memory of
Adolph S. Oko
(1883-1944)
Librarian and Scholar
and
Jacob Rader Marcus
(1896-1995)
Historian and Archivist of American Jewry

The publication of this catalog was made possible by
generous contributions from Susanne and Paul Kester
and the Skirball Foundation.

Distributed by the
University of California Press
Berkeley   Los Angeles   London

Copyright ©1996 by the Skirball Cultural Center
All rights reserved.

For information contact the publisher at
2701 North Sepulveda Boulevard
Los Angeles, CA 90049

Library of Congress Card Number: 96-67646

ISBN 0-9651640-0-4 (softcover)

ISBN 0-9651640-1-2 (hardcover)

Printed in Hong Kong

FRONT COVER: Statue of Liberty Hanukkah Lamp, Manfred Anson, 1985

BACK COVER: *Sabbath Afternoon,* Moritz Oppenheim, ca. 1860

ENDSHEETS: Detail, Torah Mantle, Italy, 17th-18th century, HUCSM 60.2

PAGE 1: Detail of Plate 118

PAGE 2-3: Detail of Plate 19

PAGE 6: Detail of Plate 122

CONTENTS

VISIONS
AND
VALUES   *Culmination and*
Beginning

W E HAVE LIVED to see the challenges of the past decade culminate in the opening of the Skirball Cultural Center. It is a joy to welcome the opening of the museum component's Core Exhibition entitled "Visions and Values." The Core Exhibition, with its survey of some four thousand years of Jewish historical experience and its strong emphasis on Jewish life in North America, is quite distinctive in the museum world; it will be a source of instruction and enjoyment for untold numbers of visitors, including each year hundreds of thousands of school children and their teachers.

The dream which undergirds the Skirball Cultural Center began with Jack and Audrey Skirball. Jack, sadly, did not live to see this culmination of the dream, but everyone "present at the creation" is thankful to have Audrey Skirball-Kenis with us for the inauguration of the Cultural Center. I do take great pleasure in acknowledging the proud contribution of the Skirball Foundation, its President Morris Bergreen and its Trustees, to the work of translating the dream into the realm of reality. The Skirball Cultural Center would not have been possible without the Foundation's support.

It is also a pleasure and a privilege to acknowledge the indispensable generosity of a great many other foundations and individuals whose embrace of the Cultural Center dream has been—and continues to be—utterly essential to the viability of this effort. I would find it hard to exaggerate the importance I attach to their confidence and encouragement.

The architectural design Moshe Safdie has fashioned for the Cultural Center speaks eloquently enough for itself. To have had the force of his genius—and his friendship as well—must be regarded as an ongoing inspiration and blessing.

Those who have been directly involved in the creation of the Core Exhibition and of this inaugural catalogue can look on their achievement as a splendid gift to American culture in general and Jewish education in particular. There are no words adequate to thank them for their labors.

To what end this prodigious effort? To the end that America and American Jewish life both be enriched and elevated, made more conscious of their complexity and potential, and more determined to realize their best, most humane values—an appreciation of the pluralist character of American society, a wish to encourage a balance between individual prerogative and collective need. What can the Skirball Cultural Center do through its exhibits and its programs to encourage a commitment to these values? This question is to be our great preoccupation: We have only begun!

It is truly a wonderful privilege to have had a share in the building of this new institution.

URI D. HERSCHER, President
Skirball Cultural Center

Plate 1. *Plum Street Temple*, Henry Mosler, 1866

A WONDER
TO
CONTEMPLATE

ONE OF THE HISTORIC OPPORTUNITIES to advance the cause of Jewish education and culture given me as President of the College-Institute was the ability nearly twenty-five years ago to arrange for the Hebrew Union College Museum to be transferred to our then brand-new campus in Los Angeles adjacent to the University of Southern California. The museum became known there as the Skirball Museum and flourished mightily. Indeed its success inspired the need for larger, more accessible quarters so that even fuller, richer service could be offered the North American community. Now, after years of arduous planning and striving, that need has been met in the form of the Skirball Cultural Center and Museum in Sepulveda Pass, midway between West Los Angeles and the San Fernando Valley.

The Center is wonderful to contemplate—a jewel-like complex of buildings housing as its core component one of the few truly significant Judaica collections in the Western Hemisphere.

The Core Exhibition of the Skirball Cultural Center must be recognized as extraordinarily and admirably innovative and will in its own right inspire new chapters of American and Jewish cultural history.

The founders, planners, and designers of the Skirball Cultural Center and their predecessors who nurtured the museum's collection deserve our highest praise. They have created a marvel, and I am delighted with this chance to invite a large and varied public to enjoy, study, and absorb the treasures to be experienced in the exciting Sepulveda Pass setting.

ALFRED GOTTSCHALK, Chancellor
Hebrew Union College-Jewish Institute of Religion

PREFACE

IN 1996 THE SKIRBALL MUSEUM, a component of the Skirball Cultural Center, opens a new set of doors to a new era and is more ready than ever to fulfill its potential for cultural and educational impact. When the museum was established in Los Angeles in 1972, there was energetic growth among the city's cultural institutions, and the Skirball took its place as the first Jewish museum. As the museum reopens within the multifaceted new Skirball Cultural Center, it is committed to exploring the complex nature of American Jewish life in the context of American society as a whole. It is hoped that all Americans will find personal meaning in the dynamic interplay between America and her varied religious and ethnic communities.

The Skirball Museum is fortunate to enjoy an exquisite natural and architectural environment in its new location, as well as vastly expanded space and facilities, which will increase visitors' opportunities for education and enjoyment. The long-term interpretive core exhibition, "Visions and Values: Jewish Life from Antiquity to America," utilizes a multitude of both traditional and state-of-the-art display resources and strategies. This exhibition, which presents the historical experiences, beliefs, and values of the Jewish people, integrates historical artifacts and art objects from the museum's excellent, extensive and specialized collections into environmental and contextual settings utilizing media, music, simulations, and interactive computer programs. The Discovery Center invites children of all ages to explore ancient Near Eastern history and archaeological themes through participatory exhibits and hands-on activities. An outdoor activity center simulates an Israeli archaeological site, which invites "digging" as an exciting learning methodology. This reinforces the themes of the Discovery Center. Other galleries have been handsomely designed for temporary exhibitions. The Skirball Museum's changing exhibitions will focus on artists and subjects illuminating the Jewish experience. A new dedication to American Jewish exhibition subjects will often explore connections to other cultures as well. In order to make more of the Skirball's significant collections and, most prominently, its recently acquired Project Americana objects accessible to the public, the museum has created a Visible Storage space. Visitors will enter the museum's behind-the-scenes chambers to view selected objects from the collection usually available only to curators, researchers, and conservators. Classrooms, a resource center, and an auditorium, as well as courtyards and restful garden spots, offer visitors myriad

Plate 2. Rothschild Hanukkah Lamp,
Johann Heinrich Philip Schott and Sons, ca. 1850

opportunities to relax and learn by filling the mind and enriching the spirit.

Along with the Jewish Museum in New York, the Skirball Museum holds one of the largest collections of Jewish art and material culture in America, with objects of art and history that reveal much about daily life, beliefs, customs, worship, values, human yearnings, historical experiences, and artistic achievement from biblical to contemporary times. The collection —some 25,000 objects and still growing—spans not only time but space, as the museum's holdings reflect Jewish life in virtually every corner of the globe.

The collections include: archaeological materials from biblical and later historical periods illuminating early Jewish life; an extraordinary body of Jewish ceremonial art ranging over the last five centuries of Jewish life; an important assemblage of coins, medals, and seals; an extensive group of objects exemplifying Jewish historical experience; the more recently formed Project Americana collection, items that document the everyday life of ordinary people during three centuries of American Jewish life; and the stellar fine arts holdings, which comprise thousands of graphics, paintings, sculptures, and other works of art in a variety of media. The one factor that unifies this wide-ranging collection is that every object relates to the Jewish experience either directly or indirectly. An ancient Jewish coin depicting the Temple in Jerusalem; an elegant silver Hanukkah lamp commissioned by the German branch of the Rothschild family in the mid-nineteenth century; an early oil landscape by the French Impressionist Camille Pissarro, an artist of Jewish birth; a contemporary work on a Holocaust theme by a non-Jewish artist—each of these enhances this collection, which exists to preserve a heritage and further understanding about Jewish life and its interaction with the larger society.

This catalogue is the first truly representative handbook of the collection ever published. The museum's origins are discussed in the essay, "Visions, Revisions, and Reverberations: The Evolving Hebrew Union College Skirball Museum." Each of the essays, ably written by curators of the Skirball Museum and invited scholars, illuminates the museum's collections. Each illustrates a selection of objects from different museum collection categories, with an essay describing that part of the collection: its range, its meaning, its unique and important treasures. Many of the objects selected for illustration are also included in the inaugural exhibition of the Skirball Cultural Center, which this catalogue documents and expands upon to bring a deeper understanding of its subjects. The Skirball Museum plans to produce other educational materials to broaden the public's knowledge of its collections and to provide exciting alternative ways to explore the ideas and objects in the "Visions and Values" exhibition, including a video catalogue, CD Roms, and discovery and activity kits for youth.

In 1972, with the generosity of the Skirball Foundation providing initial support, the museum's collections moved from Cincinnati, Ohio, to the new Hebrew Union College-Jewish Institute of Religion campus in Los Angeles. While the stewardship of the collections was centralized in Los Angeles at the now-renamed Skirball Museum, the collections have always been available to galleries on the Cincinnati and New York campuses of HUC-JIR. This arrangement mirrored the established tradition of the Klau Library and the American Jewish Archives on the Cincinnati campus. These central repositories were committed to lending books and documents where they were needed for use on other HUC campuses.

Following the move to Los Angeles, the museum benefited greatly from the exceptional talent, energy, advice, and leadership of numerous individuals. We are thankful for the generous financial contributions from individuals, foundations, corporations, and government granting agencies which have assisted the museum in its rapid growth.

It was my good fortune as Skirball Museum Director to know Jack H. Skirball, of blessed memory, and to have worked with Audrey Skirball-Kenis for many years. The hopes Jack and Audrey cherished for the Skirball Museum and their advanced vision for the Skirball Cultural Center, with the museum as its central component, have given all of us involved with the project a sense of privilege in helping to create what they so significantly helped to launch.

NANCY M. BERMAN,
Director, Skirball Museum

SECTION ONE

THE HEBREW UNION COLLEGE

SKIRBALL MUSEUM

AND ITS COLLECTIONS

Detail of Plate 32

Plate 3. Ancona Ketubbah, 1692

VISIONS,
REVISIONS,
AND
REVERBERATIONS

*The Evolving
Hebrew Union College
Skirball Museum*

NANCY M. BERMAN

THE SKIRBALL MUSEUM, housing the Hebrew Union College-Jewish Institute of Religion's rare and specialized collections of Judaica, has existed in several locations across America—in Cincinnati, Ohio, in downtown Los Angeles, and as of 1995 in the Sepulveda Pass at the crest of the Santa Monica Mountains, on the Westside of Los Angeles. With each move, the museum has continually expanded its meaning and purpose in a changing society. In this relocation of the museum to the elegant and energetic building designed by architect Moshe Safdie, the Skirball has been given its most monumental physical form as the central component of the new Skirball Cultural Center. Once again the museum has added to its mission and increased its collections, specifically to focus through acquisitions and exhibitions on American Jewish life of the past, present, and future. This reshaped Skirball Museum now takes its place as the largest Jewish museum in America dedicated to understanding the American Jewish experience in the full range of Jewish culture, history, belief and expression on the one hand and American patterns and values on the other.

The Skirball Museum has a long history as one of the oldest Jewish repositories in America. Its transformation within the Skirball Cultural Center is a logical and compelling next step in its role of educating a diverse public about the Jewish experience.

During its century-long existence, the museum has lived through two dramatically distinct stages, each reflecting profound changes in its mission and scope. The evolution of Hebrew Union College itself determined the museum's first phase. The American museum movement, which has been radically transformed in the last generation, provided the context for showcasing the museum's rich collections in increasingly accessible, public spaces in Los Angeles since 1972.

The museum was developed initially as both a Jewish museum and a college museum. It was not unusual for collections, amassed by members of the nobility and the mercantile and scholarly classes in Europe, and later by educated and wealthy Americans, to find their way eventually into colleges and universities, following the tradition initiated by the Ashmolean Museum at Oxford University in 1683. It was, and still is, in the university setting that objects of art, history, and science are understood and ideally utilized as resources for the advancement of knowledge to which the university is dedicated. It seems inarguable that the acquisition of collections and the concomitant research and scholarship on museum objects would benefit the educational and academic life of colleges and universities.[1]

Hebrew Union College's goals have always been the advancement of Jewish knowledge and the perpetuation of Judaism. HUC (which in 1950 merged with the Jewish Institute of Religion to form HUC-JIR) has realized these goals through its dedication to scholarship and its establishment of professional degree programs preparing candidates for Jewish careers. These purposes are spelled out in the College's 1926 Articles of Incorporation, "to prepare students to become rabbis, Jewish religious teachers and social workers; to promote the study of Jewish religious history and literature, and otherwise to foster and perpetuate Judaism and to disseminate knowledge thereof..."[2]

Broad principles of scholarship and education have always guided the College and its museum. Different stages in the museum's development have reflected change at HUC-JIR. As Dr. Alfred Gottschalk wrote in 1976 on the occasion of the College's centennial, "The College-Institute has a mission stemming from its founding days, but strongly enlarged since."[3] Of the many ways to define a museum's mission, the most universal and essential is that a museum exists to advance knowledge, preserve heritage, and promote understanding.

The first stage in the museum's development lasted for nearly a century, beginning sometime after the College opened its doors in 1875 in Cincinnati and concluding only in 1972 when the museum moved to Los Angeles. The actual moment of the collection's birth in Cincinnati is unknown. There is no documentation of the exact date when the first objects were officially accepted by the College's incipient library, which early on accepted some objects along with donations of books. In its long first phase, the museum's emphasis and practice was almost exclusively on acquiring collections and researching them. It was primarily through the vision and efforts of HUC's brilliant librarian, Dr. Adolph Oko, that the College, in the first quarter of the twentieth century, amassed a collection of Judaica whose quality and quantity rank it even today as one of the two most extensive and important Jewish art and material culture collections in the United States.

The traditional and profound belief that "a museum is only as good as its collections" testifies to the incomparable power of objects to open people's eyes to life, history, culture, civilization, and nature. In addition, collections of depth and breadth in a field offer the largest range of learning possibilities for both scholars and the public. Based on that principle, the founders of the original museum at Hebrew Union College had the vision, confidence, and good fortune to take the steps necessary to establish a Jewish museum of superlative quality and meaningful quantity.

Not until the 1920s did the College begin adding aggressively to the collections, which since 1875 had been acquired in a passive way through the acceptance of gifts. Dr. Oko then began purchasing significant private European collections of Judaica including, in 1925, the famed collection of six thousand objects amassed by German businessman Salli Kirschstein and formerly displayed in a private Jewish museum adjoining his villa near Berlin. Also purchased by Oko were the Joseph

Hamburger collection of coins and metals (1921), the Anglo-Jewish collections of Israel Solomons (1924), and Dr. Louis Grossman's graphics, medals, and seals collection. These collections were housed on the Cincinnati campus in what was called the Union Museum. Instituted in 1913 with the assistance of the National Federation of Temple Sisterhoods, it was the first formally established Jewish museum in the United States. Its institution coincided with large-scale growth in American museums, a time when throughout the country all types of museums (private, public, university/college, municipal, encyclopedic, specialized, etc.) were being developed. Establishing collections to gather the resources to further educational roles was the first order of business among the numerous museums opening in the late nineteenth and early twentieth centuries, just as it was at HUC's Union Museum in that period. Some American museums even conducted full-scale excavations in the Eastern Mediterranean region. A portion of the exotic treasures that were unearthed entered the great collections at such museums as New York's Metropolitan and Chicago's Field Museum, as well as university museums including those at Yale and the University of Pennsylvania.

That the first Jewish museum in America should have emerged at Hebrew Union College, an institution of higher Jewish learning, makes preeminent sense. The College, the academic arm of American Reform Judaism, was originally and exclusively a modern rabbinical seminary, where learning was predicated on the principle of *Wissenschaft des Judentums*, "the scientific study of Judaism." These academic principles, originally developed in nineteenth-century Germany, applied objective scholarly methods to Jewish history and thought. This same scientific intellectual approach formed the basis of its museum's collecting efforts and informed the development of Jewish museums in Europe as well. The collecting of Jewish objects throughout the nineteenth century represented a radical change in the collective sense of self that developed among liberal Jewish thinkers, who more systematically analyzed and historicized the Jewish people and their culture. The desire to collect, preserve, and study specimens of Jewish heritage, whether religious or ethnographic, grew out of a combination of forces related to the emancipation and enlightenment of European Jewry. With emancipation breaking down barriers and social differences between Jews and the rest of European society, many Jews participated in activities and adopted attitudes that had become popular in the larger society. Since the eighteenth century, it had been the practice of both royalty and wealthy aristocrats in Europe to acquire and display ancestral portraits and *objets d'art* or at least to possess a "cabinet of curiosities crammed with natural and artistic marvels."[4] Such collecting practices became the impetus for the birth of Jewish museums throughout Europe from London to Saint Petersburg.

Exemplifying this attitude, Julian Morgenstern, then President of HUC, spoke in 1926 of the Union Museum as "unique in American Jewry and as invaluable for historical and ritualistic research in the science of Judaism." Librarian Oko wrote, regarding his purchases of large fully formed collections, "There have been brought to America all of the important collections of Judaica which exist in the world... the student who would delve into any phase of Jewish history can find unequaled opportunity for research here... the center of Jewish culture has crossed the sea; now for the first time, the whole story of the Jews' culture and religious history can be written."[5] In other words, the collecting and research of objects for scholarly purposes was deemed fully congruent with the academic agenda and pedagogic style of Hebrew Union College.

Oko's vision of museum objects as the basis for Jewish studies was an academic attitude, which HUC supported. However, Oko's vision of the objects as the

Plate 5. *Portrait of Artist's Wife and Granddaughter*, Max Liebermann, 1926

basis for the "writing" of Jewish history denoted an authentic and traditional museum attitude, in keeping with the character and purposes of American museums of that era. In his view, the collections existed primarily for the purpose of scholars, who would distill the essence from the objects for the sake of increased knowledge. Learned museum curators studied objects and filtered their interpretations to the public through exhibition labels, lectures, and scholarly publications. The use of collections for traditional scholarship and exhibitions remains an important goal, but by today's standards for museum education, it is too limited.

From the 1940s through the 1960s, the curators of the Union Museum, first Dr. Franz Landsberger, a German refugee who had been the former Director of the Berlin Jewish Museum, and later Dr. Joseph Gutmann, now Professor Emeritus of Art History at Wayne State University and a contributor to this catalogue, reinforced the museum's priorities of collecting, research, and most significantly scholarship and publication about the collections. In 1946 Landsberger published a book entitled *A History of Jewish Art,* which was the first comprehensive survey of Jewish art ever written in English.

The College had by then established a healthy and well-researched Jewish museum collection, which proved an essential foundation for its transition to Los Angeles. At that same moment in the early 1970s, many American museums, whether large or small, municipal or university, underwent radical changes. In the case of the Skirball Museum, the change was dramatically facilitated by the museum's physical move in 1972 to the College-Institute's Los Angeles campus near the University of Southern California. This change of location provided the opportunity for a new vision of the museum and its scope, which could respond to the demands the American public now made of its museums that had become "part of a popular movement in which more Americans attended cultural events than sports." [6]

The most distinctive aspect of this second stage in the Skirball Museum's life was its primary orientation toward the public, both Jewish and non-Jewish. Expanding its original educational emphasis of serving faculty and students, the museum now sought to serve multiple audiences: adults, schoolchildren, senior citizens, tourists, Jews and non-Jews. Located as it was in the country's second-largest metropolitan area, which has the second-largest Jewish population center in the United States, the museum saw its mandate to serve the general and Jewish public more comprehensively. Because a high-priority goal was to establish the HUC Skirball Museum in Los Angeles as a valuable public resource, the initial focus of museum work, at this stage, centered on large public exhibitions and outreach through museum education and public programming. The emphasis on collecting and research during the museum's early phase in Cincinnati now served the relocated museum well as it provided a solid foundation for efforts in exhibition and education. The collection in Cincinnati had grown substantially through the years, and by the time of its move to Los Angeles, it comprised a wide variety of Jewish art and material culture objects including the Nelson Glueck archaeological collection, objects from European Jewish museums redistributed after the Holocaust by the Jewish Cultural Reconstruction, and thousands of historical and fine arts works purchased from or given by hundreds of individuals.

The growing practice of presenting large-scale popular exhibitions to attract "blockbuster" crowds transformed the public's understanding of what museums could offer for learning, leisure, and entertainment. The Skirball Museum staff, recognizing this opportunity for increased public service and education, adopted the new populist attitude that was electrifying the museum world. A museum's exhibitions are its "primary means of communication and the most prominent aspect of its public face," [7] and since 1972, the Skirball Museum has organized three major exhibitions of its core collections and more than one hun-

Plate 6. *Joseph's Coat of Fate*, Dina Dar, 1990

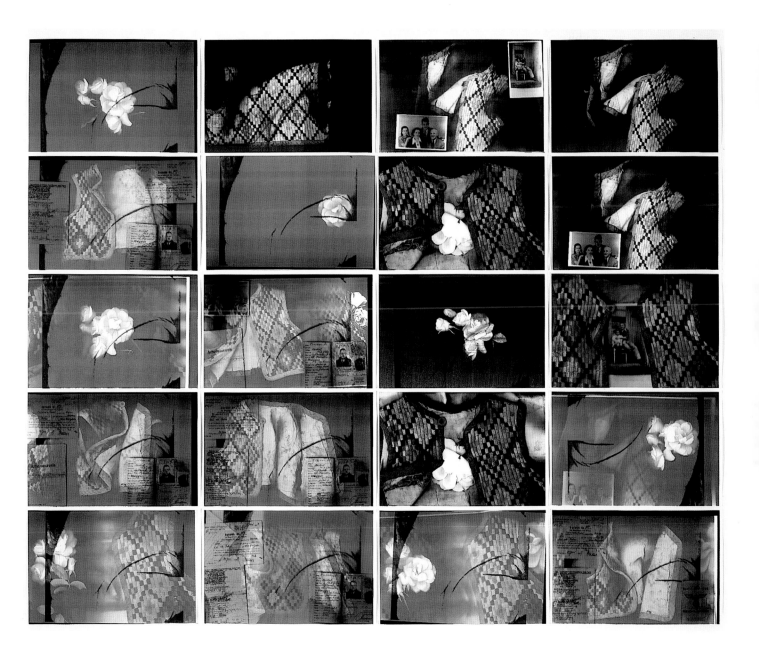

dred temporary exhibits, both large and small, on a wide range of topics reflecting Jewish art, historical and cultural experiences. Exhibits, with their extraordinary power to convey messages through objects and other types of displays, have become the museum's most powerful tool for public education.

Recognition that education is, properly, one of a museum's highest priorities has brought profound change to contemporary museum practices. The contemporary view is that education should be integrated into every aspect of the museum's offerings to realize the goals best expressed in the Smithsonian Institution's charter as "the increase and diffusion of knowledge." In a museum's formative years, curatorial scholarship aided the "increase" of knowledge. In our time, museum curators and educators take seriously the responsibility of "diffusion," attempting to promote increased understanding in museum visitors of all ages and backgrounds.

The Skirball Museum has realized its educational role by creating such programs as docent-led tours, lecture and film series, and family festivals that foster an appreciation of Jewish history, culture, and traditions. In response to the new "museum education" agenda, innovative approaches and programs were created in the museum's early years in Los Angeles. Espousing the principle that museum learning experiences could be stimulated and enhanced by an exhibit's style or environment, the museum in its first long-term core exhibition, *A Walk Through The Past* (1974), presented objects in a visual and physical context based on a theme which would dramatically and effectively convey information about the objects and ideas in the exhibit. The exhibition presented an overview of ancient Jewish history as well as Jewish religious beliefs and ceremonies as manifested in life cycle events, holidays and prayer. One exhibit case suggested an archaeological "tel," the earth hill that archaeologists peel away to discover material remains of various cultures, including ancient Israelite artifacts. The result was an educa-

tionally effective exhibit in which complex historical ideas could be easily transmitted to people of all ages and backgrounds. This attitude reflects an educational orientation in the display of museum objects, which foreshadowed the approach taken in the new core exhibit, *Visions and Values: Jewish Life from Antiquity to America,* of the Skirball Cultural Center.

An ambitious and effective educational effort, undertaken by the museum in conjunction with the College-Institute's Rhea Hirsch School of Jewish Education, began in 1976: the MUSE (Museum Utilization for Student Education) project was created with a large grant from the National Endowment for the Humanities as well as funding from the Jewish Community Foundation of Los Angeles. The museum-school partnership program was the first in which a Jewish museum in America developed a multicultural program for public school children. The program demonstrated the effectiveness of museum objects and hands-on experiences as learning tools, serving more than one hundred public and Jewish school classes every year in Southern California. We look forward to offering it again with the reopening of the museum at the Skirball Cultural Center.

While the museum focused on developing effective educational resources, the necessary museum functions of acquisition, conservation, research, and publication continued. Numerous historical, ceremonial, and fine arts objects were offered to the resituated museum, and a high percentage came from its new constituency in the western United States. A 1982 exhibition, *New and Renewed,* celebrated the museum's tenth birthday in Los Angeles by displaying numerous objects acquired in that decade as well as long-held items which had been given renewed life through conservation treatment. In the early 1980s, as the Skirball Cultural Center, with its emphasis on American Jewish life was conceptualized, the museum created Project Americana to enlarge its collections of American artifacts and art to serve its future needs. Throughout the

1970s and 1980s, the museum embarked on conservation efforts to survey its entire collection systematically and then to procure professional treatment for critical objects entrusted to its care. A full-scale textile preservation project commenced with the set-up of a studio for on-site technical treatment. Exhibition and collections catalogues, published to further the museum's mission of advancing scholarship and promoting understanding, included *Ketubbah: Jewish Marriage Contracts of Hebrew Union College Skirball Museum and Klau Library*, a 400-page, fully illustrated scholarly publication.

Serving an ever-growing public was what the Skirball Museum understood as its expanded mission during the 1970s and 1980s. This attitude also reflected changes in the life of its parent institution, the College-Institute, which has itself evolved since its founding, while adhering to its original mission of contributing to Jewish scholarship, heritage, and understanding. To respond to changes in society and to the changing needs of the Jewish people, HUC-JIR has found it necessary at different stages of its history to revise its own interpretation of how best to serve American Jewry. Thus, over time, it has enlarged its vision of what a Jewish professional is, adding to its original rabbinic program the professional training of Jewish educators and social workers. In this way, HUC-JIR has come to serve in a multiplicity of effective ways a much larger American Jewish public.

This evolving College-Institute vision parallels the Skirball Museum's orientation toward a wider public. Underlying programs and activities carried on by both HUC-JIR and the museum is the critical need to meet the challenge of preserving Jewish identity and its continued vitality. As the quality of Jewish life in America can be enhanced through the establishment of graduate schools of Education and Communal Service, which train professionals to meet contemporary Jewish needs, so can it be enhanced by stimulating inquiry into one's Jewish roots through museum exhibitions and programs. The College-Institute has continued to define its role as a major force in advancing Jewish knowledge, preserving Jewish heritage, and promoting Jewish understanding among a larger Jewish population. The Skirball Cultural Center and Museum is a significant way in which these same goals can be effectively realized.

From a national perspective, the Skirball Museum reflects the phenomenal growth in the country's cultural and ethnic museums. In the aggregate, these museums contribute to our collective understanding and sense of self as Americans. The Skirball Museum, by providing all Americans with a sense of Jewish life and history, and by exploring important cultural relationships of Jews and others in this country, offers visitors a place to contemplate and to nurture America's constantly changing identity. As the museum of the Skirball Cultural Center opens, it is poised for a new era with two richly evolved phases behind it.

In this next stage, the Skirball Museum will serve American society through the opportunities for understanding it provides all Americans. It will also be a major force in the strengthening of Jewish life in America for generations to come.

NOTES

1. George Heard Hamilton, "Education and Scholarship in the American Museum," *On Understanding Art Museums* (Englewood Cliffs, N.J.: Columbia University, Prentice-Hall, Inc., 1975), p. 101.

2. Hebrew Union College, *Articles of Incorporation*, January 6, 1926.

3. Alfred Gottschalk, in Samuel E. Karf, ed., *At One Hundred Years* (Cincinnati: Hebrew Union College Press, 1976), p. 483.

4. Karl E. Meyer, *The Art Museum: Power, Money, Ethics* (New York: William Morrow Company, Inc., 1979).

5. Excerpt of untitled, unreferenced article by Oko, in "Report of National Committee," National Federation of Temple Sisterhoods Proceedings, October 31, 1926.

6. Hamesh Maxwell, "Foreword" to *Museums for a New Century*, a report on the Commissions on Museums for a New Century, Joel B. Bloom and Earl A. Powell, III, eds., (Washington, D.C.: American Association of Museums, 1984), p.9.

7. *Museums for a New Century*, p. 63.

CREATIVITY

AND

SPIRITUALITY

*The Aesthetic Impulse
in Jewish Ceremonial Art*

JOSEPH GUTMANN

IN 1926, BY ACQUIRING 6,174 objects from the private museum of Berlin businessman Salli Kirschstein, Hebrew Union College in Cincinnati became the owner of the largest and finest collection of Judaica in America at that time. Kirschstein's collection had, since he purchased it around 1908, comprised the exquisite items amassed by Heinrich Frauberger, the Catholic director of the Industrial Arts and Crafts Museum (*Kunstgewerbemuseum*) in Düsseldorf, Germany, who was truly the pioneer in the study of Jewish ceremonial art.[1]

Individuals began collecting Judaica in the second half of the nineteenth century and Judaica items began to appear at international expositions in the closing decades of that century, but no public Judaica museums were established until the early twentieth century. Prior to the nineteenth century, the ceremonial objects of Judaism primarily served religious functions in synagogues and homes. Only with the emancipation of Jews and their integration and assimilation into the dominant societies of nineteenth-century Europe were these pieces seen in a nonreligious context; only then did their historical and aesthetic framework begin to be considered. Nostalgic yearning for a fast-disappearing pietistic Jewish world and the desire to create a positive visual image of Jewish culture (and thereby fight latent anti-Semitism) were factors that also stimulated the collecting and study of Jewish ceremonial art.[2]

Most of the Judaica objects in the Skirball Museum are linked to synagogal and Jewish home celebrations. The synagogue has been the most significant Jewish institution for roughly the last 2,000 years. Prior to the rise of the synagogue, the Temple in Jerusalem was for close to a thousand years a centralized and, for the most part, the sole cultic shrine of ancient Israel. The Temple, considered the House of God, was served by priests whose function was to insure the fertility of the land through animal sacrifices. The

Plate 7. Torah Finials, Johann Jacob Leschhorn, 1769–1787

Plate 10. Torah Crown, 1771

Plate 11. Torah Crown, 1758–1802 >

synagogue, on the other hand, has functioned historically as the house of the Jewish people, with God's presence invoked through prayers and *mitzvot* (ethical acts), deemed to aid the individual Jew as well as the community by assuring a promised salvation in the world to come and resurrection at the end of days. The cultic objects in the Jerusalem Temple differed radically in form, function, and meaning from those which developed in the synagogue, although the same terms that designated the cultic Temple vessels were often maintained in the synagogue in an effort to imply an unbroken chain of tradition from Temple to synagogue. Thus the ark (*aron*), which contained the stone tablets of the Ten Commandments in the Temple, became the repository of the Torah

(Pentateuchal) scrolls in the synagogue. The ark cover (*kapporet*), which had been associated with atonement rituals in the Second Temple, became in the synagogue a valance, also called *kapporet*,[3] hung over the Torah ark curtain (*parokhet*). The seven-branched cultic *menorah* of the Temple, administered by the priesthood, also found its way into the synagogue, but in the late Middle Ages this lampstand, still called *menorah*, received two additional light arms and came to be identified with and used at Hanukkah in Ashkenazi synagogues and homes.[4]

Although Jewish ceremonial items are mentioned in early rabbinic literature, the oldest securely dated ceremonial pieces extant are a pair of silver *rimmonim* (Torah finials) from fifteenth-century Sicily, then

under Aragonese rule. These *rimmonim,* now kept in the Cathedral Treasury of Palma de Mallorca in Spain, are well documented and there can be little doubt about their authenticity and antiquity.[5] On the other hand, triangular Hanukkah lamps,[6] Sabbath lamps,[7] spice boxes,[8] Seder plates,[9] and marriage rings,[10] which have been dated to the Middle Ages, raise many questions. Thorough investigation is needed to prove conclusively and convincingly that these items actually stem from medieval Europe. Their attribution, rarely questioned or subjected to critical research, rests largely on endless repetitions by scholars through which the objects have come to be accepted as truly dating from the Middle Ages.

The Skirball Museum possesses some outstanding and unique Judaica items, most of which date primarily from the seventeenth century on. These include the early eighteenth-century tower-form silver *rimmonim* made by the Frankfurt master craftsman Johann Jacob Leschhorn[11] (Plate 7), as well as the silver-gilt neoclassical *rimmonim* and Torah shield, which were probably crafted by the Christian silversmith Georg Zeiller in Munich about 1828 (Plate 8). A silver-gilt Torah shield, one of several similar Torah shields, may be from eighteenth-century Nuremberg (Plate 9). It features two running unicorns and the double-headed eagle, symbolic of the Holy Roman Empire of which Nuremberg was an integral part. A rare and splendid silver-gilt Torah crown was made in the late eighteenth century in Upper Franconia, Germany, and is clearly modeled on crowns of royalty (Plate 10). Surmounted by a rampant lion holding an oval finial, it may allude to the lion of Bavaria. An eighteenth-century silver-gilt Torah crown from northern Italy is an open cylinder, typical of Italian Torah crowns of that period (Plate 11).[12]

The cylindrical and octagonal *tik,* a container for holding the Torah scroll, is at home primarily in Islamic Jewish communities and may have been inspired by cabinets for storing Qur'ans. Sixteenth-century metal Torah cases have survived from Samaritan synagogues.[13] A rare wooden cylindrical *tik,* surmounted by a flame-shaped knob, comes from the no-longer-existing synagogue at Kaifeng in Honan province, China (Plate 12). It is one of two extant Torah cases from that community and may date from the seventeenth century.[14] The appearance of the *tik* in China is probably due to its introduction by Jewish merchants from Islamic Western Asia.[15] A handsome silver *tik* from India is dated 1916 (Plate 4).

A satin velvet Torah ark curtain with metallic appliqué from Bohemia is dated 1697 (Plate 13). Although similar to Bohemian Torah ark curtains on display at the Jewish Museum in Prague, it is probably the oldest Bohemian Torah ark curtain in this country and one of the few seventeenth-century examples that survived the Holocaust.[16] The earliest Torah ark curtain extant is dated 1592 and comes from Prague. The embroidered Torah ark curtain, dated 1785, from Menden, Germany, is a splendid example of extant eighteenth-century curtains (Plate 115). The unique and beautiful velvet Torah valance (*kapporet*), with its embroidered crown flanked by two cherubim wings and surrounded by Tabernacle/Temple implements, was donated in 1724 by the women of the Hohe Synagogue in Prague (Plate 14).[17]

The Skirball Museum possesses what is perhaps the oldest surviving Hanukkah candelabrum made for a synagogue, that at Aschaffenburg, Lower Franconia, Germany, in the early eighteenth century (Plate 17). During the Middle Ages, it had become customary in Europe to set up a large Hanukkah lamp in the synagogue, and by the seventeenth century, the synagogue lamp had adopted the shape of the ancient Temple *menorah* but with two additional light arms. This lamp was placed to the south or right of the Torah ark in memory of the ancient Temple *menorah* that stood to the south. It was lit in the synagogue to "enable the ignorant to hear the blessings recited correctly" and to

34

"spread the miracle [of Hanukkah] in public."[18] This large, handsome bronze candelabrum has a central shaft from which spring eight hands supporting eight of the branches.

Synagogue lamps, in smaller format, had also appeared in Jewish homes by the eighteenth century. An unusual silver-gilt Hanukkah lamp of this type (Plate 19) was produced in Galicia (South Poland) about 1800. In format it is an oak tree chased in bark pattern; its naturalistic oak leaves and acorns give rise through its six subordinate branches to eight candle sockets. On the tree trunk is a bear climbing toward a honey pot with a bee on it; below is a man with a gun aimed at the bear.[19] Another splendid Hanukkah lamp of this genre, made by Johann Heinrich Philip Schott and Sons in Frankfurt-am-Main, Germany, is from the mid-nineteenth century (Plate 2). Its base proudly displays the baronial Rothschild coat of arms, which was granted in 1822. It may have been a wedding present of Wilhelm Carl von Rothschild to his Viennese bride Hannah Mathilde von Rothschild.

Hanukkah lamps using architectural forms ap-peared in the eighteenth century. The Skirball Museum has a unique German specimen in the neoclassical style, dating from 1814 (Plate 18). In shape it is a resplendent classical building with columns, pediments, and lampposts. Its owner may have been named Samuel Hirsch, because the pediment features two stags (in German, *Hirsch*) on whose bodies are inscribed the Hebrew name Samuel. Whether the two triple triangular symbols on the pediment allude to the Masonic order deserves further investigation.[20]

The exquisite late seventeenth-century silver-gilt star-shaped Sabbath lamp with a three-tiered graduated shaft is one of several surviving silver objects made in the late seventeenth or early eighteenth century for wealthy Jews residing in the *Judengasse* (ghetto) of Frankfurt-am-Main (Plate 15). They come from the workshop of such master craftsmen as Johann Valentin Schüler, his brother Michael, and their relatives.[21] They may have been wedding presents given at the ceremony called *Spinnholtz* or *Spinholz* —among German Jews a celebration held on the Friday preceding the actual wedding or on the Sabbath before the nuptials.[22] An

35

ordinance passed by the Frankfurt Jewish Council in 1715 specifically mentions that only three gifts of silver are permitted to be displayed on that occasion—a *Tisch-Becher* (a [*kiddush*?] table cup), a *Leuchter* (a [Hanukkah?] menorah) and a *Lampe* (a [Sabbath?] lamp).[23]

An elegant four-tiered circular silver Seder container in the collection is a unique neoclassic Passover ceremonial piece that appears to have been introduced in the eighteenth century (Plate 22). The top tier has seven screwed-on figural ornaments, which hold or carry vessels for the symbolic Passover Seder foods. The center features a large figure of Moses supporting on his head a cutout silver stand for the cup of Elijah. This container was made around 1815 in Vienna. A fifteenth-century illuminated Italian Passover Haggadah with 64 round pendant leaves, which are so joined together that they can be folded up, is a unique specimen of Haggadah illustration (Plate 106).

An unusual *omer* calendar, made of silver and glass, comes from mid-nineteenth-century France

(Plate 24). Whether the entire piece was originally intended to serve as an *omer* calendar is not certain. It carries the signature of Maurice Mayer, gold and silversmith and jeweller to Emperor Napoleon III.[24]

Aside from pieces made by master Christian craftsmen, the Skirball Museum collection features embroidered items made by skilled, loving Jewish hands. These folkloric items are usually the handiwork of women, who made them especially to celebrate birth, the Sabbath, and Passover. A remarkable folkloric Passover towel, dating from 1821 in Alsace, France, reveals a pipe-smoking man, perhaps Abraham Blümche, whose name is embroidered on the towel, leading the Passover lamb on a rope (Plate 23). A beautiful multicolored embroidery on white silk tafetta from late nineteenth-century Germany shows the two prescribed Sabbath *ḥallot* (called *Barkhes* or *Berkhes*) in the center surrounded by the name of the maker, Marianna Kirschstein, and the blessing over the Sabbath loaves (Plate 16). She was the wife of the collector Salli Kirschstein.

The Skirball Museum contains one of the largest extant collections of *Wimpeln* (Torah binders). It became customary around 1500 in southern Germany to take the swaddling cloth upon which a boy had been circumcised, wash it, and cut it generally into four sections, which would be stitched together and embroidered to make a *Wimpel*. Aside from the boy's Hebrew name, that of his father and the day, month, and year of his birth according to the Hebrew calendar, it carried the pious formula: "May he grow up to study Torah, get married and perform good deeds."   By the eighteenth century this South German custom had spread to other German-speaking areas. A finely embroidered example in the Skirball Museum is dated 1733 from Halberstadt, Saxony (Plate 26). Though the origin of this custom is not clear, it may have been adapted from a purported similar practice among South German Catholics to have pious statements embroidered on the *Taufwindel* (baptismal swaddling cloth). The oldest surviving *Wimpel*, dated Wednesday, 11th of Kislev 5369 (November 10, 1608), was recently found in the former synagogue of Westheim in Lower

Franconia.[25] The collection also contains precious metal amulets, among them an eighteenth-century example from Italy, placed on the baby's crib to ward off evil spirits (Plate 94). A wooden Chair of Elijah, on which the *sandak* (a sort of godfather) sat while he held the child to be circumcised, is dated 1803 and comes from Rheda, Westphalia, Germany (Plate 25).

Several hundred *ketubbot* (marriage contracts) in the Skirball Museum are among the finest extant in Judaica collections. These have been researched and published.[26] The decoration of *ketubbot* appears to have had its origins in eleventh- and twelfth-century Islamic Egypt and Syro-Palestine. The geometric and floral decor in the extant fragments of Jewish marriage contracts from that period appears to follow the artis-

tic patterns established in contemporary Islamic marriage contracts.[27] When Islam's imperial center in the Middle East underwent decline, the custom of the illustrated *ketubbah* may have spread west to Islamic Spain, although there is as yet no supportive evidence for this conjecture. Ornamented *ketubbot* made in the thirteenth to fifteenth centuries in Christian Spain do exist, and the practice spread to Italy and Turkey with the dispersion of the Sephardi Jews following their expulsion in 1492. It was in Italy, however, that the golden age of *ketubbah* decoration emerged in the seventeenth and eighteenth centuries, and the Skirball Museum has splendid examples of this practice. The earliest known *ketubbah*, employing a lavish figural and decorative program, is dated 1649 from Venice (Plate 111). These

40

ketubbot sometimes carry biblical scenes alluding to the Hebrew name of the groom, like that of Aryeh Samuel Hai ha-Cohen from Ferrara in 1775, which depicts the prophet Samuel (Plate 27). Other contracts, such as the one from Pisa in 1790, incorporate common Italian motifs like a nude reclining Venus as well as allegorical figures (Plate 28).

The Holy Society for Visiting the Sick held an annual festive banquet where all members of the *hevra* (society) drank from a special large silver beaker or had wine poured from it into their cups. The names of the members are engraved on the splendid beaker in the Skirball collection made by Daniel Matignon in Berlin in 1779 (Plate 29).

A sizable collection of decorated Esther scrolls

(*megillot*) is to be found in the Skirball Museum and in the Klau Library on the Cincinnati campus of Hebrew Union College. These *megillot* have yet to be researched. Esther scrolls began to be decorated in late sixteenth-century Italy, and the style flourished during the seventeenth and eighteenth centuries in Italy, Germany, and the Netherlands. These scrolls have lavish floral and animal ornamentation, their text is frequently separated by columns, and their upper and lower margins have illustrations that relate the story of Esther. Two of the Skirball's *megillot*, one made in Venice in 1748 by Arye Loeb ben Daniel, a traveling copyist originally from Poland (Plate 20), and the other by the popular scribe Aaron Wolf Herlingen from eighteenth-century Gewitsch, Moravia (Plate 103), are typi-

Plate 22. Tiered Seder Plate, Franz Strobl (?), 1814

Plate 23. Passover Towel, 1821

cal of popular *megillah* ornamentation.[28] An unusual, well-preserved set of twelve faience plates, specially made "in accordance with the custom of exchanging gifts on Purim" (Esther 9:22), dates from 1785 in Amsterdam (Plate 21).

Only in the nineteenth century are Jewish artists freed from the jurisdiction of the Jewish community and the restraints imposed by Christian guilds; only then are they enabled to assume a major role in Jewish life. The Skirball Museum possesses one of only two known oil paintings from the series *Traditional Jewish Family Life* by Moritz Oppenheim, one of the first Jews to paint such scenes. Entitled *Sabbath Afternoon*, it was made around 1860 and reveals a sentimental genre rendering of bourgeois happiness and well being (Plate 37). It shows the father in deep slumber while a young child recites the Hebrew lesson he has mastered. The mother is reading a book and ignores the innocent flirtation between her daughter and the visiting yeshivah student. The twisted *hallah* loaves and the *kiddush* cup are on the table and the *Judenstern* (Sabbath lamp) is suspended from the ceiling. Oppenheim, dubbed in his time "the painter of Rothschild and the Rothschild of painters," was the first major Jewish artist to record Jewish religious observances—customs he recalled from his own orthodox childhood in Hanau, Germany. In a secular German environment of rapid integration and assimilation, these paintings undoubtedly were for him and many German Jews nostalgic reminders or anchors of a vanishing world that had once flourished amid the pieties of the close-knit Jewish ghetto.[29]

Most of the well-crafted ceremonial implements in the Skirball Museum were made in Western Europe prior to the present century by such Christian master silversmiths as Valentin Schüler, Georg Zeiller, and Jeremias Zobel, as Jews were banned from Christian guild organizations and were not permitted to establish their own. However, some ceremonial items pro-

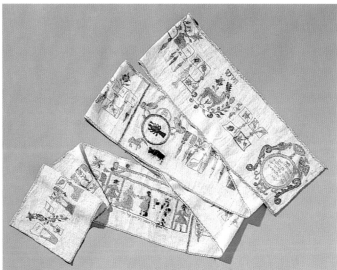

duced in Eastern Europe are the work of Jewish crafts-men, for in such countries as Poland Jews were permitted by the seventeenth century to organize their own craft guilds, known as *hevrot*. Before the nineteenth century, these craftsmen were generally unidentifiable, as Jews were still forbidden to affix a maker's mark to their objects. In Islamic communities where metalsmithing was often considered an inferior occupation, Jews were active as smiths and probably produced their own ceremonial objects.[30]

In the twentieth century there has been a revival in the crafting of Jewish ceremonial art. Artisans reinvented the medieval Jewish tradition by fashioning highly original and exciting new ceremonial objects. Artists represented in the Skirball collection include Ludwig Wolpert (Plate 30), Otto Natzler (Plate 36), and Hana Geber (Plate 33), who all trained in Europe before World War II, the Israelis Zelig Segal (Plate 31) and Arie Ofir (Plate 34), and the American architect Richard Meier (Plate 35). The simple and elegant twentieth-century silver Torah crown by Moshe Zabari departs from traditional forms and testifies to the contemporary striving for daring and novel interpretations (Plate 32).

The specific forms, styles, and decorations of the objects reflect the dynamic involvement of Jews with the host Christian and Islamic societies. Thus, for instance, spice containers in tower form are adaptations by Christian smiths of Christian monstrance and reliquary containers. European *rimmonim* often show recognizable contours of spires and turrets of local churches, and a pair of *rimmonim* from Morocco echo the patterns of Islamic architecture (Plate 117). Torah crowns were modeled on royal crowns or crowns of the Christian Madonna. Torah cases appear to be adaptations of metal or wooden cabinets for storing Qur'ans. *Kiddush* cups were frequently secular table-ware utensils made to serve Jewish purposes through the addition of Hebrew inscriptions. Sugar bowls and soap dishes also became containers for the *etrog* (citron), used in the fall harvest Sukkot festival, by adding a Hebrew inscription or symbol.

Just as some forms of Jewish ceremonial objects were inspired by those found in the dominant non-Jewish environment, decorative elements likewise may reveal the artist's perspective on society. Thus, as the double-headed eagle on the Nuremberg Torah shield simply expressed Jewish loyalty to the leadership of the

Plate 27. Ferrara Ketubbah, 1775

Plate 28. Pisa Ketubbah, 1790

< Plate 29. Beaker of the Holy Society for Visiting the Sick, Daniel Matignon, 1779

Plate 30. Hanukkah Lamp, Ludwig Y. Wolpert, ca. 1960

Plate 31. Laver, Zelig Segal, ca. 1980

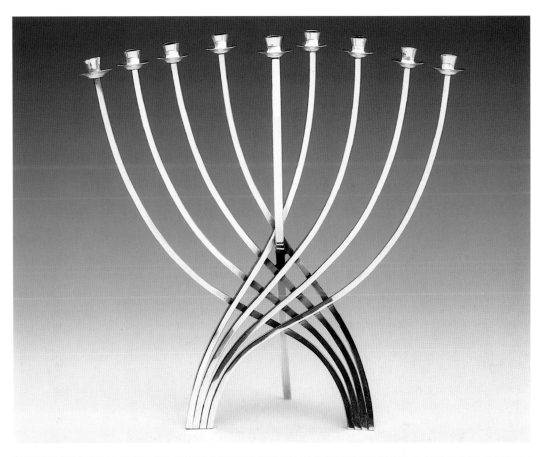

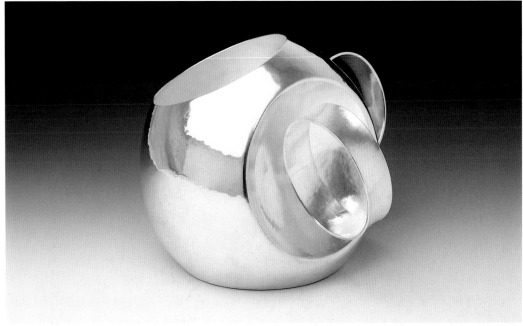

Plate 34. Candlesticks, Arie Ofir, 1990

Plate 35. Hanukkah Lamp, Richard Meier, 1990

Plate 36. Hanukkah Lamp, Otto Natzler, 1988 >

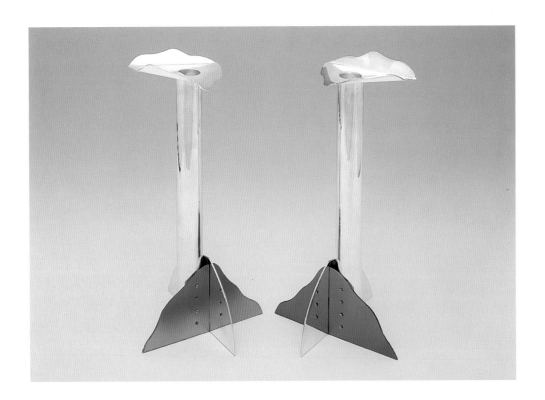

Holy Roman Empire, so the lion on the Torah crown made in Upper Franconia need not refer exclusively to the lion of Judah, but equally to the lion of Bavaria; this Torah crown may very well bespeak Bavarian Jewry's respect for their country and its rulers.

The styles of some items in the Skirball Museum reflect Jewish involvement with the many majority cultures in which they lived: utensils from Islamic countries evince the Islamic predilection for abstract decoration; seventeenth-century ceremonial items from Europe show the dramatic baroque style, which gives way in the eighteenth century to the more delicate and whimsical rococo style; in the late eighteenth and early nineteenth centuries, the majestic yet severe neoclassic style predominates. Although many objects in the Skirball Museum collection reveal the use of Christian forms and styles, there is a fundamental difference in the way each religion regards these vessels. In Catholic worship, the objects involved in the sac-

rament are regarded as sacred in that they help invoke and impart the redeeming power of the actual divine presence. In Judaism, the sacramental aspect is absent, and the main purpose of the implements is aesthetic, to enhance worship of the invisible deity. The objects in themselves impart no sanctity but are simply a means to help approach divinity; they are not instruments through which the divine becomes manifest.

Given the multifaceted involvement of Jews in Islamic and Christian communities, it is not surprising to find a rich diversity in the use of objects in different Jewish communities. Fashioning the *Wimpel*, for instance, appears to be unique to German-speaking Jewry and is a practice unknown in Eastern Europe and in Islamic communities. Likewise, most Ashkenazi countries preferred covering the Torah scroll with a textile mantle and placed the Torah scroll flat on the reader's desk, whereas many Islamic communities enclosed the Torah scroll in a cylindrical or octagonal *tik*, a case made of metal and/or wood; the case is opened and its Torah scroll is usually read while standing upright on the reader's rostrum.[31]

In sum, the objects discussed reveal in style and form the unique involvement of Judaism with both Islamic and Christian cultures over the last several hundred years. They reflect the Jewish desire to worship God with aesthetically pleasing objects and to stress not only the beauty in holiness but the holiness of beauty. They demonstrate great Jewish creativity and ability to adapt new forms and styles to ever-changing conditions. They suggest not so much the unity of Judaism as a rich diversity varying from one Jewish community to another and from one country to another.

NOTES

1. J. Gutmann, "The Kirschstein Museum of Berlin," *Jewish Art* 16/17 (1990/91), 178.

2. Cf. G. Grossman, "Judaica at the Smithsonian: Cultural Politics as Cultural Model," doctoral dissertation, Hebrew Union College-Jewish Institute of Religion, Los Angeles, 1994, 1-190; R. I. Cohen, "Self-Image Through Objects: Toward a Social History of Jewish Art Collecting and Jewish Museums," in J. Wertheimer, ed., *The Uses of Tradition: Jewish Continuity in the Modern Era* (New York, 1992), 203-42; and J. Gutmann, "Is There a Jewish Art?" in C. Moore, ed., *The Visual Dimension: Aspects of Jewish Art* (Boulder, 1993), 1-5. The following may be added to p. 14 of the last article: Jacob Epstein, the noted sculptor, said: "I, for the life of me, cannot see why my bronzes in this exhibition were particularly Jewish, any more than the works of Rembrandt...." Cf. S. Gardiner, *Epstein: Artist Against the Establishment* (New York, 1993), 244-45.

3. Cf. J. Gutmann, "The History of the Ark," in J. Gutmann, *Sacred Images: Studies in Jewish Art from Antiquity to the Middle Ages* (Northampton, 1989), IV, 22-30; J. Gutmann, "Return in Mercy to Zion: A Messianic Dream in Jewish Art," Gutmann, *ibid.*, XVII, 218-19. Cf. also J. Gutmann, "An Eighteenth-Century Prague Jewish Workshop of *Kapporot*," *Visible Religion* 6 (1988), 180-90.

The following corrections and additions can be made to this last article: p. 181, line 28 should read: bearded winged youths; p. 182, line 31: Whether the creation of *kapporot* originated in Bohemia-Moravia or Germany is, in light of new evidence, still open to question. An early *kapporet* similar to the ten *kapporot* described in my article has just come to my attention. It is in the Prague State Jewish Museum (Inv. No. 37.385) and was donated by Gadel ben Esriel (Azriel) Schames (Shammash) [Zappert], and his wife Jentele bat Pesach Brandes Segal in the year 1707. I am indebted to Drs. Arno Parík and Alexandr Putík for this information. Cf. C. Benjamin, *The Stieglitz Collection. Masterpieces of Jewish Art* (Jerusalem, 1987), for an illustration of this *kapporet* on p. 15 of the Hebrew section; p. 184, n. 27, line 7 might read Genendel; p. 184, n. 33, the Torah ark curtain does not match the *kapporet*, cf. I. Benoshofsky and A. Scheiber, *The Jewish Museum of Budapest* (Budapest, 1987), p. 167.

4. Cf. J. Gutmann, "A Note on the Temple Menorah," in Gutmann, *Sacred Images*, V, 289-91 and J. Gutmann, *The Jewish Sanctuary* (Leiden, 1983), 14. The following corrections and additions should be made: p. IX, BEMPORAD...should read arte cerimoniale; CASSUTO... should read Costruzione; p. X JEWISH ART TREASURES ... should read Gallery; p. XI should read Piattelli; POSEN...should read Toraschrein Vorhaenge; p. 1, line 16 should read Jehoiakhin; p. 8, line 27 should read Meisel; p. 10, line 13 on the use of the word *tappuhim*, cf. D. Thon, "*Tappuhim*: Torah Finials from Morocco," *The Israel Museum Journal* 7 (1988): 87-95; p. 11, line 35 should read Sephardi and Islamic synagogues; p. 14, line 35 add: *Polisch, Polischen* ; p. 14, line 36 add *Schemeskastl*; p. 14, line 41 add: *kuppat ha-tzedakah, Pushke*; pp. 20-22 add: W. Gunther Plaut, *The Magen David* (Washington, 1991) for additional information; p. 24, plate VIIIa, the Torah mantle may be from the Rhineland or Bavaria; p. 25, plate XI Torah mantle should read: Miniature from Rothschild *mahzor*, Passover service; plate XI Torah shield should be dated 1606. It was made for Yaakov and Rachel Tirado by the silversmith Leendert Claesz; p. 26, plate XVI, line 4, Torah shield should read: Thalmessing 1848; p. 27, plate XIX, line 9 should read circunstancias; p. 30, plate XXXIII, line 8, Gunteles (?) (rather than Gautel); p. 31, plate XXXVIII, Torah ark curtain may be from Lorraine or Germany. It is now in the Jewish Museum of New York, Inv. No. F 5210; p. 32, should read plate XXXIXb (not XXXIb).

5. Gutmann, *Jewish Sanctuary*, p. 27, plate XIX.

6. Cf. J. Gutmann, in A. Plous, ed., *Feast of Lights: Art and Tradition of Hanukkah Lamps* (Detroit, 1992), 8. The dozen or so oil burning lamps, attributed to the Middle Ages, deserve detailed scrutiny. A bronze Hanukkah candelabrum does not come from fifteenth-century Italy, as Landsberger maintained, cf. J. Gutmann, ed., *Beauty in Holiness: Studies in Jewish Customs and Ceremonial Art* (New York, 1970), XX.

7. The German Sabbath lamp, dated fourteenth century, in N. L. Kleeblatt and V. B. Mann, *Treasures of the Jewish Museum* (New York, 1986), 30-31, is probably from a later time. Cf. F. Landsberger, "The Origin of the Ritual Implements for the Sabbath," in Gutmann, ed., *Beauty in Holiness*, p. 177, n. 18.

8. It is doubtful that a spice box, reproduced in M. Narkiss, "Origins of the Spice Box," *Journal of Jewish Art* 8 (1981), 28-29, can be attributed to thirteenth-century Spain as the spice box appears to have originated in Germany. Furthermore, no depictions of spice boxes are found in medieval Spanish miniatures and the use of the *hadas* (myrtle leaf) during the *havdalah* ceremony was the established custom in medieval Spain. Cf. J. Z. Lauterbach, "The Origin and Development of Two Sabbath Ceremonies," in Gutmann, ed., *Beauty in Holiness*, 220-21.

9. V. B. Mann, "Forging Judaica: The Case of the Italian Majolica Seder Plates," in L. Mendelsohn and R. I. Cohen, eds., *Art and its Uses: The Visual Image and Modern Jewish Society*, VI (New York, 1990), 201-24, has convincingly shown that these plates do not stem from the late Middle Ages, as previously assumed.

Cf. also A. Moldovan, "Foolishness, Fakes, and Forgeries in Jewish Art," in Moore, *Visual Dimension*, 105-19.

10. Some 300 extant marriage rings deserve critical, scholarly examination. Cf. G. Seidmann, "Jewish Marriage Rings," *Jewellery Studies* 1 (1983-84), 41-44 and J. Gutmann, *The Jewish Life Cycle* (Leiden, 1987), 15. The following corrections and additions should be made in this book: p. 4, line 37 should read: Senoi, Sansenoi, Sanmangeloph/ Samangeloph (the same correction should appear on p. 5, line 3, and p. 23, plate IIa-b), cf. J. Schudt, *Jüdische Merckwürdigkeiten* (Frankfurt, 1714), Zweiter Teil, Book VI, Chap. 26, p. 7; p. 4, line 42 add *Scheimestafel* and *Hamalostafel*; p. 5, line 10 add *veglia* (in Italy), cf. E. Horowitz, "The Eve of the Circumcision: A Chapter in the History of Jewish Nightlife," in D. B. Ruderman, ed., *Essential Papers on Jewish Culture in Renaissance and Baroque Italy* (New York, 1992), 554-87; p. 12, n. 11 on the Islamic influence on the decoration of Jewish marriage contracts, cf. J. Gutmann, "Jewish Medieval Marriage Customs in Art: Creativity and Adaptation," in D. Kraemer, ed., *The Jewish Family: Metaphor and Memory* (New York, 1989), 55; p. 15, line 9 add: H. H. Pollack, "Why the 'Erusin and the Nissu'in were Combined: A Study in Historical Causation," in *Proceedings of the Ninth World Congress of Jewish Studies*, Division D (Jerusalem, 1986), 47-54; p. 15, line 15 should read: "you are set apart for me"; p. 16, line 32 add: D. Davidowitz, "Breaking a Cup on the Wedding Stone," in *Israel, People and Land*, 4 (1986-87), 253-67 (in Hebrew); p. 19, lines 6-7 add: R. L. Wilken, *The Land Called Holy* (New Haven, 1992), 303, n. 95 on the practice of placing soil from Eretz Israel in a coffin; p. 23, plate IIIb add: also known as *Krasmesser* — "a witch shall not live" is from Exodus 22:18; p. 27, plate XXb line 5 should read A 380/II; p. 28, plate XXc should read 5152; p. 29, plate XXIIb, line 2 should read: son of Moses Judah — line 3 should read Jacur; p. 29, plate XXIII, change to Sepill on line 2; plate XXIIIb, line 11 change to Gradisca; p. 30, plate XXIVb change to Elia Tagliacozzo; plate XXVb, line 2 change to Fiorenzuolo; plate XXVIa, line 1 change to parchment, line 7 change to *hakham*; plate XXVIb, line 2 change to — son of Benzecki and line 3 daughter of Shalom, son of Abraham Benyunes; p. 31, plate XXVIIb, line 1 change to August 16. All of the above marriage contracts are now discussed in S. Sabar, *Ketubbah: Jewish Marriage Contracts of Hebrew Union College Skirball Museum and Klau Library* (Philadelphia, 1990). p. 32, plate XXXIb, line 3, eliminate "...have the beginning Hebrew letters of Psalm 118:20."

11. These were long attributed to Jeremias Zobel. Cf. V. B. Mann, *A Tale of Two Cities: Jewish Life in Frankfurt and Istanbul 1750-1870* (New York, 1982), 94-95.

12. Gutmann, *Jewish Sanctuary*, 8-11, 26-29.

13. *Ibid.*, 6, 23 and R. Pummer, *The Samaritans* (Leiden, 1987), 13, 37.

14. The second Torah case from China is in the Royal Ontario Museum in Toronto.

15. Cf. Gutmann, *Jewish Sanctuary*, 6, 23-24.

16. *Ibid.*, 30-32.

17. Cf. Gutmann, "Eighteenth-Century Prague Jewish Workshop of *Kapporot*," 180-90 and *supra*, n. 3.

18. Quoted from sixteenth-century Rabbi Mordecai Jaffe, *Levush, Orah Hayyim, Hilkot Hanukkah 671:8*) and thirteenth-century Lunel rabbi, Abraham ben Nathan Hayarhi *Sefer ha-Manhig 105a,* cited in Gutmann, *Jewish Sanctuary*, 14.

19. The topmost candleholder (*shammash*) and the three-lobed tray that supports the tree may have been added later. This lamp deserves detailed scholarly examination. Cf. F. Landsberger, "Old Hanukkah Lamps," *Beauty in Holiness*, 283-309.

20. Cf. N. M. Berman, "The Hirsch and Rothschild Hanukkah Lamps at the Hebrew Union College Skirball Museum," *Journal of Jewish Art* 6 (1979), 86-97, and A. M. Greenwald, "The Masonic Mizrah and Lamp: Jewish Ritual Art as a Reflection of Cultural Assimilation," *Journal of Jewish Art* 10 (1984), 92-93.

21. V. B. Mann, "The Golden Age of Jewish Ceremonial Art in Frankfurt: Metalwork of the Eighteenth Century," *Leo Baeck Institute Year Book* 31 (1986), 389-403.

22. Cf. J. Gutmann, "Christian Influences on Jewish Customs," in L. Klenicki and G. Huck, eds., *Spirituality and Prayer: Jewish and Christian Understandings* (New York, 1983), 133. The following additions and corrections should be made to this article: p. 133, line 20 ought to be velamen; p. 134, line 37 insert: Again, the custom of reciting the ancient *kaddish* as a prayer for the dead has its roots in the presence of the congregation....; p. 135, n. 4 read: *Reconstructionist*; p. 138, nn. 31 and 33 add: W. Jacob, *American Reform Responsa* (New York, 1983), 377-79 and 393-95 (on the *kaddish* and *Jahrzeit*).

23. Cf. A. Weber, "Splendid Bridal Gifts from a Sumptuous Wedding Ceremonial of 1681 in the Frankfurt Judengasse," *Jewish Art* 19/20 (1993-94), 169-79 and G. Schoenberger, "Silberne Sabbath- und Festtagslampen aus Frankfurt am Main," *Kunst in Hessen und am Mittelrhein* 9 (1969), 63-72.

24. A silver Torah case made by Maurice Mayer is in the Jewish Museum of New York, cf. Kleeblatt and Mann, *Treasures of the Jewish Museum*, 154-55. Mayer also made several Torah shields, cf. V. Klagsbald, *Jewish Treasures from Paris* (Jerusalem, 1982), 27-29.

25. Cf. J. Gutmann, "Die Mappe Schuletragen: An Unusual Judeo-German Custom," *Visible Religion* 2 (1983), 167-73; F. Wiesemann, *et al.*, *Genizah — Hidden Legacies of the German Village Jews* (Vienna, 1992), 213.

26. S. Sabar, *Ketubbah: Jewish Marriage Contracts.*

27. Cf. J. Gutmann, "Jewish Medieval Marriage Customs in Art," 155-56.

28. Cf. J. Gutmann, "Estherrolle," *Reallexikon zur deutschen Kunstgeschichte* 6 (1973), 88-103.

29. Oppenheim is best known for his 20 grisaille paintings of Jewish family celebrations, which were often reproduced. Cf. E. Cohen, *Moritz Oppenheim: The First Jewish Painter* (Jerusalem, 1983) and A. Werner, *Moritz Oppenheim: Pictures of Traditional Jewish Family Life* (New York, 1976).

30. Cf. M. Wischnitzer, *A History of Jewish Crafts and Guilds* (New York, 1965) and I. Pataky-Brestyanszky, "The Becker Family: Silversmiths of Bratislava," *Jewish Art* 19/20 (1993-94), 181-93.

31. Cf. J. Gutmann, "The Precious Legacy: Judaic Treasures from the Czechoslovak State Collections," *Rotunda. The Magazine of the Royal Ontario Museum* 18 (1985), 17-23.

Plate 37. *Sabbath Afternoon,* Moritz Oppenheim, ca. 1860

EXPRESSION AND MEANING IN THE JEWISH VISUAL ARTS

Fine Arts in the Skirball Museum Collection

BARBARA C. GILBERT

EWISH MUSEUMS are usually perceived as cultural institutions that collect and exhibit objects used in Jewish rituals and ceremonies or that illustrate the distinctive nature of Jewish communities worldwide. In addition to these traditional Judaic and ethnographic materials, works of art either by Jewish artists or by non-Jews on Jewish themes are an important and ever-growing component of many such collections. Often the historical prints, paintings, and sculptures within exhibits in Jewish museums provide the most cogent illustrations of Jewish ideas, ritual practices, and daily life.

Almost from its inception, the Union Museum of Hebrew Union College included paintings, sculpture, and graphic arts among its many holdings. When Hebrew Union College was negotiating the purchase of the Salli Kirschstein Collection of Berlin, the paintings were described in more specific detail than the Jewish ritual objects.[1] About twenty-five years later, when Dr. Franz Landsberger, the postwar curator of the Union Museum, selected objects to be acquired for the museum through the Jewish Cultural Reconstruction, an organization established to redistribute Judaica and Jewish art objects confiscated by the Nazis, key paintings from the former Jewish Museum of Berlin, where

he had served as Director during the 1930s, were included at the top of his request.

Over the years, the fine arts segment of the collection has grown exponentially in comparison to the rest. The growth in the fine arts collection can be attributed in part to the increasing rarity of historical examples of Jewish ceremonial art and the relatively modest output of contemporary Judaica, but even more important, beginning in about 1970 artists have in greater numbers begun to grapple with Jewish ideas and issues in their works.

There were significant examples of paintings, prints, and even sculpture within the general Judaica collections, including the Salli Kirschstein Collection, mentioned previously, and the Louis Grossman Collection, acquired for the college by Dr. Adolph Oko in the 1920s. A few collections dedicated almost exclusively to paintings and sculpture have been acquired, including those of Ben Selling of Portland (1940s) and Mr. and Mrs. Jack Cottin of New York (1958); ivory reliefs from the workshops of the Bezalel Academy in Eretz Israel formed the core of Joseph Schontal's collection; outstanding examples of contemporary Israeli art from the Frederick R. Weisman Foundation (1988); and works on paper on Jewish themes or by Jewish artists were donated by Rabbi William R. Kramer (1993). The museum has, through purchase and donation, also acquired many significant individual artworks.

Today about one-third of the Skirball Museum collection is dedicated to fine arts, including at least five thousand pieces which comprise the collection of historical prints and other works on paper. The majority of the prints came to the collection as part of larger collections purchased in the 1920s, such as the above-mentioned Kirschstein and Grossman Collections as well as the Anglo-Jewish Collection of Israel Solomons. Originally inexpensive, these prints were collected for antiquarian rather than artistic value. In general, these collectors were motivated by any printed material that illustrated the Jewish experience: portraits of well-known Jewish figures; depictions of synagogues, private residences, or other communal buildings; genre scenes recording Jewish rituals and customs; biblical subjects; current events that affected the Jews; and anti-Semitica. Kirschstein and Grossman collected prints that referred to Germany and Central Europe, while Solomons specialized in prints that illustrated the Jewish experience in Britain from the late seventeenth century (when Jews were readmitted to England) to the late nineteenth century. Not originally intended as individual artworks, these prints were produced as broadsides or as illustrations in books. The

artists and craftsmen were generally non-Jews. As is characteristic of the print media, each work is by two people: the artist responsible for the original drawing and the engraver or lithographer. The prints are an important resource to the museum, providing the historical and sociological contexts for understanding Jewish life at earlier times.

The several hundred paintings, drawings, and sculptures in the collection range from the sixteenth century to the present and exhibit the varying regional and period art styles represented in that span of time. Since Jews did not have open access to professional art training until the late eighteenth and early nineteenth centuries, earlier works in the collection usually represent non-Jewish interpretations of biblical and other Jewish themes. Among the Jewish subjects that had special appeal to non-Jewish artists was the Book of Esther, an especially popular subject for religious commissions in the sixteenth and seventeenth centuries in present-day Belgium and Holland. Esther was perceived as a prefiguration of the Virgin Mary, and her story thus was characteristically used in church altarpieces and individual paintings.[2] The Skirball Museum has a rare pair of oil paintings on wood panel (Plate 38) illustrating the triumph of Mordecai by the Belgian artist Lambert Lombard (1501–1566), who spent a year in Rome, where he was exposed to antique sculpture and murals by Raphael in the private rooms of the Vatican. Both sources are apparent in the costumes and figural compositions of the Skirball Museum paintings. The two panel paintings in the collection may have originally been part of Lombard's chief work painted in Liège after his return from Italy, the now-dismembered high altar of the Church of St. Denis. The early date attributed to the panels suggests that Lombard may have been responsible for the visual transmission of the story of Esther from Italy to the Low Countries.

Religious tolerance in seventeenth-century

Plate 39. *Vanitas Still Life*, Evert Collier, 1696

Holland, coupled with the Dutch Reform Church's Hebraist interests, fostered a respect for biblical and other Judaic themes. A painting in the collection that exemplifies Dutch Hebraism is a *Vanitas Still Life* (Plate 39) by Evert Collier (died c. 1702), an artist who spent much of his career in Leyden. The tradition of Vanitas still lives, paintings that convey a moral message through the use of specific symbols refering to the transience of human existence, were common in Holland during the period. Instead of the customary signs of an opulent lifestyle, Collier focused on the transitory nature of learning. The dominant motif is a large, open volume of a seventeenth-century publication in English of the writing of the first-century C.E. Roman-Jewish historian Flavius Josephus. His books *The Jewish War* and *The Jewish Antiquities*, both written in the decades after the destruction of the Second Temple, were the only sources of knowledge during Collier's time of the Second Jewish Commonwealth Period. Josephus's historical documentation became increasingly important as a Protestant proof text for the Bible. Furthermore, Josephus's *Antiquities*, a retelling of Old Testament stories with Jewish legends, was an important source of iconographical inspiration for Dutch artists. The inclusion of a portrait of the humanist scholar Erasmus, who participated in the Latin translation of Josephus in 1524 and was among the first Christian theologians to revive the study of the Bible in the original Hebrew, adds further relevance to the implied Jewish content of the painting. Stylistically, the painting is a remarkable example of a Dutch still life with its emphasis on contrasting textures, verisimilitude, and dramatic contrasts of dark and light.

The Emancipation that spread throughout Europe in the post-Napoleonic period gave Jews the opportunity to gain skills as artists within the established system of the academies. The concurrent change in emphasis from religious to secular subjects—such as portraiture, landscape, and genre painting—provided a more comfortable environment for non-Christian artists. Portraiture was an area of specific importance for fledgling, academically trained painters, and it was in this area that many Jews excelled. The collection contains portraits by numerous Jewish artists of the period including Anton Graff (1736–1813); the Henschel Brothers (August, d. 1829; Friedrich, d. 1837; Moritz, d. 1862; and Wilhelm, d. 1865), four Jewish brothers from Breslau who specialized in portrait painting; Edouard Bendemann (1811–1889), who served as director of the Düsseldorf Academy; and Philip Weber (active mid-nineteenth century).

The greater familiarity that many Jews enjoyed with the culture outside the Jewish community gave rise to many of them having their portrait painted by both Jewish and non-Jewish artists. An unusual example in the collection (Plate 40) is the likeness of Sarah Lyons (d. 1808), an elderly British-Jewish woman who lived in East Anglia and sat for her portrait at the age of 101 for the later-to-be-celebrated British landscape painter John Constable (1776–1837). Early in his career, Constable's parents encouraged him to paint portraits in the hopes of his someday becoming a fashionable portrait painter. About one hundred of his portraits, falling within two types of portrayals, are known: intimate likenesses of friends and family members and more distanced presentations of humble laborers and other residents of the area such as Mrs. Lyons, his only identified Jewish sitter.

The practice of having one's portrait painted was especially popular in Germany between 1816 and 1848 during what is called the Biedermeier period, an era of emphasis on family and domestic values. It is understandable that Jews sought out painters from their own community for their portrait commissions. The museum has in its collection many examples of portraits of German Jews from this period, commissions that served a purpose similar to present-day photography. Several of the sitters can be identified by name. Some

are companion portraits of a husband and wife, undoubtedly intended for the family home. Others are portraits of well-known people such as Karl Ludwig Boerne and Moses Mendelssohn. There are portraits of famous rabbis as well as unidentified men whose traditional Jewish dress implies that they are scholars or rabbis. There are also examples of artist self-portraits and informal likenesses of family members. The range in demeanor and dress of all portraits in the collection reflects the various degrees to which Jews before the middle of the nineteenth century retained their ties or moved away from the Jewish community. A head covering of the type characteristically worn by observant Jewish women identifies Frau Ottinger (Plate 41) in her portrait by the little-known artist Samuelssohn. Painted in 1838, when many women were casting off traditional Jewish dress, Frau Ottinger's likeness attests to her adherence to Jewish laws and customs while at the same time taking part in the more secular and modern interest in documenting one's image.

By the mid-nineteenth century, many artists turned to subjects from everyday life, a trend that provided further enriching opportunities for Jews in the arts. Realism, a movement that emphasized a truthful and impartial representation of the real world and a meticulous observation of everyday life, started in France with such artists as Jean-François Millet (1814–1875) and Gustave Courbet (1819–1877) and spread throughout Central and Eastern Europe. In an effort to democratize the subjects for art, artists painted a wide range of scenes from everyday life from studies of peasant life and labor to the growing urban experience, all with a focus on ordinary people. In an era of growing industrialization and urbanization, much of

Plate 42. *Mourning,* Moritz Oppenheim, 1876–1877

this art concentrated on simple and religious rural life, seen by artists as symbolic of a purer, more reverent past.

Nostalgia for the past provided an especially effective tool for numerous Jewish artists to paint works on Jewish genre themes. Most, if not all of these artists, were a part of the cosmopolitan art world and yet, regardless of their degree of removal from it, looked to the former Jewish ghetto as fertile subject matter. Moritz Oppenheim (1800–1882), known as "the first Jewish painter," represented Jewish life and customs in the genteel, refined manner identified with the earlier Biedermeier period in the hope of improving the image of the Jew in the outside world. In his painting *Sabbath Afternoon*, c. 1860 (Plate 37), one of a series of works on Jewish family life and customs, Oppenheim revisited his youth in the pre-Emancipation Hanau ghetto, depicting his family discussing the weekly Torah portion following their Sabbath-day meal. He was also active as a book illustrator, repainting his famous genre works in grisaille and also illus-

trating books by contemporary German authors. A mourning scene (Plate 42), depicting customs surrounding the traditional seven-day observance of the death of a parent or child, is one of a series of eight paintings in grisaille on wood panel intended to illustrate the *Stories from Jewish Family Life*, a group of short fictional accounts by Solomon Hermann Mosenthal that feature the conflicts between traditional Jewish life and modernity and emancipation.

Religious genre paintings in the collection show the range of the nineteenth-century Jewish religious experience: a series of twenty-two illustrations in gouache by the little-known Polish artist K. Felsenhardt document observant Jewish life in Poland at the end of the century (Plates 43, 44); a more refined presentation of Jewish synagogue ritual in the painting *Cantor and Choir in the Synagogue* (Plate 45), by the Alsatian-born artist Edouard Moyse (b. 1827, active c. 1850–1881), may have been a study for a large-scale painting of a French synagogue service for the Paris Salon. The

Plate 45. *Cantor and Choir in the Synagogue,* Edouard Moyse, ca. 1860

American Jewish artist Henry Mosler (1841–1920) celebrated the 1866 inauguration of Temple Bene Yeshurun (Plum Street Temple) in Cincinnati (Plate 1) with a portrayal of the elaborate exterior of this famous landmark of Reform Judaism in America. The building was the first Moorish-style synagogue built in America and set the standard for other similar grand structures. Mosler, who lived for most of his career in Paris and was known for his paintings of Breton genre, during his years in Cincinnati had established ties with Rabbi Isaac Mayer Wise and other leading Jews of the city, associations that undoubtedly influenced his commemoration of the important new structure.

Jewish artists have rarely concentrated solely on Jewish subject matter, and most, if not all, have interpreted subjects similar to those of their non-Jewish colleagues. At times works on secular subjects by Jewish artists suggest a Jewish interpretation. The Dutch painter Joseph Israels (1824–1911) sometimes portrayed life in the Jewish quarter of Amsterdam but more often focused on the situation of humble peasants and fishermen in villages on the coast near Amsterdam. His painting of a peasant woman sewing at a table by a window (Plate 46), patiently and fearfully waiting for the return of her husband from the sea, reveals the artist's keen ability to capture the pathos of the human situation.

The British painter Simeon Solomon (1840–1905) was associated with the PreRaphaelite Brotherhood, a late nineteenth-century British art movement inspired by the simplicity of Italian art prior to Raphael and known for painting Christian, historical, and literary themes in a stylized but realistic manner. While Solomon sometimes portrayed biblical themes and the sensitive faces of young rabbis, he is known as well for his depictions of allegorical female figures with wistful, sad expressions. Among his most powerful works are colored chalk drawings such as *Young Woman* (Plate 47), a tender portrayal from late in his career that re-

Plate 47. *Young Woman*, Simeon Solomon, 1889

veals his unique ability to blend influences from the Italian Renaissance and the PreRaphaelites.

Camille Pissarro (1830–1903), a prominent French Impressionist who painted both rural and urban subjects, was born in St. Thomas to a Sephardic businessman who had emigrated to the West Indies from Bordeaux. At the age of twelve Pissarro was sent to school in France, where he lived with his relatives who were practicing Jews. While none of his paintings reflect his Jewish heritage, he never denied his background and, at the time of the Dreyfus Affair, decried those of his colleagues who took an anti-Dreyfusard position. *Pond at Montfoucault* (Plate 48) is a subject that Pissarro painted at different seasons over several years. Montfoucault was a small, isolated farm in South Brittany that belonged to the family of his friend Ludovic Piette, and his paintings of the enclosed agricultural community represent the first of Pissarro's detailed studies of rural life.

A tremendous efflorescence of Jewish participation in the arts during the first decades of the twentieth century occurred almost simultaneously in art centers worldwide: in France, Germany, the United States, and Russia. Jews became leaders in various aspects of the art world from painters and sculptors to dealers, leading critics, and collectors. While occasional references were made to their Jewish heritage, on the whole, most of the work was completely secular in nature, reflecting the thematic and stylistic interests of the general art community. This time period is well represented in the collection.

Jews were particularly active in the many art centers of Germany prior to World War II. Max Liebermann (1847–1935), in the course of his stellar career, studied in Berlin, Weimar, and Paris, spent his summers in Holland, and by 1884 had returned to his native city of Berlin, where he subsequently became a founding member and later president of the Berlin Secession, the association of modern-leaning artists who

gave the city its reputation for artistic innovation. Liebermann himself was a fairly traditional artist known for landscapes, rustic peasant genre scenes, and paintings of modern life. He now and then portrayed peasant Jewish life as a parallel to his studies of the Dutch peasant experience. It was primarily in his portraits, both commissioned and of friends and relatives, that his painting took on a more modern and psychological dimension. *Portrait of Artist's Wife and Granddaughter* (Plate 5) is one of his more intimate portrayals of family members. The painting, which has a distinguished history, was in a private collection when exhibited at the Prussian Academy of Art in 1926; it was next in the Berlin Jewish Museum where it was confiscated by the Nazis; it came to the Skirball Museum in the postwar era through the Jewish Cultural Reconstruction.

Plate 48. *Pond at Montfoucault*, Camille Pissarro, late 1860s

Plate 49. *Viki,* Oto Gutfreund, 1960 cast of 1913 sculpture

Plate 50. *Kaddish,* Joseph Budko, 1930

The sculptor Oto Gutfreund (1889–1927), who spent most of his professional career in Prague, was one of the few Jewish artists in the Expressionist movement associated with pre-World War I Germany. The bronze bust entitled *Viki* (Plate 49) is a cogent example of his forward-thinking approach to sculpture, which he conceived as the interaction of dynamic planes rather than as static mass. Like many of his fellow Czech artists, Gutfreund achieved a synthesis of the rational analysis of Cubism, the mystical and expressive elements of Gothic art and architecture, and the theatricality of Baroque art. Joseph Budko (1880–1940) represents the second generation of German Expressionism of the twenties and thirties. He was one of the few Jewish artists who focused on Jewish themes, primarily in illustrating traditional Jewish texts such as Genesis, the Psalms, and the Passover Haggadah and works on Jewish themes by such contemporary authors as Isaac Leyb Peretz, Sholem Asch, Sholem Alechem, and Hayyim Nahman Bialik. His painting *Kaddish* (Plate 50) was painted in 1930, just three years before he left Germany for Eretz Israel. In this work, Budko evoked the bleakness of the ghetto of his childhood in Eastern Europe and in the foreboding expressions of the men even seems to predict the future destruction of Jewish life in Germany.

Paris had a reputation as an international art center from the nineteenth century, and from 1905 until 1941, Jewish artists flocked there from many parts of the world: the United States, Germany, Eastern Europe, and even Eretz Israel. They congregated in the Montparnasse area, many living in studios in the ramshackle building known as La Ruche ("Beehive") and participating in the vibrant cafe life of the district. At one point there were forty-three Jewish artists as part of the community. Although they were always perceived as a "Jewish" group, only the paintings of Marc Chagall and Mane Katz offered much Jewish content. Many studied with Matisse and were aware of his expressive

70

use of color and exaggeration of form; most knew Picasso, seeing firsthand his daring breakthroughs in the Cubist analysis of form. Like these mentors, the artists in the School of Paris, including the Jewish artists, concentrated on generalized subjects such as portraiture and still life while experimenting with style and technique.

The museum collection includes paintings by Jewish artists from diverse backgrounds who were brought together in Paris because of their Jewish heritage. Jules Pascin (1885–1930) was born in Bulgaria to a prosperous Sephardic merchant and, having the fi-

nancial means, was sent for art training to Vienna and Munich, where he established himself as an illustrator of such modernist journals as *Simplicissimus* and *Jugend.* Pascin was one of the first to come to Paris, arriving in 1905, and eventually became a leader of the close-knit group of Jewish artists there. Although painted just a few years before he took his own life, *Girl in Boots* (Plate 51), a portrayal of a scantily dressed young woman with her gaze directed at the viewer, reveals Pascin's lifelong compassion for prostitutes and other lowlife or marginal subjects. The painting technique — contours sketchily drawn in charcoal com-

Plate 53. *Portrait of Bialik*, Chana Orloff, 1926

Plate 54. *Jacob and the Angel* [maquette], Jacques Lipchitz, 1931

bined with smokey, soft tones of turpentine-diluted oil —further intensifies Pascin's ability to probe the inner emotions of his subjects.

Pinchus Krémègne (1890–1981) was one of many Russian Jews who had first studied in Vilna and then came to Paris prior to World War I. He originally intended to become a sculptor but switched to painting in 1913. *Still Life of Fish and Fruit* (Plate 52), painted circa 1928, with its emphasis on the inherent flatness of the picture plane and the use of expressive, unnatural colors, reveals Krémègne's debt to Fauvism. A more immediate source for his expressive handling of paint and the emotional intensity of a seemingly benign subject

would have been Chaim Soutine (1893–1943), a leader of the Jewish artists in Paris with whom Krémègne had studied in Vilna.

Although the emphasis within the Circle of Montparnasse was on painting, the Skirball has an unusually strong collection of sculpture from this group of artists. The *Portrait of Bialik* (Plate 53), a bronze bust of the Hebrew writer by Chana Orloff (1881–1968), epitomizes Orloff's dual interests: her love for Eretz Israel and her debt to Cubist sculpture. Born in the Ukraine, Orloff emigrated to Eretz Israel in 1905 and in 1910 came to Paris to study drawing and sculpture. She was one of the few women who participated

Plate 55. *Bust of Jacob Kramer,* Jacob Epstein, ca. 1920

in the School of Paris and more specifically in Cubist experiments in form. Beginning in 1919, she began to specialize in portraits, receiving commissions for likenesses of cultural leaders and artists in Paris and in Eretz Israel, which she visited throughout her career. Bialik probably sat for this bust during her trip there in 1925. The first of her sculptures done in a moderate Cubist style, this work embodies the stripped-down forms and concentration on the personality of the sitter that are the two most distinguishing features of her portraits.

Jacques Lipchitz (1891–1973) is recognized as the sculptor who most successfully translated the Cubist idiom into sculptural form. Born in Lithuania, the son of a wealthy banking family, Lipchitz came to Paris in 1909. His early works were subjects more typical of Cubist painters: harlequins, musicians, mu-

sical instruments, and still lifes. *Jacob and the Angel* (Plate 54) is a maquette for a four-foot-high sculpture cast in bronze in 1932 that is considered one of his greatest works. It represents a change—to biblical subjects and to a more fluid and baroque sculptural form—that persisted through the rest of Lipchitz's long and prolific career. Lipchitz looked to the Bible for guidance to understand the tragic events of his own time, and he turned to convulsive, tormented forms in anticipation of the terrible future for the Jews of Europe.

Sir Jacob Epstein (1880–1959) was born in New York to immigrants from Poland. The early years of his career typify the experience of immigrant Jewish artists in New York, and his stint in Paris, from 1902 to 1905, was quite brief. He then moved to London, where he built a reputation as one of England's avant-garde artists, often criticized in his early years there for the crudeness of his directly carved, wood sculptures. *Bust of Jacob Kramer,* c. 1920 (Plate 55), represents his change in medium to bronze and to a more conservative style characteristic of his portraits beginning in the 1920s. Epstein was a close friend to Kramer (1892–1962), who was a painter, and successfully captured his sitter's intense personality.

The circle of Jewish artists in Paris ended abruptly in 1941 with the Nazi invasion. Many sought refuge in the south of France; a few were saved through the efforts of Varian Fry, an emissary in France of the United States Emergency Committee; many perished in the camps. Jewish artists gradually returned to France in the postwar period. Some, including Hannah Orloff, had found refuge in Switzerland; Marc Chagall had spent the war years in the United States. The Polish-born artist Maryan [Pincas Burstein] (1927–1977), who survived the horrors of labor camps, ghettos, and concentration camps, arrived in Paris in 1950 after having spent time in displaced persons camps and in Israel. His personal experiences, coupled with the pre-

Plate 56. *The Drillers*, Aaron Goodleman, 1933

vailing fascination by artists such as Jean Dubuffet with art of the insane and disturbed, had a strong impact on the oeuvre of Maryan. *Kapparot* (Plate 57), a bold and expressive visualization of the custom practiced by some Orthodox Jews in which the sins of a person are symbolically transferred to a fowl, was painted in 1952 during the time that Maryan concentrated on overtly Jewish themes. From 1960 until he took his own life, he painted imaginary, tormented figure types termed "personnages" that, although he denied it, grew out of his Holocaust experiences.

The large number of Jewish immigrants and children of immigrants who became professional artists bespeaks the wider opportunities available in the United States at the turn of the century. Most came from poor families without previous exposure to the visual arts. Large numbers of young Jews studied together at New York's Educational Alliance School in the Lower East Side, established by German Jews to Americanize the East European newcomers. Many were involved in Yiddish secularist culture that dominated so much of Jewish life including the visual arts. Aaron Goodleman (1890–1978) is one of many Jewish artists of the period influenced stylistically by such modernist movements as Cubism, which he used as a vehicle for liberal social content. His sculpture *The Drillers* (Plate 56) glorifies labor, a subject that fascinated such other American artists of the depression era as Louis Lozowick and Charles Sheeler. Goodleman went on to create empathetic images, first of those Americans left homeless by the depression in America and then in memory of those Jews who perished in the Holocaust.

Peter Krasnow (1887–1980) was an East European immigrant artist who chose a different path by settling in 1922 in Los Angeles, where he was one of the few modernist artists. Working in isolation as an artist and cut off from the large Jewish community of the East Coast, Krasnow concentrated on subjects from the Hebrew Scriptures and Jewish life in Eastern Eu-

rope. In *The Wanderers*, 1927 (Plate 58), a self-portrait and a portrait of his wife Rose, Krasnow imagined being forced to leave their home, perhaps revisiting the pogroms of his childhood. The Skirball Museum has especially strong holdings of works representative of the various periods of his career, donated by Krasnow just before his death. Godfrey Frankel (b. 1920) is one of several American photographers who, in the vein of Social Realism, focused on images of everyday America. In the years just after World War II, Frankel captured the essence of the Lower East Side in New York with a series of nostalgia-laden storefront scenes, such as *Scissors Shop* (Plate 59).

The art of modern and contemporary Israeli artists is another important focus of the collection. While aware of international art currents, many of these artists select subjects and forms that relate specifically to issues of concern to modern-day Israel. Anna Ticho (1894–1980) formed the nucleus of a group of German artists who trained as Expressionists in Europe and emigrated between 1912 and 1930. One of Israel's foremost graphic artists, she focused throughout her career on the landscape of Jerusalem, capturing its unique sublimity as in this late drawing, *Judean Hills*, ca. 1970 (Plate 60). Moshe Gershuni (b. 1936) is a native-born Israeli who translates his passionate emotions for his country and the Jewish people to his art. *Little Angels*, 1987 (Plate 61), speaks of the void caused by the Holocaust and the potential for renewal with the State of Israel. Gabi Klasmer (b. 1950) represents the generation of Expressionist artists in Israel who came of age in the 1980s. In his aggressively painted diptych *Shimshon*, 1982 (Plate 62), Klasmer uses the persona of the famous biblical figure to address the uncertainty and confusion he feels about the Land of Israel and its destiny. Zvi Goldstein (b. 1947) was born in Roumania and although he emigrated at the age of eleven, his background in a Communist country has influenced his art in both idea and form. He has

Plate 59. *Scissors Shop*, Godfrey Frankel, 1946

Plate 60. *Judean Hills*, Anna Ticho, ca.1970

Plate 61. *Little Angels*, Moshe Gershuni, 1987

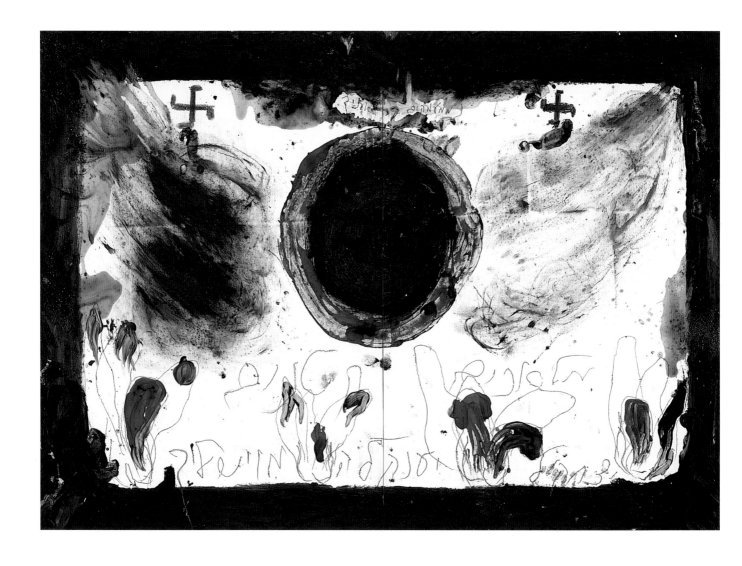

Plate 62. *Shimshon*, Gabi Klasmer, 1982

Plate 63. *Element C-15*, Zvi Goldstein, 1985

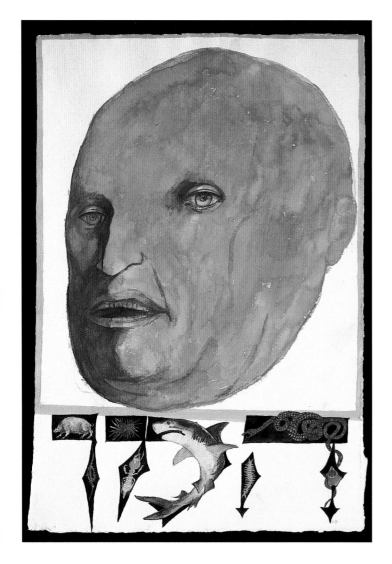

Plate 64. *Haman*, Leonard Baskin, 1980

taken his cue from political events staged by Constructivist artists during the Revolution. *Element C-15*, 1985 (Plate 63), is one of a series of works from the 1980s in which Goldstein invented a potentially menacing public arena comprised of propagandistic wall texts and mysterious metal, three-dimensional floor objects, perceived interchangeably as searchlights, megaphones, or abstract metal sculptures.

The category in the collection that has experienced unprecedented growth is that of contemporary works relating to the Jewish experience, many of them either inspired by Judaica in the collection or motivated by support from the museum director or curators. With this encouragement from culturally specific museums, artists since the 1970s have become less self-conscious about delving into their own background — in this case, their Jewish heritage — for thematic, symbolic, and stylistic sources. While the subject range and conceptual bases of these paintings, graphics, and sculptures are vast, the work can be organized into broad categories: Jewish texts and rituals; Jewish history; the Holocaust; personal Jewish experiences; and the pursuit of spirituality.

Leonard Baskin (b. 1922) is an artist with a thorough grounding in Judaism who has often turned to Jewish themes and Hebrew texts as source material to express his own humanist convictions. His insightful interpretation of *Haman* (Plate 64) is one of thirty-seven images from a commission by the Central Conference of American Rabbis to illustrate the Five Scrolls or *Megillot* (the Scrolls of Ruth, Esther, Ecclesiastes, Song of Songs, and Lamentations). Using his characteristic figurative, expressive style, he convincingly conveyed the idea of evil with associations to both ancient and modern experiences.

Jewish history, traditions, and the idea of a sacred Jewish place are concepts that have intrigued many contemporary artists. Seattle-based photographer Harry Zeitlin (b. 1952) is known for his enig-

Plate 65. *The Past: The Great Synagogue of Danzig*, Ruth Weisberg, 1983

Plate 66. *Collage,* Hannelore Baron, 1981

matic examinations of the tension and balance of the natural world. His black-and-white photograph, *The Western Wall at Night,* 1982 (Plate 69), is one of a series of close-up, detailed views of the monumental remains of the Temple in Jerusalem, which has been a powerful symbol to artists since the nineteenth century. With its sharp angle cutting the composition almost in half, Zeitlin suggests the minimalist aesthetics of early twentieth-century Russian Suprematism; yet, the close-up details of scrubby plants emerging from the Wall on the left and a full moon at the upper right imply an actual environment.

The Holocaust has become a major factor of Jewish identity to many of today's Jewish artists. For some, it is an inquiry into their own dreadful experiences. For many American-born Jewish artists, it was confronting the historical facts of the Holocaust that led them to explore their own backgrounds. Hannelore Baron (1926–1987) was born in Germany and fled to the United States with her parents after *Kristallnacht.* A self-taught painter, collage artist, and sculptor, her goal was to transcend her own experiences and make art about the human condition. *Collage,* 1981 (Plate 66), is an excellent example of her small, fragile collages comprised of rice paper, scraps of cloth, and stamped symbols. While the symbols can be read to refer to her own traumatic experiences, the horizontal, scroll-like format can be understood as a metaphor for a Torah scroll. Dina Dar (1939–1995), a pioneer in the medium of electrography, overtly explores her life as a child in Poland during the Holocaust when she and her family hid out as Christians. *Joseph's Coat of Fate,* 1990 (Plate 6), is one of several works that resulted from a trip she took to Portugal to meet the *Conversos,* people in that country who had been forced to convert to Christianity at the time of the Inquisition but have somehow revived their links to Judaism; she asks whether she would have retained her Judaism if forced to conceal herself as a Christian for decades or even generations. Using a format of multiple freeze frames to tell her story and ask her questions, Dar interweaves flowers nurtured in her own garden, family photographs and documents, and a personal garment, a wool vest that her mother made for her from a pillow. Ruth Weisberg (b. 1942) is an American-born artist who has great respect for history and tradition: for Judaism, art history, and the history of women. In *The Past: The Great Synagogue of Danzig,* 1983 (Plate 65), a painting on unstretched canvas, Weisberg combined historical fact from the Holocaust with elements of

Plate 67. *Holy, Holy, Holy Is The Lord of Hosts*, Laurie Gross, 1984

personal illusion, blending time and memory. By including an image of herself as a child within the circle of European Jews of the 1930s who stand in front of the Great Synagogue of Danzig, which was sold to finance the Jewish community's mass exodus from the city, she becomes the witness and the victim. Less than a decade later, Weisberg completed one of the masterpieces of contemporary Jewish art expression, now in the museum collection, *The Scroll*, a ninety-foot drawing in scroll form that interweaves Weisberg's life story, her evolution as a knowledgeable Jew, and the meanings and traditions of the Jewish life cycle.

Several artists have been motivated to use their art for one of the most difficult and elusive purposes, to explore and communicate the Jewish spiritual experience. Laurie Gross (b. 1952) started her career as a weaver but as her commitment and understanding of Judaism grew, she likewise infused her artwork with serious Jewish thought and interpretation. Continuing to use the medium of weaving, Gross moved from functional items to woven sculptures that operate on the level of visual biblical commentary. *Holy, Holy, Holy is the Lord of Hosts*, 1984 (Plate 67), was inspired by a nineteenth-century Torah valance, a textile placed above the Torah Ark in the synagogue, that she saw in the museum collection. Gross transformed the image of sheltering wings on the valance to abstract forms that likewise convey the sense of protection and holiness. Bill Aron (b. 1941) is a celebrated photographer who has throughout his career concentrated almost exclusively on Jewish themes. *Learning*, 1995 (Plate 68), is one of a series commissioned by the museum for the Skirball Cultural Center's core exhibition, "Visions and Values." The pair of hands, one old and the other young, that together grasp the Torah pointer as the man guides the child through the reading provide a succinct and poignant message that has resonance for many Jews of our time—the challenge of carrying on honored traditions and values of the Jewish religion.

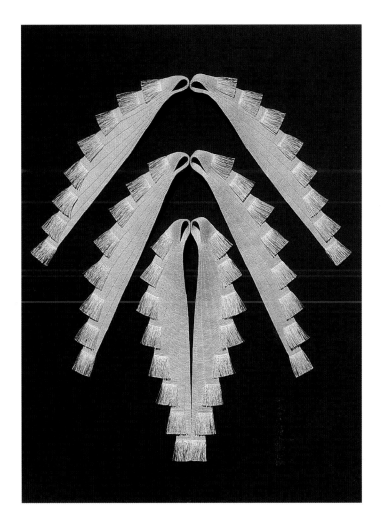

NOTES

1. Correspondence between Salli Kirschstein and Dr. Adolph Oko, Librarian of Hebrew Union College, 1925-1926, Skirball Museum Archives.

2. For background on the iconography and development of the Book of Esther in art with its culmination in seventeenth-century Holland, see Madlyn M. Kahr, "The Book of Esther in Seventeenth-Century Dutch Art," Doctoral Dissertation, New York University, 1966.

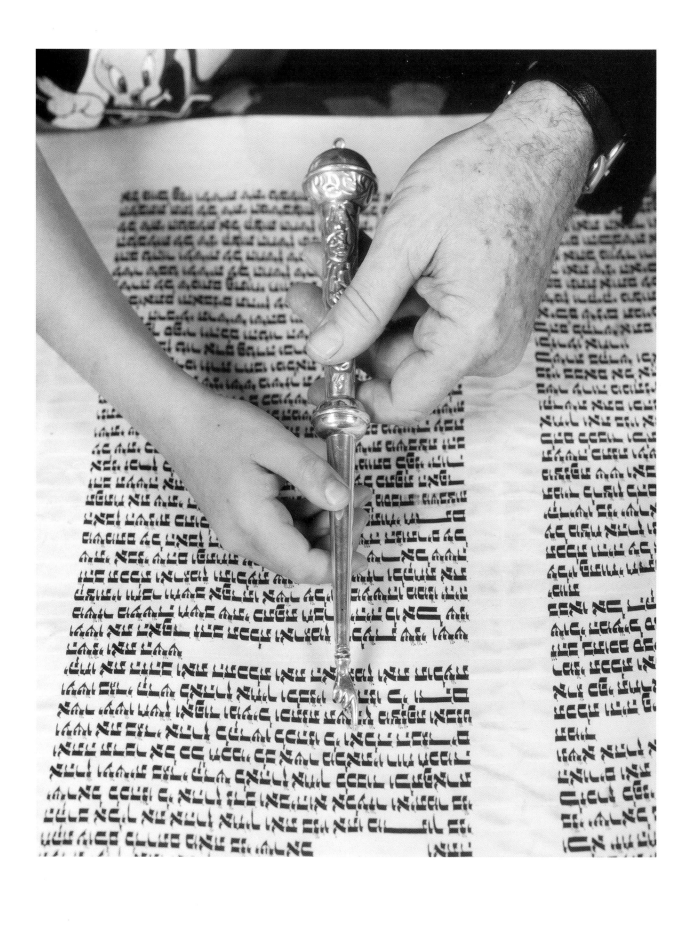

Plate 69. *Western Wall at Night*, Harry Zeitlin, 1982

PROJECT
AMERICANA

*Collecting Memories and
Exploring the American
Jewish Experience*

GRACE COHEN GROSSMAN

S OME EIGHTY YEARS AGO, Professor Gotthard Deutsch, who taught history and philosophy at Hebrew Union College, was an early advocate of the museum as a repository of social history. "What Belongs in the Union Museum" reflects his perspective.

> Few people know what a Museum stands for. It is a collection of historic monuments. There was a time when people considered only works on history, political documents and objects connected with prominent people as illustrations of history. We know differently now. History is made by the masses, as it affects the masses. It, therefore, must illustrate the life of the people. Any object, giving us an insight into this life, a letter written by plain people on the average concerns of their life, the tools of a mechanic, an article used in the household, the implements of worship, the furniture of a schoolroom and similar objects show us how people lived. The collections of articles illustrating the life of the Jews must be the object of a Jewish museum...[for they] give us a picture of Jewish life.

Deutsch's comments were accompanied by an appeal: "Many objects that were held in high esteem by those who were familiar with its use are today to be found hidden in garrets. You can redeem them from this oblivion by presenting them to the [Union] Museum."[1]

Recognizing the continuing validity of Deutsch's perspective and appeal, Project Americana was developed during the planning process for the Skirball Cultural Center. Through a broad array of exhibits, public programs, and educational resources, the Cultural Center will explore the American Jewish experience and the millennial tradition to which it is bound. Focusing on the ideals, realities, and challenges of American Jewry, it will explore the rich tapestry of religious and ethnic diversity that has thrived in this country.

To further the Center's objectives, Project Americana was established in 1985 as a concerted national effort to collect and preserve objects of Jewish history and ceremony, memorabilia from everyday life, folk art, and fine art—all of which document the spectrum of Jewish life in America. As a resource, Project Americana complements the Skirball Museum's already-existing major collection, which is primarily European in origin, as well as the wealth of documents and photographs available in the American Jewish Archives and the vast holdings of the Hebrew Union College-Jewish Institute of Religion libraries.

Project Americana was launched under the chairmanship of Mark C. Levy with the acquisition of a 1912 can of Rokeach Scouring Powder, found in mint condition in LaPorte, Indiana. The red, white, and blue label emblazoned with a prominent image of a six-

Plate 70. *Shiviti*, Phillip Cohen, 1861

pointed star is a quintessential example of how every-day objects used by ordinary people can trigger personal and collective memories for American Jews (Plate 90).

The first task undertaken was a survey of historic items of Americana already in the Skirball Museum's collection. Among the objects so identified was a miniature portrait of Bernard Gratz (1738–1801) by Charles Peale Polk (1767–1822) (Plate 71). Gratz was a merchant who supported the American Revolution and actively worked against the practice, common in some of the former colonies, of requiring public office holders to take an oath of allegiance to Christianity. A sampler made by Sarah Peixotto, daughter of Moses Levi Maduro Peixotto, a *hazzan* (clergyman) of Congregation Shearith Israel in New York, the oldest American synagogue, also dates from the early nineteenth century. Like other young girls, Sarah Peixotto was taught to do needlework at an early age; samplers, with the alphabet, numbers, sometimes a text, and often the girl's name and the date, were typical of their handicrafts. A rare illustrated marriage contract (Plate 81) from New York, dated 1820 and witnessed by M. L. M. Peixotto, is to date Project Americana's oldest acquisition.

Also located in the survey are portraits of Judah P. Benjamin (Plate 72), his wife Natalie, and baby daughter Ninette. Judah P. Benjamin (1811–1884), who served as a United States Senator from Louisiana before the Civil War, became Secretary of War and later Secretary of State for the Confederacy. The Rev. Ferdinand Sarner, who immigrated to the United States in 1859, served in the Civil War on the Union side as one of the first Jewish chaplains. After being wounded at Gettysburg, Sarner left the Army and returned to the pulpit. A lovely Victorian water service presented to him in 1878 by the Confirmation class of Temple Beth-El Emeth in Memphis, Tennessee, was later given to the museum (Plate 73). Another student tribute is a Torah shield and finials presented to Isaac Mayer Wise

(1819–1900), founder of Hebrew Union College, on the occasion of his eightieth birthday (Plate 75). The democratic process of nineteenth-century Jewish organizational life is represented by a ballot box of the International Order of B'nai B'rith, founded in 1843, the first and still largest Jewish service organization.

Adaptability has long been a hallmark of the Jewish experience. Wherever they settled, whatever the political, economic, and social environment, Jews managed to find a way to adjust, even as they maintained strong ties to tradition. Typically Jewish ceremonial objects were influenced by the cultural milieu in which they were created, taking on the stylistic form and often the symbolic content current in the majority culture. Exemplifying this phenomenon is a *mizraḥ*, documented in the survey, made in 1850 in Cincinnati by Moses H. Henry (Plate 74). A *mizraḥ*, from the Hebrew word meaning east, is a marker placed on the eastern wall as a symbolic orientation for prayer toward Jerusalem in remembrance of the Holy Temple. For this reason, images of the Temple are often used in *mizraḥ* designs. This highly complex *mizraḥ* is also an

omer calendar, used to count the forty-nine days between the holidays of Passover and Shavuot. It combines biblical text, images from Jewish ritual, references to the Temple, and, very prominently, the patriotic motif of the American eagle perching astride a shield and bunting of the "stars and stripes." The text also includes the standard Prayer for the Government, variants of which were recited by Jews on Sabbath mornings in synagogues to honor the national governmental leadership. Particularly noteworthy is the meshing of Jewish symbols with such Masonic emblems as the plumb line, compass, trowel, and chisel. Masons use building images because their ceremonies refer to God as the "Great Architect of the Universe." During the nineteenth century Jews commonly joined Masonic lodges in tribute to a liberal organization that aimed to promote brotherhood and foster morality. Many Jews believed that the United States provided the best environment to foster Reform Jewish and Freemason ideals.[2]

A similar reference to the ancient Jerusalem Temple combined with a patriotic motif is found on a *shiviti* made by Phillip Cohen in 1861 (Plate 70). The

term *shiviti* comes from the phrase *shiviti Adonai le-negdi tamid*, "I have set the Lord always before me" (Psalm 16:8). Cohen used the standard text and visual references to the Temple, but set an American flag atop each of the columns. The American flag is also used as a motif on a Torah binder made in 1890 in Trinidad, Colorado, to mark the birth of Gilbert Sanders (Plate 78). This *Wimpel* represents the transmission of a tradition from Central Europe to the United States. In seventeenth-century Germany, it became customary to make a Torah binder from the swaddling cloth (*Wimpel*) used to wrap the eight-day-old infant boy at his circumcision ceremony. The binder was made by cutting the cloth into three or four sections and sewing them together to form a long band. The binder was then embroidered or painted with the child's name and birthdate and the blessing recited at the circumcision ceremony in the hope that the child would grow up to study Torah, marry, and do good deeds. *Wimpels* were typically made by the mother or grandmother and were frequently personalized with symbolic motifs.

These and other objects located during the initial survey not only provided the nucleus for exhibit planning but helped formulate a wish list reflecting many facets of the American Jewish experience from colonial to contemporary times. Using this guideline, which broadly covered the topics of immigration, family and home, synagogue, community organizations, education, occupations, and the arts, the next task of Project Americana was to ascertain which types of objects were generally saved and could likely be acquired by the museum.[3] The response to this quest of finding the often-hidden treasures of the American Jewish experience has been tremendous. As the project progressed, specific themes emerged as focal points for collecting, yet the museum was also able to collect broadly following the original guidelines. Hundreds of individuals have given their personal heirlooms and shared their cherished memories, so that, in turn, the Skirball Museum can present them to the wider community. Items have also come from synagogues and other Jewish institutions and organizations, some through such Project Americana rescue efforts as expeditions to various crawl spaces, basements, and attics, to collect and properly preserve historical materials.

One area of special concentration covers items that interweave American and Jewish imagery. These form a fascinating index to nuances of American Jewish identity. Though changes are evident in recent years, the historical examples all represent the message that American and Jewish ideals are congruent, and they underscore the hopeful promise of American liberty.[4] Just as combined American and Jewish imagery is found on *mizraḥ* plaques and Torah binders from the nineteenth century, dozens of later examples which merge these symbols have been located, documenting every sphere of the American Jewish experience. Among the ceremonial objects are marriage contracts with American and Zionist flags; a *hallah* cover for the Sabbath with an American flag; a Statue of Liberty Hanukkah lamp crafted by Manfred Anson to commemorate the centennial of the Statue (Plate 120); a Torah mantle made by Peachy Levy, with the flag and the verse "Proclaim Liberty Throughout the Land" (Leviticus 25:10) inscribed on the Liberty Bell (Plate 121); and as a memorial tribute to Judith Resnick, astronaut on the ill-fated Challenger space shuttle, a contemporary prayer in the form of a medieval Hebrew manuscript illumination by Darrie Schlesinger. There are objects from Jewish organizations, such as the charter of the Southern California Brotherhood Association from 1936, which includes an American eagle and both five- and six-pointed stars; and from the Jewish National Fund, a card school children used in the 1950s to collect their dimes for the purchase of a tree in Israel, on which the American holidays of Thanksgiving and July Fourth are represented along with the dates of Jewish festivals.

Articles of popular culture include Yiddish sheet music with the title song "Long Live the Land of the Free" and the image of Columbia, gowned in stars and stripes; and an advertisement for Mogen David Cherry Wine with the likeness of George Washington (Plate 85). Objects demonstrating Jewish patriotism include a fund-raising poster issued by the Jewish Welfare Board, ironically dated the week the Armistice was signed in November, 1918, depicting soldiers engaged in the heat of battle and captioned "Civilians When We Go Through This We Need All the Help We Can Get." During World War II a "V" for Victory flag, in red, white, and blue, with prayers for the United States and President Roosevelt, written in Hebrew, English, and Yiddish, was proudly hung in Jewish homes (Plate 87). During the Bicentennial of the American Revolution, many objects reflected the merging of symbols including a Bicentennial Haggadah. This collection continues to grow.

The premise of Project Americana is that everyone has a valuable story to tell and that objects play an important role in the preservation of those cherished stories. In the process of collecting for Project Americana, it has been fascinating to see what has been saved and what has become a family heirloom. Because many of the Skirball Museum's exhibits explore the identity and collective memory of the Jewish people, Project Americana has become a way of collecting memory of American Jewish life. Whenever an object is acquired by the museum, every effort is made to record background information on the maker and user. For example, Jewish weddings, and especially the clothing worn at weddings, have mirrored the taste of the general population. When a wedding gown is acquired, we also try to document information about the bride and groom and the wedding itself, as well as collect other objects related to the event: a photograph, an invitation, a pressed bouquet, a memento from the celebration. All of these help recapture a moment to be

shared with later generations, providing a cultural context for the exhibit. The museum has been able to acquire items representing Jewish marriages of every decade since 1890.

These accounts are a most valuable aspect of the interpretation of objects in Cultural Center exhibits and programs. While, at times, little can be learned about the history of the acquisition, it is fortunate that numerous individuals have had much to communicate about their individual experience and personal contributions, telling stories connected to the objects and the particular meaning of objects preserved. Thus, the ongoing oral histories, undertaken as a part of Project Americana, which we hope to expand greatly in the Cultural Center, are a means of furthering understanding of a variety of personal experiences.

Many people preserved objects they or their forebears had brought with them to America. Hopes and

dreams, as well as the circumstances under which Jews left their Old World homes, are reflected in the personal keepsakes and household effects immigrants brought with them to the New World. These objects reflect the choices people could and did make when they left their homes and embarked on what was, even under the best of circumstances, physically arduous and emotionally trying. The journey to America was a voyage of change, and except in rare instances, there was no looking back. For the immigrants, the momentum was always forward, toward the promise of America.

It is fascinating to discover what people have saved from their journeys—trunks and suitcases, passports and family records, a special suit of clothes, and treasured personal items. The first Jewish settlement on the North American mainland was in the Dutch colony of New Amsterdam in 1654, when twenty-three Jews arrived from Recife, Brazil; the Jewish popula-

tion grew slowly until there were about two thousand Jews living in America at the time of the Revolution. The earliest immigration-related objects to be discovered by Project Americana date from the substantial mid-nineteenth-century immigration of Jews seeking to escape political and social upheaval in Central Europe. When teenaged Marcus Jonas set off from his native Germany in the 1860s to seek his prospects in California, his father entrusted him with the family *shofar,* the ram's horn used on the High Holidays. Arriving in America, Jonas carefully crafted a special box, fashioned to echo the form of the *shofar,* to protect the revered ceremonial object (Plate 76).

The vast majority of American Jews trace their ancestry back to the great wave of immigrants, including some two million Jews, who arrived from Eastern Europe between 1880 and 1920. Many East European immigrants brought along ritual objects, typically brass candlesticks and silver kiddush cups, as well as practical domestic items such as hand-embroidered bed linens and copper kitchenware. Pillows and bedcovers were needed because they knew from relatives that only wooden bunks were provided for steerage-class passengers. Familiar kitchenware gave the homemaker a fast start in the new land with the right pot to cook the family's favorite delicacy. Surprisingly, many immigrants from Eastern Europe also brought along samovars for making tea (Plate 86). Though large and cumbersome, these were a way to maintain old customs in a new land. The lingering nostalgia for kitchenware, even after families had been settled for decades in the United States, enabled the museum to outfit an entire kitchen, which incorporates both objects brought from Europe and those purchased in America before World War II (Plate 88).

While the typical pattern for East European immigrants was to travel westward across the Atlantic, other routes were taken as well. Revan Komaroff's family went eastward via Shanghai before coming to the United States and settling in California. Komaroff, who celebrated his Bar Mitzvah in Shanghai in 1904, brought with him the tallit (prayer shawl) and tallit bag beautifully embroidered for him in China (Plate 96).

The turn of the century also saw a significant immigration of Sephardic Jews, many from Turkey and the island of Rhodes. In order to help preserve customs and traditions brought by Sephardic Jews to America, Project Americana has embarked on a special effort to acquire objects reflecting the Sephardic heritage. A recent addition to the collection is a *tavla de dulsé,* used to serve sweets in welcoming guests to a home (Plate 93). A *tavla de dulsé,* typically included by the bride in her trousseau, was an integral part of Sephardic culture in these Eastern Mediterranean communities.

Preparing to leave for America was very different for those who fled Nazi-threatened Europe in the 1930s. Some who left early were able to take many household goods, so even though they felt a tremendous sense of dislocation, they could begin to reestablish themselves surrounded by the familiar trappings of home. Others left only with what they could pack in a few suitcases. Teenaged Marion Stiebel Siciliano left Germany in April 1938, for what her mother told her was to be a vacation in Italy. Instead, they made for Portugal, then travelled to France, and finally arrived in the United States that year in September. She saved the suitcases from her trip, along with her tennis racket and little accordion, with its warm memories of a happy childhood. Her mother saved the typewriter she had taken along, which had stood her in good stead when she arrived in the United States and used it in her work to help support the family.

Very poignant are the few objects Holocaust survivors have given the museum. These include the yellow badges that Jews were forced to wear as a mark of identification, which some survivors saved to bear witness to what they had experienced. Benjamin Pinkowitz left Frankfurt after *Kristallnacht* in November, 1938,

and went to the Netherlands, which he, like many others, thought would be a safe haven. During the war, he and other family members were deported to Westerbork and then to Theresienstadt. Somehow, he managed to keep hidden and to use clandestinely the family's Scroll of Esther, which later came to the museum through his son. A very special memento of the renewal of the human spirit is a chess set made by children in a Displaced Persons camp after the war and given to Project Americana by a friend of the art teacher who had worked with the children.

In the postwar era, a significant number of Jewish immigrants came to the United States, many of them because of political conditions in their native country. More recently, there has been a great influx of Jews from the former Soviet Union, Iran, and South Africa. An effort is being made to collect items from these newcomers as well.

A natural extension of the focus on "coming to America" is the phenomenon of "starting over." What was the acculturation process like? How did people cope? What forces influenced their ability to succeed? What many an immigrant learned on arrival was that America was not a guaranteed *goldeneh medineh*, a golden land, and that acculturation would by no means prove easy. By 1910, there were large Jewish-immigrant populations in New York, Chicago, Detroit, Cleveland, and Boston. During World War I, at a time when many Jews lived in poverty in the new ghettos of these cities and many newly arrived young men were serving in the war effort, the U.S. Department of Agriculture issued a poster, printed in several languages, sternly cautioning the immigrants, "Food Will Win the War - You Came Here Seeking Freedom. You Must Now Help to Preserve It. Wheat is Needed for the Allies. Waste Nothing" (Plate 122).

The acculturation process was a very harsh reality for many. In the cover illustration of the Yiddish sheet music for "A Brivele Dem Taten" (A Letter to the Father), the father forlornly bids farewell to his son about to depart from Europe and, in the words of the song, asks him to write to ease his loneliness; later he greets his son in America and looks at him, in his new American clothes, as if he is a stranger (Plate 84). Similarly, the cultural differences are immediately recognizable, in a painting by Marlene Zimmerman entitled *First Wedding in the New Land: Mama, Papa and the Kids,* based on an actual wedding photograph. No one seems very comfortable: older members of the family still wear the old-fashioned garb of the "Old Country" while the younger members are all dressed in contemporary American style (Plate 80).

The immigrants did their share, they worked hard and many of the immigrants from Eastern Europe—and certainly their children—took advantage of the possibilities for advancement afforded through free public education.[5] They succeeded by blending the values and skills they brought with them and the unique opportunities provided in America.

An important factor in the acculturation process was the Jewish community and its manifold resources. From the earliest years of Jewish settlement in America, efforts were made to establish a strong community: synagogues were established and schools were founded. Social action was a phenomenon evident early on as Jewish organizations mobilized in response to the needs of Jews in other countries as well as participating in philanthropic causes at home.

< Plate 80. *First Wedding in the New Land:*
Mama, Papa and the Kids,
Marlene Zimmerman, 1972

Plate 81. New York Ketubbah, 1819

Sometimes there was ambivalence. In the face of the great wave of immigrants from Eastern Europe, many of the German Jews, already well-established in America, were less than enthusiastic about the influx of their less modern coreligionists. The challenge was met by creating institutions meant to aid new immigrants and foster Americanization. Though the motivation may have been less than meritorious, the results were nonetheless commendable, with many new immigrants benefitting from the services made available to them. The range of Jewish organizations in existence by the early years of the twentieth century is phenomenal, from hundreds of *lantsmannshaftn,* benevolent societies of people who came from the same town or region in Eastern Europe, to Jewish Masonic lodges, and from conservative German Jewish groups to Socialist labor groups. Religious life also evolved, so that by the late nineteenth century, rabbinical schools had come into existence for traditionalist and modernist Jews. Several hundred items related to Jewish organizations and institutions have been acquired by Project Americana, reflecting the broad spectrum of interests and concerns of American Jews.

A key topic explored by Project Americana is occupations. What did Jews do when they came to America? How did they make a living? While it is common to cite the promise of American liberty as a motivation for new immigrants, it is also important to stress the economic opportunity America represented. While none of the work-related objects found date any earlier than the late nineteenth century and are thus primarily representative of the East European

Plate 82. Synagogue Lions, Marcus C. Illions, early 20th century

immigration, the Levi Strauss & Co. Archives presented the museum with a reproduction of the earliest Levi jeans as well as some of the company's early advertisements (Plate 123). Levi Strauss immigrated to the United States from his native Bavaria in 1848 and in 1850, during the California Gold Rush, started a dry-goods business in Sacramento.[6] Strauss represents an entrepreneurial spirit characteristic of many of the German Jewish immigrants of the mid-nineteenth century, many of whom arrived as young single men and forged out on their own to the South and West to seek their fortunes.

Many of the objects acquired relate to what might be termed the service-based economy of the neighborhood. "Tools of the Trade" as represented in Project Americana recalls the baker, the barber, the butcher, the carpenter, the dry-goods merchant, the grocery store owner, the iceman, and the jeweler. But the most

widespread occupation of those arriving from Eastern Europe, including young unmarried women, was to work in the garment industry. Many individuals saved their tailoring tools, many even kept old manual sewing machines (Plate 89). The conditions in the infamous sweatshops led to the formation of unions, in which Jewish labor organizers played a significant role.

Some individuals were able to transfer skills they had learned in the "Old Country" and transform them into an economically viable trade in America. Such was the case with Marcus Charles Illions, born in Vilna in 1865 and apprenticed at age nine to a carving shop. He left Vilna for England as a teenager, arrived in the United States in 1888, and soon became known as a master carver with his own shop in Coney Island. Illions gained renown as a maker of carousels. The same deftness and vitality evidenced in his carousel

Plate 83. Memorial Papercut, 1901

Plate 84. *A Brivele dem Taten* Sheet Music, 1911

animals are found in a lively pair of synagogue lions made by Illions for a Brooklyn synagogue and acquired by the museum (Plate 82). The museum was also fortunate in conducting an oral history with Illions's youngest son Barney, who worked with his father as a "painter of the ponies" and made possible the acquisition of fifty photographs from the Illions workshop.

As time went on, some enterprising individuals turned to more risk-taking occupations such as distilling and cigarmaking, both represented in the collection. The film industry, also a speculative endeavor, was also largely pioneered by Jews. The museum has begun planning a future exhibit on Hollywood, the film industry, and the image of Jews in the movies, for which objects are being sought to add to the collection.

By the second generation, the children of the East European immigrants were working in different oc-

cupations. Many young women became teachers and social workers. Many became professionals. The museum has acquired the equipment Jacob Paley used in his "Sunrise Pharmacy" in New York and the optometry implements of Dr. Reuben Greenspoon, an innovator in the field of contact lenses, who worked in Beverly Hills. Greenspoon worked with many actors in the film industry, using contact lenses to help achieve special makeup effects.

A concentrated effort has been made to collect advertisements and promotional items that highlight the important role Jewish businesses and Jewish consumers played in maintaining Jewish identity and ritual practice. These objects include products that demonstrate an awareness by general food suppliers of the Jewish market, such as early twentieth-century cookbooks like Crisco's "Recipes for the Jewish Housewife," in English and Yiddish. Perhaps the most famous example of this genre is the Maxwell House Coffee Haggadah, the text for the Passover seder, which has been published and distributed as seasonal advertising by the coffee maker for decades. Specially packaged items labelled "Kosher for Passover" are now routinely collected from major food suppliers by Project Americana. Advertisements have also been acquired representing such purveyors of kosher foods as Manischewitz, Streit's, and Rokeach.

Objects of popular culture, which reflect the leisure-time activities of American Jews, have been collected and will continue to be a focus. Included thus far are such items as Yiddish sheet music from the turn of the century and the memorabilia of Raasche Rips, who was a member of Mickey Katz's famous "Borscht Capades" troupe from the 1950s. Among the objects related to sports, Project Americana was able to acquire quite fortuitously a Detroit Tigers cap that belonged to the legendary baseball hero Hank Greenberg.

A special focus of the collection are objects that document the role of Jews in American politics. As

Plate 85. Mogen David Cherry Wine Advertisement, 1970s

part of this effort, a pilot project to identify related items in other institutions nationwide was initiated with a survey sent in 1992 to all Jewish historical societies in the United States. More than 75 percent of these surveys were returned to the museum, an incredible response, establishing a vital resource for future research in this field. Information has now been indexed on hundreds of individuals who have served in city, state, and federal government. The museum has gathered all types of campaign material including buttons, bumper sticker, posters, and various giveaways. A special category is memorabilia with Yiddish or Hebrew used by public officials to appeal to Jewish groups. In 1990 Project Americana began requesting relevant campaign material from contemporary candidates for Congressional office.[7]

Many fascinating pieces in the Project Americana collection reveal the immigrants' efforts to maintain Old World customs in America. Some American-crafted items were done in traditional styles, such as a folk art amulet for Samuel Hade in New York about 1922; it was made probably by the *effendi* (caretaker) of the synagogue as was the practice of Jews from Rhodes (Plate 108). A paper-cut memorial, dated 1901, from Scranton, Pennsylvania, done in the technique of East European examples, is also in the collection (Plate 83). A glass box, its use unknown, was made in Chicago, perhaps at a Settlement House, around the turn of the century. The imagery is typical of items of the period reflecting not only the continuity of such Jewish symbols as the seven-branched menorah but also the use of the Hebrew word "Zion" within a six-pointed star, a symbol of the Zionist Movement, which had held its first Congress at Basel, Switzerland, in 1897 (Plate 79).

Of course, many customs and traditions have been transformed by being adapted to the American context. This is perhaps most pronounced in the celebration of Bar and Bat Mitzvah, whose changing char-

Plate 86. Samovar, 1847

Plate 87. Military Trunk, World War II >

acter in twentieth-century America is documented through invitations, photographs, and memorabilia from the ceremony itself and the attendant celebrations. In the early twentieth century, it was typical for a boy to pose for a portrait proudly wearing his tallit. There are no such photographs of girls, because the first official Bat Mitzvah ceremony did not take place until the 1920s, when Judith Kaplan Eisenstein, daughter of Mordecai Kaplan, founder of the Reconstructionist Movement, celebrated her coming of age in a formal synagogue service. Some Bar and Bat Mitzvah memorabilia indicate the evolution of social action efforts—by providing part of one's gift monies to food banks or other charitable causes as an element of the experience; the idea of "twinning" with Soviet Jewish Refuseniks, symbolically sharing the honor of the day with a counterpart who could not then openly participate in a Jewish ritual, became de rigueur in the 1970s and 1980s. The elaborate Bar/Bat Mitzvah souvenirs and theme mementoes demonstrate a more questionable, frivolous aspect of the ritual of becoming a Jewish adult.

A major goal of Project Americana is to encourage awareness of the importance of preservation. To further this goal in the larger community, the Project Americana staff worked with Wilshire Boulevard Temple in Los Angeles to develop a preservation project meant to serve as a prototype for other congregations. An exhibit was developed with "Precious Heirlooms" of synagogue members. As much as possible, stories about the objects were documented and included in the exhibit text. A year-long series of activities was planned in conjunction with the exhibit for every age level and special interest group in the congregation. Individuals were taught how to care for their family's memorabilia. Subsequently, a Precious Heirlooms workshop was developed to share the planning process, which was taught to representatives from synagogues all over the United States.[8]

S. Dillon Ripley, former Secretary of the Smithsonian Institution, wrote on the occasion of the American Bicentennial in 1976: "The American has come to be a multiple person, with allegiances here and sympathies to a past which somehow seems essential to one's quest for personal identity."[9] The objects that the Skirball Museum collects for Project Americana give witness to the past and in a highly distinctive way help preserve that past and help interpret it for future generations.

NOTES

1. G. Deutsch, "What Belongs in the Union Museum," *Union Bulletin* 5, no. 9 (1915), np.

2. For a discussion of Freemasonry and an analysis of the use of Masonic images on the Moses Henry *mizraḥ,* see Alice M. Greenwald, "The Masonic Mizraḥ, and Lamp: Ritual Art as a Reflection of Cultural Assimilation," *Journal of Jewish Art* 10 (1984), pp. 87-101.

3. The development of Project Americana benefitted from consultation by many individuals including Richard E. Ahlborn, Curator in the Division of Cultural History at the National Museum of American History, Smithsonian Institution; Abraham Peck, Executive Director of the American Jewish Archives in Cincinnati; and Neil Harris, Professor of History at the University of Chicago. Barbara Kirshenblatt-Gimblett, Professor in the Department of Performance Studies at New York University, recommended a three-fold plan to be carried out simultaneously: "reconnaissance" of objects generally available both in the general community and by approaching scholars who were working on a specific topic in American Jewish life and could facilitate acquisitions; identification of possible exhibit themes and programmatic goals and collection of objects to meet those goals; and development of a collection policy that enables the museum to prioritize areas of special effort, while still maintaining the flexibility to acquire objects which incidentally become available to the museum. Dr. Kirshenblatt-Gimblett presented a seminal paper on models of collecting entitled "American Jewish Life: Ethnographic Approaches to Collection, Presentation, and Interpretation" at the Annual Meeting of the Council of American Jewish Museums held in New York in December, 1984. The expertise and boundless energy of Lynne Gilberg, founding coordinator, contributed enormously to the success of Project Americana.

4. Professor Jonathan D. Sarna, Joseph H. and Belle R. Braun Professor of American Jewish History at Brandeis University, previously was on the faculty of Hebrew Union College in Cincinnati, and served for a number of years as a consultant on the Core Exhibit of the Skirball Museum at the Cultural Center. The intellectual framework he proposed for the exhibition also impacted the Project Americana collecting efforts. The topic of American and Jewish imagery is a subject that

both became a focus of the museum's research and that Dr. Sarna continues to investigate as well. Dr. Sarna presented a paper exploring this theme, entitled "The Cult of Synthesis in American Jewish Culture" at the World Congress of Jewish Studies, Jerusalem, June, 1993. The analysis of the attempt to establish a "synthetic" whole is cited from an unpublished draft of Dr. Sarna's paper.

5. An investigation of the topic of education is one of the projected focus areas of Project Americana as we move into the Cultural Center. The issues to be explored include both education in the secular sphere and its impact, especially on the occupations of American Jews, and the ongoing decision process of "what shall we teach our young" as regards Jewish education in America. To date, acquisitions related to education have been limited, but include such objects such as primers and educational games.

6. *Encyclopaedia Judaica*, s.v. Levi Strauss, 15:434-435.

7. Bruce Phillips, Professor of Sociology at the Irwin Daniels School of Jewish Communal Service on the Los Angeles campus of Hebrew Union College, was especially helpful in developing the survey.

8. These sessions were conducted at Biennial conventions of the Union of American Hebrew Congregations and the National Federation of Temple Sisterhoods.

9. S.D. Ripley, "Foreword" in *A Nation of Nations* (New York: Harper and Row, 1976), xiii.

SECTION TWO

The Inaugural Exhibition

of the

Skirball Cultural Center

Detail of Plate 98

JEWS IN AMERICA *Seize the Day!*

STANLEY F. CHYET

A COLLECTION OF ARTIFACTS or *objets d'art* exhibited to suggest the shape of a particular theme or experience inevitably suggests much else as well. The items exhibited have not selected themselves but been selected and not only by the exhibitors; ultimately and significantly they have been selected by the cultural and social environment in which the planners of the exhibit live, and so this collection, these objects, will reflect larger and more intricate patterns than the exhibitors may have consciously intended.

The core exhibit created for the new Skirball Cultural Center is a case in point. Meant to limn how Jews have lived at specific times and in specific places, the exhibit cannot be fully appreciated unless one takes into account the context—the nation, the community, the time—in which the preparations for this new institution went forward. The century now drawing to a close has not been a model of serenity; at the least it has been one of radical change, ongoing and cacophonous, some of it terribly troubling, some of it remarkably uplifting. The American nation developed more than one new economy and more than one new social, legal, and political shape in the course of this century—in addition to fighting a number of major and minor wars, absorbing (if not always welcoming) millions of immigrants, and expanding its cultural and aesthetic horizons (not invariably in ways that all Americans understood, appreciated, or considered edifying). American Jewry has followed suit, becoming (for better and for worse) increasingly integrated into American society and culture, increasingly subur-

banized, increasingly composed of holders of university degrees, increasingly removed from ancestral outlooks and memories—while at the same time reflecting the force of some distinctive influences: the ebb and flow of anti-Semitism here and overseas, the Nazi Holocaust, the Stalinist tyranny and its aftermath, the rise of the Third Jewish Commonwealth in the Middle East, and the (at least until recently) never-less-than-bruising confrontation between Israeli and Arab national movements.

But change has been a constant as American Jewry has adapted from its mid seventeenth-century communal beginnings to its new context: politically, from Dutch to British to American (and during the 1860s in some instances to Confederate) loyalties; demographically, from dominance by people of Sephardic background to those of Central European antecedents to an unprecedentedly large mass of East European ancestry; religiously and culturally, from orthodoxy (at first Sephardic, then Ashkenazic) to various manifestations of non-orthodoxy (emerging Re-

Detail of Plate 75

form, Conservative, Reconstructionist, and Humanist perspectives), agnosticism and atheism (including socialist and other left-of-center attachments); socially and economically, from typically petit-bourgeois status and kindred pursuits to occasional vaults up the social and economic ladder and from a proletarian, trade-unionist milieu to upper middle class and, not uncommonly, upper class circumstances.[1] Under Governor Stuyvesant in Dutch New Amsterdam, Jews had to struggle for a grudging recognition of their civil rights;[2] three hundred and fifty years later individuals of Jewish background composed nearly 10 percent of the United States Senate, two Jews sat on the United States Supreme Court, Jews and individuals of Jewish origin were serving as Secretary of the Smithsonian Institution, as Chief of Naval Operations, as Director of the CIA, as Presidents of several "Ivy League" and comparable academic institutions, and even as chief executives of corporations not so long ago suspected of nourishing anti-Jewish sympathies.

A Jewish patriot in Georgia—who had apparently been reading Tom Paine's Crisis Papers—was sure at the end of the Revolutionary War that "we have the world to begin again,"[3] but it's improbable that he dreamed his coreligionists could ever aspire to positions of the highest honor and dignity in American life. George Washington, recently elected President of the United States, might declare to the Jews of Rhode Island in 1790: "It is now no more that toleration is spoken of as if it was by the indulgence of one class of people that another enjoyed the exercise of their inherent natural rights."[4] In the post-Revolutionary generation, however, a North Carolina politician found his Jewish origins arousing colleagues to seek his expulsion from the state legislature. He argued in his defense that "intolerance in matters of faith" was among "the severest torments by which mankind could be afflicted" and affirmed Judaism as a religion which "inculcates every duty which man owes to his fellow men;

... the practice of every virtue, and the detestation of every vice"; how could the North Carolina state constitution be called on to support his expulsion from the state legislature on religious grounds? The Federal Constitution certainly endorsed his argument—but again he is not likely to have placed an invincible reliance on its guarantees, still of limited or uncertain influence in American society.[5] That generation also saw an American diplomat of Jewish background dismissed from government service on the ground that "the religion which you profess would form [an] obstacle to the exercise of your consular function."[6] The first significant victory of Federal Constitutional principles where Jews were concerned was the struggle culminating in 1826 in Maryland's "Jew Bill," which conferred on Jews in that state the political equality hitherto denied them by the state constitution.[7]

Nearly four decades later, during the Civil War, Jewish communities in the Ohio and Mississippi valleys could be threatened by a Union commander with a medieval-like edict of expulsion.[8] Throughout his lengthy nineteenth-century career on American shores Isaac Mayer Wise, a major Jewish religious leader, never saw any reason to cease railing against attempts to "baptize the Constitution."[9] In short, nineteenth-century Jews could never deem it a foregone conclusion that Jewish emancipation would be complete in this land, and the twentieth century failed to begin on a more auspicious note—witness the message Theodore Roosevelt's Secretary of State, John Hay, wished conveyed to Rumania in 1902:

> The condition of a large class of the inhabitants of Roumania has for many years been a source of grave concern to the United States. I refer to the Roumanian Jews, numbering some 400,000...by the cumulative effect of successive restrictions, the Jews of Roumania have become reduced to a state of wretched misery.... Human beings so circumstanced have virtually no alternatives but submissive suffering or flight

to some land less unfavorable to them. Removal under such conditions is not and cannot be the healthy, intelligent emigration of a free and self-reliant being. It must be, in most cases, *the mere transplantation of an artificially produced diseased growth to a new place....*

Jews possess in high degree the mental and moral qualifications of conscientious citizenhood.... *But when they come as outcasts, made doubly paupers by physical and moral oppression in their native land, and thrown upon the long suffering generosity of a more-favored community, their migration lacks the essential conditions which make alien immigration either acceptable or beneficial.*

...Putting together the facts now painfully brought home to this Government, during the past few years, that many of the [Jewish] inhabitants of Roumania are being forced by artificially adverse discriminations to quit their native country; that the hospitable asylum offered by this country is almost the only refuge left to them; that they come hither *unfitted by the conditions of their exile to take part in the new life of this land under circumstances either profitable to themselves or beneficial to the community,* and that they are objects of charity from the outset and for a long time—the right of remonstrance against the acts of the Roumanian Government is clearly established in favor of this Government. [Emphases added.]

Emma Lazarus, too, in her famous "New Colossus" sonnet hailing Bartholdi's Statue of Liberty, had evinced some ambivalence about the "wretched refuse" fleeing Europe for America. She seems not to have recognized that these "huddled masses" and "homeless, tempest-tost" possessed any rich cultural heritage to offer the New World, but Lazarus, unlike Secretary Hay, had a faith in America's alchemy: the New World would transform European dross into American gold.[10]

If a few years later Jewish pressure could induce the Taft administration to cite human rights in de-

nouncing the longstanding Russo-American Trade Treaty, a nervous post-World War I Congress, moved by a racialist agenda, effectively curtailed Jewish (and in general non-"Nordic") immigration and, with the onset of the Great Depression a few years later, withdrew into an isolationism which opposed offering even a modest number of Jewish refugee children any hope of asylum in America.[11] The post-World War II decade saw the rise of an internal anti-communist crusade, a witch-hunt which many Jews feared or experienced as a hunt for *Jewish* witches: Hollywood screenwriters, Judith Coplon, Harry Dexter White, the Rosenbergs, J. Robert Oppenheimer, et al.[12]

All the more astonishing, then, to contemplate the degree of integration and social as well as economic success American Jews were able to achieve in the 1960s and thereafter. Jewish involvement in American life is often measured in economic terms, and it is a fact—actually of minor demographic significance—that Jews are disproportionately represented in "Fortune 500" ranks. More salient is the educational and cultural role Jews have been playing in the post-World War II generation.

It is their educational and cultural achievements that have given Jews a telling impact on contemporary American life. Individuals of Jewish background have in any number of ways come close to defining twentieth-century American artistic endeavor, even before World War II. We may forego a catalogue of distinguished names and rest content with the truism that American art in our century—literature, drama, criticism, music, painting, sculpture, architecture, photography—would in the absence of Jewish creators have been far less distinguished than it is. Much the same can be claimed for American science and for the American academic scene, and it is scarcely less the case for producers and purveyors of American popular culture.

It is improbable that any other ethnic component of the American population can claim comparable es-

Plate 91. Statue of Liberty New Year's Greeting, early 20th century

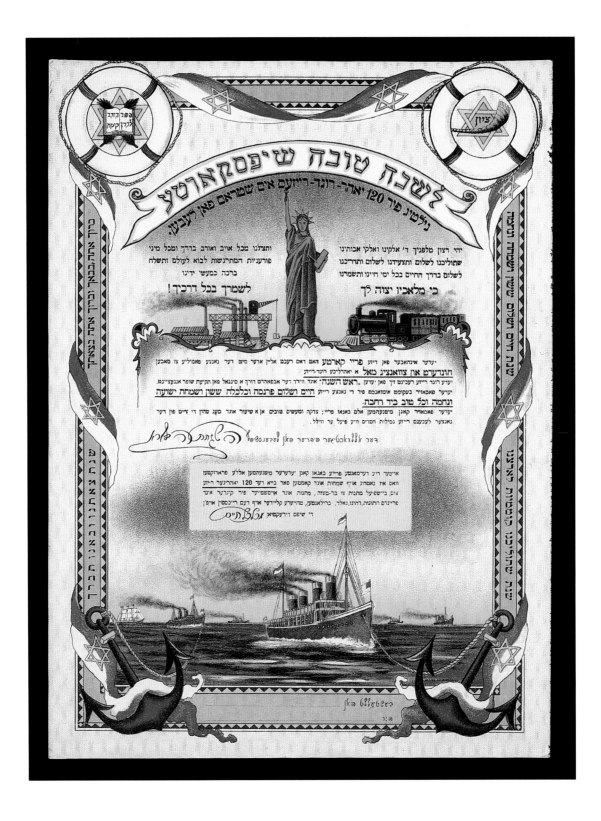

thetic and intellectual scope and influence in the century coming to an end. Such a claim could not have been put forth in previous centuries and may very well not be replicated in the twenty-first century, but the Jewish impact on twentieth-century cultural productivity—again both for good and for ill—appears incontestable. It is in this century, its second half in particular, that Jews have found themselves well positioned to take advantage of the country's geography of opportunity. The urban concentration of the Jews has clearly had a great deal to do with this complex phenomenon. There can be scant doubt, too, that the phenomenon has owed something to the larger society's post-Holocaust guilt, to the unfolding of a stable Jewish state in the Middle East, and to the overridingly bourgeois character of American Jewry (Theodor Herzl in *Der Judenstaat* saw all Jews of European background as "a bourgeois people," and American Jewry would seem a case in point).[13]

A significant factor in the mid and late twentieth-century American Jewish success story is, of course, America's expanding postwar economy and widening cultural horizons. From an historical perspective the story has taken shape so rapidly that American Jewry's heritage of insecurity remains largely intact. It is all but inevitable that some Jews—and, if for different reasons, how many non-Jews?—will regard this story as a "countercultural" saga and perhaps seriously problematic as such. Still, America in this checkered century has offered Jews as well as others a peerless chance to escape the restraints and disabilities of the Old World past, and the century has seen Jews seize the day: *Carpe diem* with a vengeance! At least for well-educated, ambitious individuals, post-World War II America has continued to be economically and socially synonymous with opportunity, and that is to a very large extent what the American Jewish success story rests on, even amid the fluctuations and downsizings of the 1990s.

NOTES

1. See Jacob R. Marcus' masterly studies: *The Colonial American Jew, 1492–1776*, 3 Vols. (Detroit: Wayne State University Press, 1970) and *United States Jewry, 1776–1985*, 4 Vols. (Detroit: Wayne State University Press, 1989–1994). I've attempted my own summary in "American Jews: Notes on the Idea of a Community," in *American Jewish History* 81 (l994), pp. 331–39.

2. See J.R. Marcus, *The Jew in the Medieval World* (Cincinnati: Union of American Hebrew Congregations, 1938), Ch. 15: "The Settlement of the Jews in North America, 1654–1655," and *The Colonial American Jew*, Vol. I, pp. 215 ff.

3. Mordecai Sheftall, Savannah, Ga., to Sheftall Sheftall, Charleston, S.C., 13 April 1783: see J.R. Marcus, *Early American Jewry* (New York: Ktav, 1975), Vol. II, p. 373.

4. See Paul R. Mendes-Flohr and Jehuda Reinharz, eds., *The Jew in the Modern World: A Documentary History* (New York: Oxford University Press, 1980), p. 363.

5. Jacob Henry represented Carteret County in the North Carolina House of Commons in 1808 and was re-elected in 1809: see Morris U. Schappes, ed., *A Documentary History of the Jews in The United States, 1654–1875* (New York: Citadel Press, 1952), pp. 122–25. See also S.F. Chyet, "The Political Rights of the Jews in the United States: 1776–1840," in *American Jewish Archives* 10 (1958), pp. 14–75.

6. James Monroe, U.S. Department of State, to Mordecai M. Noah, Tunis, 25 April 1815: see Jonathan D. Sarna, *Jacksonian Jew: The Two Worlds of Mordecai Noah* (New York: Holmes & Meier, 1981), p. 26.

7. See Schappes, *op. cit.*, pp. 168–71, 607.

8. In December 1862, Gen. Ulysses S. Grant issued his General Orders No. 11, expelling the Jews "as a class" from the territory in the Ohio and Mississippi valleys under his military control: see Schappes, *op. cit.*, pp. 472–76.

9. See Dena Wilansky, *Sinai to Cincinnati: Lay Views on the Writings of Isaac M. Wise* (New York: Renaissance Book Co., 1937), pp. 37 ff., 53, 211 ff.; J.R. Marcus, *United States Jewry*, Vol. III, pp. 69, 218.

10. See "Jews in American Diplomatic Correspondence," in *Publications of the American Jewish Historical Society* 15 (1906), pp. 58–60; Emma Lazarus, *The Poems of Emma Lazarus* (Boston: Houghton, Mifflin, 1895), Vol. I, pp. 202–3.

11. See Naomi W. Cohen, "The Abrogation of the Russo-American Treaty of 1832," in *Jewish Social Studies* 25 (1963), pp. 3–41; *American Jewish Year Book* 27 (1925), pp. 422–45, and Vol. 28 (1926), pp. 439–68; Howard M. Sachar, *A History of the Jews in America* (New York: Alfred A. Knopf, 1992), pp. 483–501. See also David S. Wyman, *The Abandonment of the Jews: America and the Holocaust, 1941–1945* (New York: Pantheon, 1985), pp. 5–9.

12. Sachar, *op. cit.*, pp. 623–41.

13. See Theodor Herzl, *The Jewish State (Der Judenstaat)*, trans. Harry Zohn (New York: Herzl Press, 1970). See also my "American Jews: Notes on the Idea of a Community," *op. cit.*

Visions and Values: Jewish Life from Antiquity to America

The Core Exhibition of the Skirball Museum

ROBERT KIRSCHNER

THE INTERPRETIVE MISSION of the Core Exhibition is to document and describe the historical continuity of Jewish culture across continents and centuries, culminating with the experience of the Jews in America. The exhibition combines the display of museum artifacts with interactive computer technology and multimedia production. Occupying more than 15,000 square feet, it is divided into a series of galleries depicting different chapters and dimensions of Jewish life.

The first half of the exhibition treats Jewish history and culture from biblical times to the modern era. It describes where Jews have lived over the centuries, featuring objects organized by country of origin, and how they have lived, focusing on ritual, ceremony, and custom.

In the second half of the exhibition, the American Jewish experience is explored through a variety of interpretive techniques, including artifact display, visual environments, true-to-scale replicas, and theater design. Two galleries are devoted to the impact of the Holocaust and to the establishment of the State of Israel.

Finally, the exhibition includes a separate two-level Discovery Center encouraging visitors of all ages to learn more about the science of archaeology and the material culture of ancient Israel and the Near East.

Engraved at the exhibition entry is the biblical commandment of God to Abraham, "Go forth...and be a blessing." Visitors then begin a journey from the Israelite past to the Jewish present. It begins with open and enclosed exhibits describing the origins of ancient Israel. From there visitors enter a Romanesque pavilion, representing the threshold of Jewish entry into the lands of Europe. To portray the Jewish dispersion to Asia and Africa, separate exhibits feature the Jewish communities of the Islamic world and China, conveying the variety of Jewish encounters with other peoples and cultures throughout the world.

Having described where Jews have lived, the exhibition turns next to how they have lived: the holiday customs, life-cycle ceremonies, and spiritual traditions that have characterized Jewish life in the diaspora. Organized by the conceptual categories of sacred time and sacred space, this group of galleries includes a series of interactive computer stations offering multimedia explorations of Jewish ritual and ceremonial objects, interpreting both form and function.

Jewish life in America culminates the exhibition. This new era in Jewish history is described by a sequence of three galleries, each featuring an audiovisual theater. The first gallery relates first-person narratives of Jewish immigration and the struggle for freedom and equality in the United States. The second describes Jewish enterprise and achievement in America from the late nineteenth to mid-twentieth century. The third is devoted to the contemporary American Jewish experience, focusing on how Jewish ancestral ideals have found, or failed to find, American expression.

Recognizing that the American Jewish experience must be viewed in a larger context, the exhibition also includes exhibits on the Nazi Holocaust in Europe and the establishment of the State of Israel, emphasizing the impact of these epochal events on the history and identity of American Jewry.

The introductory texts throughout the catalogue are taken directly from the exhibition. These gallery panels seek to portray the historic journey of the Jews from antiquity to America and the visions and values that they have cherished.

OLD OBJECTS, NEW FINDS

Teri B.R. Ziffren
Discovery Center

ADELE LANDER BURKE

THE TERI B. R. ZIFFREN DISCOVERY CENTER presents the Skirball Museum's archaeology collection to the public in an interactive, hands-on exhibit format geared to a youth audience. The Discovery Center grew out of a desire to utilize the museum's archaeological artifacts in order to expose young people to history in an exciting way. Visitors are able to experience how archaeologists excavate sites, thereby enriching their knowledge of past cultures.

The Skirball Museum has long had a commitment to museum education and has been a pioneer in developing creative and innovative exhibitions and educational touring programs. The museum, one of the first in the Los Angeles area to develop contextual exhibits where activity-based, youth-oriented tours were given, has from its inception served as a major resource to Jewish schools in the area of art education and offered creative family programs to the public. As an ethnically specific institution, the Skirball has, with the support of the National Endowment for the Humanities, created multicultural outreach programs to Los Angeles area public schoolchildren as well.

The core of the archaeology collection, the largest in the Western United States, is primarily Palestinian pottery that was assembled by a former president of Hebrew Union College, the respected archaeologist, Dr. Nelson Glueck. The collection was later augmented by important acquisitions of ancient glass, cuneiform tablets, and Mesopotamian cylinder seals.

This collection inspired a creative display at the former museum site, the long-term exhibit, "A Walk Through the Past," which both highlighted the archaeological process in Israel and explored the mate-rial culture of ancient Israel. This exhibit was the catalyst for a major educational endeavor undertaken in the 1970s by the museum in collaboration with the HUC Rhea Hirsch School of Jewish Education, creating a school outreach program called MUSE—Museum Utilization for Student Education. The MUSE program has been extremely successful, attracting thousands of school children to the museum each year.

As the Skirball Cultural Center began to be conceptualized, it became clear that the new museum should build on its strength in archaeology education to further its mission of outreach to Los Angeles school children. Furthermore, in recent years, demand for archaeology education has increased as the State of California's Framework for Social Studies Instruction has emphasized the role of archaeology as a means of learning ancient history, and has included the history of ancient Israel as part of the study of the foundations of Western Civilization. The youth-oriented approach of a discovery center reconciled the desire to exhibit the archaeology collection in an innovative manner with the educational needs of area school children.

Conceptual planning for the Teri B.R. Ziffren Discovery Center began in 1991 when the museum convened a team of outstanding curators, scholars, and educators knowledgeable in the archaeology of Israel as well as the principles of museum exhibition. The team was able to draw extensively on the field experience and research of the staff of the Hebrew Union College Nelson Glueck School of Biblical Archaeology in Jerusalem. This team approach to exhibit planning represented a model that has been sweeping the museum world in recent years.

The field of biblical archaeology had undergone tremendous changes in the past two decades, and this new exhibit reflects those changes as well as innovations in exhibit design. In the Discovery Center, archaeology is presented as a branch of anthropology—a means of understanding the process of human development. The exhibit emphasizes how archaeologists analyze their finds in order to learn about the past, stressing the importance of studying artifacts as they are found by recreating an archaeological site. This broad approach presents material culture over a long span of time that includes Israelite history within the context of the movements of various peoples into the region, rather than focusing solely on biblical history. The exhibit explains such archaeological principles as material decomposition, typology, dating, and stratigraphy, and explores changes over time in the areas of religious belief, social development, and technology.

Because the primary target audience is 11- and 12-year olds, the confluence of archaeological theory and methodological approach was challenging to the exhibit designers. On the one hand, a fragile and important collection could be utilized to tell the story of archaeology. On the other hand, the goal was to create an exhibit that would be highly interactive and engaging for visitors which dictated a design that allowed a hands-on approach. Therefore, unlike some discovery centers in natural history museums, where visitors can touch real objects such as skins, bones, and shells, it would not be possible for our visitors to touch the objects. The design had both to preserve the objects and to allow visitors to interact with the exhibit.

At an interactive computer station in the Ziffren Discovery Center, visitors can choose a site to excavate with the help of the delightful animated Mr. Artie Fact. They can manipulate iconic magnets on a topographic map of the Near East to see how trade brought ancient peoples together. They can touch the tools of the archaeologist, create rubbings of ancient alphabets, and try to decipher ancient Hebrew inscriptions. They can push buttons and watch how birds, pots, and daggers decay over time. They can peek into an ancient rock-cut tomb to see how artifacts look in context. And, they can engage in many exhibit-based activities and games designed for all ages in ten discovery boxes.

The hands-on, interactive experience for visitors will culminate when they participate in a simulated archaeological excavation site at the Ralph M. Parsons Outdoor Archaeological Classroom, which is adjacent to the Discovery Center. In this 1000-sq.-ft. dig, visitors, under the guidance of specially trained docents, will experience the challenges of a real excavation as they uncover the remains of an Iron Age Israelite settlement. The principles and theories explained in the Ziffren Discovery Center can be put to the test at this realistic simulation site, creating a long-lasting impression for the young visitor.

The Ziffren Discovery Center will also offer a range of adult-oriented programs in archaeology. The Skirball Cultural Center will establish relations with other institutions in the Los Angeles area to bring the latest thinking in archaeology to a broader public audience through lectures, films, and travel opportunities. Adults will have the opportunity to assist in research on the archaeological collection. The museum plans to bring changing exhibitions on archaeological themes to Los Angeles events that will complement and enhance the learning to take place in the Ziffren Discovery Center.

CATALOGUE OF THE EXHIBITION

The introductory text panels are from the exhibition script written by Robert Kirschner.

Guide to the Catalogue

The arrangement of the entries in this catalogue follows the sections of the exhibition *Visions and Values: Jewish Life from Antiquity to America.* The headings designate the cases in the exhibition. Loans to the exhibition are included according to their placement in the galleries. For conservation purposes, textiles and works on paper or parchment will be rotated. Both replacements and objects currently on display are included in this listing. A typical entry comprises the following items, in the order listed. Transliteration follows the rules set in the *Encyclopaedia Judaica*; divergence from this standard occurs only to accommodate a more common usage in English (e.g., Bar Mitzvah). Accepted English usage has been followed for biblical names.

CONSTRUCTION OF A TYPICAL ENTRY:

Name or identification of object
Artist or maker (if known)
Origin and date of object
Composition
Dimensions: height x width x depth; diameter is so indicated
Source of Acquisition
Skirball Museum (HUCSM) catalog number

BEGINNINGS

I N THE TORAH,
the first five books of the Hebrew Bible, a majestic
story unfolds: the creation of the world,
the revelation of divine law, and the liberation
of a people from slavery. From these deep roots of
tradition, the Jewish spirit has drawn its strength
and its purpose.

The Torah inspired the Jews to measure their lives
by their values. To seek justice, to show kindness,
to welcome the stranger, to protect the weak:
they accepted these ideals as God's wish and
as their responsibility.

The forms of Jewish faith have changed with time.
But the values have endured, and so has
the dream of a better world.

Plate 92. Persian Vessel

ENTRANCE

TORAH SCROLL
Germany, 19th century
Ink on parchment
38 in. (95 cm)
Kirschstein Collection
HUCSM 68.26

ANCIENT ISRAEL

ASTARTE FIGURINE
Provenance unknown
Late Bronze, 1500–1200 BCE
Clay
5½ x 2½ x 1¼ in. (14.0 x 6.4 x 3.2 cm)
HUCSM A850

WATER JUG
Beit Ulla
Iron II, 1000–586 BCE
Clay
13¾ x 11¼ in. diameter (35.0 x 28.6 cm)
HUCSM A700

BEER JUG
Provenance unknown
Iron II B-C, 900–586 BCE
Clay, slipped and burnished
9⅝ x 6 in. diameter (24.8 x 15.2 cm)
HUCSM A712

INCENSE ALTAR
Persian Period or Iron II, 1000–586 BCE
Clay, slipped and incised
3 x 3¾ in. diameter (7.6 x 3.4 cm)
HUCSM A763

FOUR-SHEKEL WEIGHT
Judea, Tel ed Duweir
Iron IIC, 800–586 BCE
Limestone
1⅛ x 1¼ in. diameter (2.8 x 3.2 cm)
Henry Kaner Memorial Purchase Fund
HUCSM A993

ONE-SHEKEL WEIGHT
Judea
Iron IIC, 800–586 BCE
Red Limestone
¾ x ¾ in. diameter (1.9 x 1.9 cm)
Henry Kaner Memorial Purchase Fund
HUCSM A996

JUGLET
Beit Ulla
Iron I, 1200–1000 BCE
Clay, slipped
4 x 2½ in. diameter (10.2 x 6.4 cm)
HUCSM A701

JUG
Khirbet el Qom
Iron IIB-C, 900–586 BCE
Clay, slipped and burnished
7⅝ x 5⅓ in. diameter (19.4 x 13.5 cm)
HUCSM A680

CHALICE BOWL
Khirbet el Qom
Iron IIA-B, 1000–800 BCE
Clay
6⅛ x 7⅝ in. rim diameter (15.5 x 19.4 cm)
HUCSM A705

ASTARTE FIGURINE
Judea, near Hebron
Iron IIC, 800–586 BCE
Clay
7¼ x 8¾ in. base diameter (18.4 x 22.2 cm)
Gift of Bella Newman Sang
HUCSM A1337

ANCIENT ROUTES

PERSIAN VESSEL *(PL. 92)*
Luristan, possibly Amlash
Date unknown
Clay, burnished
9 x 13 in. spout to handle (22.9 x 33.0 cm)
Gift of Ruth K. March from the Estate of A.L.
and Ida Koolish
HUCSM A1255

FUNERARY MASK
Provenance unknown
Roman, 2nd century
Plaster; glass inlaid eyes, painted
9 ½ x 8 x 7 in. (24.1 x 20.3 x 17.8 cm)
Anonymous donation
HUCSM A1127

ROMAN MARBLE HEAD
Provenance unknown
Roman, late 1st century
Marble, carved, and painted (originally)
12 x 10 in. (30.5 x 25.4 cm)
Anonymous donation
HUCSM A1103

JAR
Provenance unknown
Late Roman/Byzantine, 200–400 CE
Glass, blown and threaded
3½ x 3½ in. (8.9 x 8.9 cm)
Anonymous donation
HUCSM A1023

JUDEA CAPTA COIN
Struck in Rome
72 CE
1¼ in. diameter (3.2 cm)
HUCSM 65.110

JUDEA CAPTA COIN
Struck in Rome
85 CE
Copper alloy
1 in. diameter (2.5 cm)
HUCSM 65.113

JUDEA CAPTA COIN
Struck in Palestine (possibly Caesarea)
Roman, 81-96 CE
1 in. diameter (2.54 cm)
HUCSM 65.115

STELE
Palmyra, Syria
Late Roman, 2nd century CE
Limestone, carved
21 x 13 x 9 in. (53.3 x 33.0 x 22.9 cm)
Gift of Mr. and Mrs. Lester Barron
HUCSM A1251

FIGURINE
Greece
Ca. 250 BCE
Clay
7⅞ x 3½ x 2 in. (20.0 x 9.0 x 5.5 cm)
Gift of the Kershaw Family Trust
HUCSM A1352

FRAGMENT OF A MOSAIC FLOOR
Antioch, Syria
Byzantine, 324–640 CE
Stone tesserae, ceramic fragments
33½ x 29 x 1¼ in. (85.0 x 73.7 x 3.2 cm)
Gift of Joel Malter, Robert Abell, Louis Fischer
and Melvin Wank
HUCSM A982

JOURNEYS

THE STORY OF THE JEWS
begins with a journey. Across continents and centuries,
through sunlight and darkness, the Jews have traveled —
a journey as old and as fascinating as civilization itself.
From biblical times to our own, the Jews have learned from
other peoples, even as others have learned from them.
After four thousand years of cultural encounter — with
Greece and Rome, Babylon and Byzantium,
Christianity and Islam — how is it that Jews still exist?

In their long history, the Jews have spoken many languages
and lived in many places. Yet they have remained a distinct
people, a community woven by memory and hope.

SEPHARD

Citizen's Rights Certificate
The Netherlands, 1850
Printed paper and ink
19½ x 7⅝ in. (49.5x 19.3 cm)
Gift of Jacqueline Levy Fuhrman and Millicent Levy Small
HUCSM 19a.86

Shiviti *(Pl. 95)*
Maker: Solomon ben David Attias
North Africa (?), 19th century
Ink and watercolor on paper
23¾ x 17¼ in. (60.3 x 43.8 cm)
Kirschstein Collection, formerly Frauberger Collection
HUCSM 39.23

Ketubbah
Bucharest, 1831
Ink and watercolor on paper
25¾ x 20 in. (65.4 x 50.8 cm)
HUCSM 34.73

Ketubbah
Bucharest, 1854
Ink, pencil, and watercolor on paper
24¾ x 17⅞ in. (62.9 x 45.4 cm)
HUCSM 34.76

Dedication of the Synagogue of the Portuguese Jews in Amsterdam
Bernard Picart (1673–1733)
France, 1721
Engraving
15¼ x 18¾ in. (38.7 x 47.6 cm)
HUCSM 66.356

Dedication of Portuguese Jews Synagogue, Amsterdam
Bernard Picart (1673–1733)
London, 1733
Engraving, hand-colored
14⅜ x 16⅜ in. (36.5 x 41.6 cm)
Gift of Mr. Philip D. Sang
HUCSM 66.1095

Baruch Spinoza (1631–1677)
The Netherlands, 17th century
Engraving
7 x 5⅝ in. (14 x 12.6 cm)
HUCSM 66.1118

Medal of Grazia Nasi, the Younger
Maker: Pastorini de Pastorini (ca. 1508–1592)
Ferrara, Italy, 1558 (19th c. copy)
Bronze
2⅝ in. diameter (6.6 cm)
HUCSM 36.108a

Synagogue Reader's Desk Cover
Ottoman Palestine, early 20th century
Velvet, embroidered with metallic thread
36 x 34½ in. (91.4 x 87.6 cm)
Museum purchase with funds provided by The Maurice Amado Foundation at the behest of the Tarica Family
HUCSM 17.53

Synagogue Reader's Desk Cover
Ottoman Palestine, early 20th century
Velvet, embroidered with metallic thread
31½ x 30 ¾ in. (80.0 x 78.1 cm)
Museum purchase with funds provided by The Maurice Amado Foundation at the behest of the Tarica Family
HUCSM 17.54

Tablespoon
Maker: Myer Myers (active 1746–1790)
New York, ca. 1790
Silver, engraved
8¾ in. (22.3 cm)
Museum purchase with funds provided by the Gerald M. and Carolyn Z. Bronstein Fund for Project Americana
HUCSM 14.317

Woman's Caftan and Sash
Rhodes, late 19th century
Silk; cotton; and gold braid
53 in. (134.6 cm)
Gift of Diana Polichar and Family
HUCSM 25.82 a/b

Woman's Caftan
Morocco, ca. 1955
Silk brocade embroidered with metallic thread
54½ in. (138.4 cm)
Gift of Therese Chriqui
HUCSM 9.79 a/b

Tray of Sweets (tavla de dulsé) *(Pl. 93)*
Izmir, Turkey, 1920s
Silver, cast, die-stamped and pierced
Central container: 9⅝ x 5¼ in. diameter (24.4 x 13.5 cm)
Dishes: 1¾ x 6 in. diameter (4.5 x 15.2 cm)
Museum purchase with funds provided by The Maurice Amado Foundation at the behest of the Tarica Family
HUCSM 14.357a-o

ITALY

Hanukkah Lamp
Italy, 19th century
Brass, cast
5 ⅜ x 6¼ in. (13.7 x 16 cm)
HUCSM 27.19

Ketubbah *(Pl. 3)*
Ancona, Italy, 1692
Ink, gouache and gold paint on parchment
33⅞ x 27⅛ in. (86.0 x 68.9 cm)
Kirschstein Collection
HUCSM 34.109

Ketubbah *(Pl. 27)*
Ferrara, Italy, 1775
Ink, tempera and gold paint on parchment
34⅝ x 22½ in. (87.9 x 57.2 cm)
Kirschstein Collection
HUCSM 34.1

Torah Crown
Northern Italy, dated 1797
Copper, repoussé, engraved and parcel-gilt; and brass, cast
7½ x 8⅛ in. diameter (19.1 x 21.3 cm)
HUCSM 58.4

Amulet *(Pl. 94)*
Italy,18th century
Silver, repoussé, cast and parcel-gilt; and ink on parchment
4½ x 3 ⅜ in. (11.4 x 7.9 cm)
Gift of the Jewish Cultural Reconstruction, Inc.
HUCSM 2.27

Hanging Lamp
Italy (?), late 17th-early 18th century
Silver, chased
3⅞ in. diameter (10 cm)
Kirschstein Collection
HUCSM 33.42

Portrait of David Nieto (1654–1728)
Italy (?), 1720s
Painted on glass
17⅛ x 12⅛ in. (43.5 x 30.8 cm)
Gift of Mr. Ben Selling, formerly Israel Solomons Collection
HUCSM 41.461

FRANCE

Omer Calendar *(Pl. 24)*
Maker: Maurice Mayer (active 1840s–1870s)
Paris, ca. 1870
Case: silver, die-stamped, pierced, engraved and parcel-gilt; enamel; wood; glass; and amethyst
Scroll: ink, gouache and bronze paint on parchment
13¾ x 10¼ x 3 in. (34.9 x 26 x 7.6)
HUCSM 40.1

Ketubbah
Bayonne, France, 1705
Ink and watercolor on parchment
15⅞ x 13 ⅜ in. (40.3 x 34.0 cm)
Kirschstein Collection
HUCSM 34.61

Ketubbah
Bordeaux, France, 1786
Ink and watercolor on parchment
13¼ x 12⅛ in. (33.7 x 30.8 cm)
Kirschstein Collection
HUCSM 34.58

L'Etang de Montfoucault (The Pond at Montfoucault) *(Pl. 48)*
Camille Pissarro (1831–1903)
France, 19th century
Oil on canvas
12⅛ x 27 ⅜ in. (30.8 x 69.5 cm)
Gift of an Anonymous Donor
HUCSM 41.307

Portrait of Alfred Dreyfus in Vanity Fair from a Painting by Jean-Baptiste Guth
Rennes, France, 1899
Lithograph
15 x 10 in. (38.1 x 25.4 cm)
Gift of Emil Oberholzer
HUCSM 66.188

Portrait of Alfred Dreyfus in Vanity Fair
Rennes, France, 1899
Lithograph
15 x 10 in. (38.1 x 25. 4 cm)
Rabbi William M. Kramer Collection
HUCSM 66a.212

Plate 93. Tavla de Dulsé (Tray of Sweets), 1920s

THE GREAT SANHEDRIN
Damame de Martrait (1763–1827)
Paris, 1806
Etching and aquatint, printed in color
22½ x 28¾ in. (57.2 x 73.0 cm)
HUCSM 66.1152

MEDAL OF NAPOLEON AND THE GRAND
SANHEDRIN
Maker: F. Depaulis (?)
France, 1806
Bronze
1⅝ in. diameter (4.11cm)
HUCSM 36.106

GREAT BRITAIN

JEWISH SYNAGOGUE, GREAT ST. HELEN'S
T. H. Shepherd and H. Melville
London, ca 1837
Engraving
7³/₁₆ x 5⅜ in. (18.3 x 13.7cm)
HUCSM 66.237

KETUBBAH
Engraver: H. Burgh
London, 1861
Etching on parchment; and ink
16 x 12½ in. (40.6 x 31.8 cm)
Gift of Rabbi Jacob Nieto
HUCSM 34.19

PORTRAIT OF MRS. SARAH LYONS (PL. 40)
John Constable (1776–1837)
Great Britain, 1804
Oil on canvas
24 x 19 in. (61 x 48.3 cm)
Gift of Mr. Ben Selling
HUCSM 41.45

*RANDALL, THE IRISH LAD AND BELASCO, THE
JEW CHAMPION*
Charles Williams
London, 1817
Etching, hand-colored
10⅝ x 14 in. (27 x 35.6 cm)
William Rosenthal Collection
HUCSM 66.1123

*THE HOUSE OF MOSES HART, ESQUIRE:
BETWEEN TWICKENHAM AND ISLENWORTH*
Anthony Walker (1726–1765), after the drawing
by Abraham Heckell
London, 18th century
Engraving, hand-colored
10¾ x 16¹⁵/₁₆ in. (27.4 x 43.1 cm)
Israel Solomons Collection
HUCSM 66.1147

FERNANDES IN DUKE'S PLACE JAR
Great Britain, 18th century
Faience
6 ¾ x 3½ in. diameter (17.2 x 8.9 cm)
Gift of Mr. Ben Selling
HUCSM 14.41

THE FOUR ROTHSCHILDS
Richard Dighton (1785–1880)
London, 1880
Graphite and watercolor on paper
10⅛ x 7½ in. (25.8 x 19.2 cm)
Israel Solomons Collection
HUCSM 66.1105

CANDLESTICKS
Maker: Aaron Katz
London, 1895
Silver, spun, chased, pierced and parcel-gilt
15½ in. (39.3cm)
Museum purchase with funds provided by the
Henfield Foundation; the Estate of Sam Brand
in honor of Jeanne Kaufman; and Special
Acquisition Funds
HUCSM 11.54 a/b

SPICE CONTAINER
Maker: Aaron Katz
London, 1895
Silver, filigree, chased and parcel-gilt
11½ in. (29.2 cm)
Museum purchase with funds provided by the
Henfield Foundation; the Estate of Sam Brand
in honor of Jeanne Kaufman; and Special
Acquisition Funds
HUCSM 53.126

DANIEL DERONDA
Author: George Eliot; publisher: Harper Bros.
New York, 1876
On loan from the Hebrew Union College-
Jewish Institute of Religion Klau Library,
Cincinnati

CENTRAL EUROPE

DOCUMENT OF A PROTECTED JEW
Würzburg, Germany, 1798
Ink on paper
13⅛ x 8¼ in. (33.3 x 21 cm)
Gift of Rabbi Ralph Blumenthal
HUCSM 19a.6

ROTHSCHILD HANUKKAH LAMP *(PL. 2)*
Maker: Johann Heinrich Philip Schott
Frankfurt am Main, ca. 1850
Silver, cast and chased
21 x 19 in. (53.3 x 48.3 cm)
Gift of the Jewish Cultural Reconstruction, Inc.
HUCSM 27.98

Plate 94. Amulet, 18th century

Plate 95. Shiviti, Solomon ben David Attias, 19th century >

Plate 96. Chinese Prayer Shawl and Bag, 1904

TORAH SHIELD *(PL. 8)*
Maker: Georg Zeiller (active 1780–1828 or later)
Munich, 1828; dedicated 1848
Silver, repoussé, cast and gilt; rubies; white
sapphires; pearls; and glass
15⅞ x 14¼ in. (40.4 x 36.1 cm)
Kirschstein Collection
HUCSM 7.5

TORAH FINIALS *(PL. 8)*
Maker: George Zeiller
Munich, 1828; dedicated 1848
Silver, cast, chased, pierced and gilt; and rubies
14.2 x 5.3 in. diameter (36 x 13.5 cm)
Kirschstein Collection
HUCSM 47.11 a/b

KETUBBAH
Cleves, Germany, 1843
Printed on parchment; and ink
12⅝ x 8 in. (32.1 x 20.3 cm)
Gift of Grete Benedix and Grete E. Benedix in
memory of Paul and Ernst Benedix
HUCSM 34.270

JUDE SUESS
Germany, 1738
Watercolor and ink on paper; and metal case
1⅝ in. diameter folded (4.1 cm)
Gift of Esther and Jack Cagan
HUCSM 36.174

MOSES MENDELSSOHN (1729–1786)
Germany (?), 18th century
Watercolor on ivory
2 x 1⅝ in. (5.1 x 4.1 cm)
HUCSM 45.16

HIS MAJESTY KAISER WILHELM II
B. Niederland (?)
Germany, 1908
Printed on paper
11½ x 9⅜ in. (29.2 x 23.8 cm)
E. Birnbaum Collection
HUCSM 66.191

DIE SYNAGOGE ZU COELN (COLOGNE SYNA-GOGUE)
(?) von J. Hoegg
Düsseldorf, 19th century
Lithograph
18¼ x 13⅞ in. (46.4 x 35.2 cm)
HUCSM 66.2763

DIE VERWANDLUNG (THE METAMORPHOSIS)
Author: Franz Kafka
Leipzig, 1917
On loan from the Hebrew Union College-Jewish Institute of Religion Klau Library,
Cincinnati

EASTERN EUROPE

SHTETL
Issachar Ber Ryback (1897–1935); Publisher:
Farlag Shvien
Berlin, 1923
Printed paper
19¾ x 13¾ in. (50.2 x 34.9 cm)
Gift of Dorothy and Louis Danziger
HUCSM 5.191

HANUKKAH LAMP
Galicia, late 19th-early 20th century
Brass, cast
11¾ x 11⅜ x 5¾ in. (29.9 x 28.8 x 14.6 cm)
HUCSM 27.7

PRAYER SHAWL COLLAR
Poland, 19th century
Woven of metallic thread
5 x 39¾ in. (12.7 x 100.9 cm)
Gift of the Jewish Cultural Reconstruction, Inc.
HUCSM 46.20

MIZRAH-SHIVITI
Maker: Nathan Hoffman (1857–1941)
Odessa, 1890
Papercut with watercolor and ink
24 x 30 in. (76.2 x 61 cm)
Gift of Philip Hoffman
HUCSM 39.39

KETUBBAH FORM
Odessa, 1898
Printed on paper
18½ x 10 in. (47 x 25.4 cm)
Gift of Herbert A. and Nancy E. Bernhard
HUCSM 34.334

PRISONER OF CONSCIENCE BANDS
Arlington, Virginia, 1970s
Stainless steel, engraved
2⅜ in. (6.7 cm)
Gift of Ellie and Gil Somerfield
HUCSM 29.110; 29.111

THE JEWS OF RUSSIA: LET THEM GO!
New York, 1970s–1980s
Color offset lithograph
27 x 19 in. (68.6 x 48.3 cm)
Gift of the Student Struggle for Soviet Jewry
HUCSM 66a.140

LET MY PEOPLE GO!
New York, 1970s–1980S
Color offset lithograph
28¼ x 22 in. (71.8 x 55.9 cm)
Gift of the Student Struggle for Soviet Jewry
HUCSM 66a.142

ANTI-SEMITISM IS COUNTER-
REVOLUTIONARY (PL. 97)
Alexander Tyshler (1898–1980)
Moscow, ca. 1917
Lithograph
44¾ x 30 in. (113.6 x 76.2 cm)
HUCSM 66.1150

EVGENY LEVITCH PATCH
Des Plaines, Illinois, 1970s
Cotton duck embroidered with rayon thread
4⅞ x 3 in. (12.4 x 7.6 cm)
Gift of Solomon and Elaine Gluck
HUCSM 29.551

SOVIET JEWRY BUTTON
United States, 1970s
Plasticized paper on tin
1 in. diameter (2.54 cm)
Gift of Solomon and Elaine Gluck
HUCSM 29.552

AUTO-EMANCIPATION
Author: Leo Pinsker; publisher: Maccabean
New York, 1906
On loan from the Hebrew Union College-Jewish
Institute of Religion Klau Library, Cincinnati

CHINA

PRAYER SHAWL BAG
Shanghai, ca. 1920
Silk, embroidered with silk thread
8 x 9½ in. (20.3 x 24.1 cm)
Gift of Mae and Roy Friedman
HUCSM 46.103

ORT BOX AND HANDKERCHIEFS
Shanghai, 1947
Leather, painted; and silk, painted
7 x 5½ x ½ in. (17.8 x 14 x 1.3 cm)
Gift of Rose L. Rashmir
HUCSM 29.115 a-d

TORAH CASE (PL. 12)
Kaifeng, China, possibly 17th century
Wood, lacquered, and gilt; bronze; and iron
30 x 11¼ in. diameter (76.2 x 28.6 cm)
HUCSM 57.2

Plate 97. *Anti-Semitism is Counter-Revolutionary,* Alexander Tyshler, ca. 1917

IDENTIFICATION CARD
Tsingtao, China, 1938
Printed paper and ink
4½ x 3¼ in. (11.4 x 8.3 cm)
Gift of Heinz J. Pulverman
HUCSM 16.48

PASSPORT
Germany, 1938
Printed paper and ink
6½ x 4¼ in. (16.5 x 10.8 cm)
Gift of Susanne Kester
HUCSM 16.53

PRAYER SHAWL AND BAG (PL. 96)
Shanghai, 1904
Silk, embroidered with silk thread
Bag: 7 x 8¾ in. (17.8 x 22.2 cm)
Gift of Mr. and Mrs. Revan Komaroff
HUCSM 46.72 a/b

KETUBBAH FOR S.I. JACOB AND MIRIAM NISSIM
Shanghai, 1918
Printed paper and ink
26½ x 14⅛ in. (67.3 x 35.6 cm)
On loan from Rose Jacob Horowitz

SACRED TIME

IN THE ROUTINE OF LIFE, one moment may seem no different than another. But in Jewish ritual, the flow of time is noticed. Most Jewish observances — such as the Sabbath and the festivals — depend on a certain hour of the day or season of the year.

Many Jews keep track of time on two calendars, civil and Jewish. Weeks, months, and years follow two rhythms, the secular and the sacred. The cycle of each life from birth to death is also measured in Jewish time.

Judaism teaches that time has a goal: the day when suffering will end and peace will come to the world. Every moment is sacred when it is lived with justice and kindness.

Plate 98. *Zodiac Circle*, Mark Podwal, 1995

MEZUZAH
Central Europe, late 19th-early 20th century
Case: brass, pierced; iron sheet-metal; and glass
Scroll: ink on parchment
2⅛ x 2⅛ x ⅝ in. (5.3 x 5.3 x 1.6 cm)
HUCSM 37.16

ZODIAC CIRCLE (PL. 98)
Mark Podwal
Gouache, ink, and colored pencil on paper
Museum commission with funds provided in
   honor of Marian and Don DeWitt by their
   children and their families
48 x 48 in. (121.9 x 121.9 cm)
HUCSM 10.12a

LIFE CIRCLE
Mark Podwal
Gouache, ink, and colored pencil on paper
Museum commission with funds provided in
   honor of Marian and Don DeWitt by their
   children and their families
48 x 48 in. (121.9 x 121.9 cm)
HUCSM 10.12b

HOLIDAYS

THE JEWISH HOLIDAYS
are rich in tradition, symbolism, and history. There are
joyous festivals and somber holy days, family rituals and
community celebrations, special foods, songs, and prayers.

Many of the holidays originated with the cycles of nature:
the times set by sun and moon, planting and harvest.
On to these the Jews grafted the events of their own history.
Each year, in the sequence of the festivals, they relive the
journey of their ancestors from slavery to freedom and faith.

Yet the holidays are not merely pages from the past.
Every generation of Jews introduces new customs and
interpretations. These reflect the variety of Jewish life and
the vitality of Jewish culture in every part of the world.

Plate 99. Sabbath Wine Bottle, 19th century

SHABBAT

CANDLESTICKS
England, late 19th–early 20th century
Brass, cast and turned
10 7/8 x 3 3/4 in. (27.5 x 9.6 cm)
HUCSM 11.10 a/b

KIDDUSH CUP
Augsburg, 1763–1765
Silver, chased, engraved and cast
4 7/8 x 2 3/4 in. diameter (12.3 x 7.0 cm)
HUCSM 18.21

KIDDUSH CUP (PL. 33)
Maker: Hana Geber (1910–1990)
New York, 1982
Bronze, cast and silver-plated
7 1/2 in. (19.1 cm)
Gift of the Artist
HUCSM 18.40

SABBATH WINE BOTTLE (PL. 99)
Syria (?), 19th century
Etched glass
7 7/8 x 5 1/2 in. (20 x 14 cm)
Kirschstein Collection
HUCSM 33a.7

KIDDUSH CUP
Kiev, 1896
Silver, engraved
3 x 2 5/8 in. diameter (7.6 x 6.7 cm)
Gift of the Jewish Cultural Reconstruction, Inc.
(No. 6342)
HUCSM 18.13

KIDDUSH CUP
Maker: Christian Gottlieb Pintsch
Berlin, 1821–26, dated 1826
Silver, stamped and engraved
4 3/8 x 2 1/2 in. diameter (11.0 x 6.4 cm)
Gift of Mrs. Tutty Lowens
HUCSM 18.41

SET OF KIDDUSH CUPS
Maker: Yaacov Yemini (b. 1929)
Jerusalem, 1960s
Silver, filigree; and semi-precious stones
A: 5 5/8 x 3 in. diameter (14.2 x 7.5 cm)
B-G: 3 x 1 5/8 in. diameter (7.5 x 4.0 cm)
Gift of Nancy M. Berman and Alan J. Bloch
HUCSM 18.42 a-g

KIDDUSH CUP
Maker: Boaz Yemini (b. 1956)
Jerusalem, ca. 1985
Silver, gilt
3 1/8 x 2 5/8 in. diameter (8.0 x 6.7 cm)
Museum purchase
HUCSM 18.44

KIDDUSH CUP
Russia, 1880s (?)
Silver, engraved and gilt
2 3/4 x 2 5/8 in. diameter (7.0 x 6.6 cm)
Gift of Bernard and Sylvia Sayewitz
HUCSM 18.47

CANDLESTICKS
Morocco, 20th century
Brass, cast and turned
14 x 5 7/8 in. diameter (35.5 x 14. 8 cm)
Museum purchase
HUCSM 11.31 a/b

HALLAH COVER
Shanghai, 1899
Silk, embroidered with silk thread
29 x 29 in. (73.7 x 73.7 cm)
Gift of Mrs. Regina Ezra
HUCSM 33a.39

HALLAH COVER
Maker: Hilde Zadigow
Prague (?), 20th century
Silk, batik
19 1/2 x 19 1/2 in. (49.5 x 49.5 cm)
HUCSM 33a.17

WOMAN'S PRAYER
Maker: Jacob Menaḥem Halevi
Italy, 18th century
Ink and watercolor on parchment
16 5/8 x 11 1/4 in. (42.2 x 28.6 cm)
Kirschstein Collection
HUCSM 45a.15

WOMAN'S PRAYER
Italy, 18th century (?)
Printed on paper
15 1/4 x 10 1/4 in. (38.7 x 26.0 cm)
Kirschstein Collection
HUCSM 45a.16

KIDDUSH CUP
Maker: Boaz Yemini (b. 1956)
Jerusalem, ca. 1985
Silver
3 1/8 x 2 5/8 in. diameter (8.0 x 6.7 cm)
Museum purchase
HUCSM 18.45

CANDLESTICKS (PL. 34)
Maker: Arie Ofir (b. 1939)
Jerusalem, designed 1986, fabricated 1990
Silver; and titanium
9 5/8 in. (24.5 cm)
Museum purchase with funds provided by
Howard and Wilma Friedman in memory of
Emma F. Friedman
HUCSM 11.49 a/b

KIDDUSH CUP
Czernowitz, Austro-Hungary, 1851
Silver, engraved
5 5/8 x 2 1/4 in. diameter (14.3 x 5.8 cm)
Kirschstein Collection, formerly Frauberger
Collection
HUCSM 18.11

KIDDUSH CUP
Maker: Kerry Feldman (b. 1953)
Los Angeles, 1988
Hand-blown glass
9 1/8 x 3 1/2 in. diameter (23.2 x 8.9 cm)
Museum purchase
HUCSM 18.56

HANUKKAH LAMP (WITH SABBATH
CANDLEHOLDERS)
Galicia, first half of 19th century
Brass, cast
8 3/4 x 10 3/8 x 5 1/8 in. (22.3 x 26.2 x 13.1 cm)
HUCSM 27.28

SPICE CONTAINER AND CANDLEHOLDER
Maker: Georg Daniel Weiss (?)
Nuremberg, first half of 18th century
Silver, repoussé and cast
7 3/8 x 3 1/4 in. diameter (18.8 x 8.1 cm)
Gift of the Jewish Cultural Reconstruction, Inc.
HUCSM 28.4

SPICE CONTAINER
Maker: Georgia Freedman-Harvey (b. 1955)
Los Angeles, 1978
Glass, etched and sand-blasted
6 x 1/12 in. (15.2 x 3.8 cm)
HUCSM 53.114

SPICE CONTAINER
Maker: Carmel Shabi
Israel, 1984
Silver
6 x 2 1/8 in. diameter (15.3 x 5.4 cm)
Museum purchase with funds provided in
memory of Shirley Gang Melnick from loving
family and friends
HUCSM 53.120

SPICE CONTAINER
Maker: Abraham Reiner (active ca. 1851– ca.
1880)
Warsaw, 1864
Silver, die-stamped and engraved
7 1/2 x 1 3/4 in. (19.0 x 4.4 cm)
Gift of Bernard and Sylvia Sayewitz
HUCSM 53.122

SPICE CONTAINER
Brünn, Austro-Hungarian Empire, 1867–1872
Silver, filigree
10 x 3 1/8 in. (25.4 x 7.9 cm)
Gift of the Jewish Cultural Reconstruction, Inc.
HUCSM 53.77

SPICE CONTAINER
Poland, 1921–1939
Silver, cast, die-stamped and engraved
8 1/2 x 5 1/8 in. diameter (21.4 x 13.1 cm)
Gift of the Jewish Cultural Reconstruction, Inc.
(No. 62)
HUCSM 53.87

HAVDALAH CUP
Bamberg, Germany, early 18th century
Silver, repoussé and parcel-gilt
8 1/4 x 3 3/4 in. diameter (21.0 x 9.5 cm)
Gift of the Jewish Cultural Reconstruction, Inc.
HUCSM 18.25

HAVDALAH CANDLES
Maker: Hannah Kopper
United States, ca. 1900
Braided wax
15 x 2 1/4 in. (38.1 x 5.7 cm)
Gift of the Gang Family
HUCSM 28.10 a/b

SPICE CONTAINER
Maker: George Heinrich Steffen
Berlin, early 19th century
Silver, filigree
9 1/2 x 2 1/8 in. diameter (24.1 x 5.5 cm)
HUCSM 53.18

SPICE CONTAINER
Poland, mid-19th century
Silver, cast, engraved and filigree
6½ x 3⅞ in. (16.5 x 9.8 cm)
HUCSM 53.29

SPICE CONTAINER
Frankfurt am Main, early 20th century
Silver, cast
8 ⅜ x 2½ in. (21.2 x 6.3 cm)
Gift of the Jewish Cultural Reconstruction, Inc.
(No. 1346)
HUCSM 53.66

SPICE CONTAINER AND CANDLEHOLDER
Germany (?), 19th century
Wood, carved; and brass
11⅛ x 2¼ in. diameter (28.3 x 5.6 cm)
HUCSM 53.79

SPICE CONTAINER
Poland, 19th century
Wood, carved and pierced
2⅜ x 1⅝ in. diameter (6.0 x 4.1)
HUCSM 53.81

SPICE CONTAINER
Germany or Bohemia, 19th century
Pewter
2⅝ x 2⅛ x 2½ in. (6.8 x 5.4 x 6.2 cm)
HUCSM 53.92

SPICE CONTAINER
Galicia or Moravia (?), late 18th–early 19th
century
Silver, filigree and parcel-gilt
10 x 3¼ in. diameter (25.4 x 8.3 cm)
Gift of Dr. Lee M. Friedman
HUCSM 53.93

SPICE CONTAINER
Maker: Hana Geber (1910–1990)
New York, 1970s
Silver-bronze alloy, cast
4⅞ x 3 ¾ in. (12.5 x 9.5 cm)
Gift of Mr. and Mrs. Robert Kaffsky
HUCSM 53.110 a/b

HAVDALAH SET
Maker: David H. Gumbel (1906–1992)
Jerusalem, 1986
Silver; leather case
Case: 1⅝ x 2⅛ x 4⅜ in. (4.2 x 5.4 x 11 cm)
Museum purchase
HUCSM 28.9 a-d

HAVDALAH SET
Maker: Susan Felix (b. 1938)
Berkeley, 1988
Clay, kiln-fired and smoked in sawdust
4¼ x 11 x 17 in. (10.8 x 27.9 x 43.2 cm)
HUCSM 28.11 a-d

SPICE CONTAINER
Poland, early 19th century
Silver, engraved
4 x 2¼ in. diameter (10.0 x 5.7 cm)
HUCSM 53.50

SPICE CONTAINER
Germany (?), late 18th century
Silver, pierced and chased
6⅞ x 2⅝ in. diameter (17.4 x 6.8 cm)
Kirschstein Collection
HUCSM 53.12

SPICE CONTAINER
Maker: Johann Friedrich Wilhelm Borcke
Berlin, 1821–1839
Silver, cast and pierced
9 x 2⅜ in. diameter (22.9 x 6.1 cm)
Gift of Mr. Max Rudolf
HUCSM 53.100

SPICE CONTAINER
Galicia or Bohemia-Moravia, first half of
19th century
Silver, filigree
8½ x 1¾ in. (21.7 x 4.6 cm)
HUCSM 53.41

SPICE CONTAINER
Germany or Poland, ca. 1800
Brass, pierced and cast
9¾ x 3½ in. diameter (24.7 x 9 cm)
HUCSM 53.28

SPICE CONTAINER
Maker: M. Kharlap (active 1880s–ca. 1915)
Warsaw, 1891
Silver, filigree and die-stamped
9¼ x 2⅜ in. diameter (24.13 x 6.1 cm)
Gift of Mrs. Joseph Rauch
HUCSM 53.103

HAVDALAH CANDLEHOLDER FRAGMENT
Maker: Johann Valentin Schüler (active 1680–
1720)
Frankfurt am Main, 1709–1725
Silver, chased and cast
4¾ x 3¼ in. (11.8 x 8.1 cm)
Gift of the Jewish Cultural Reconstruction, Inc.
HUCSM 28.5

DER SAMSTAG (SATURDAY)
Friedrich Campe
Germany, early 19th century
Etching, hand-colored
7½ x 10½ in. (19.0 x 26.7 cm)
HUCSM 66.1144

SABBATH LAMP FRAGMENT
Germany (?), 13th–14th century (?)
Bronze, cast and traces of gilt
4⅞ x 5¾ in. (12.4 x 14.5 cm)
Kirschstein Collection
HUCSM 33.33

SABBATH LAMP
The Netherlands, 19th century
Silver, cast and engraved
37⅜ in. (95 cm)
Gift of Mr. and Mrs. Martin Retting
HUCSM 33.58

SABBATH LAMP
Italy, 18th century
Brass, cast and turned
18 x 9 in. diameter (45.7 x 22.9 cm)
Gift of Mr. Ben Selling
HUCSM 33.36

JUDENSTERN (PL. 15)
Maker: Johann Valentin Schüler (active 1680–
1720)
Frankfurt am Main, 1709–1720
Silver, cast, pierced and engraved
16 x 14 in. diameter (40.6 x 35.6 cm)
Museum purchase
HUCSM 33.18

GERMAN DINING ROOM

ḤALLAH COVER (PL. 16)
Maker: Marianna Kirschstein
Germany, late 19th century
Silk, embroidered with silk and wool thread
21½ x 21½ in. (54.6 x 54.6 cm)
Kirschstein Collection
HUCSM 33a.1

KIDDUSH CUP
Frankfurt am Main, 1720s (?)
Silver, chased and gilt
3¼ x 2¾ in. diameter (8.3 x 7.0 cm)
HUCSM 18.24

SABBATH LAMP
Germany, 19th century
Brass, chased
18⅛ x 11⅛ in. (46. 0 x 28.1 cm)
HUCSM 33.6

HAVDALAH TRAY
Germany, late 19th century
Brass, engraved
3⅛ x 7 in. (8.0 x 17.7 cm)
HUCSM 43.34

PURIM PLATE
Maker: J. N. Wiesinger
Germany (?), dated 1763
Pewter, engraved
9⅜ in. diameter (23.8 cm)
Kirschstein Collection
HUCSM 43.24

SCROLL OF ESTHER AND CASE
Germany, 18th century
Engraving on parchment; and wood
12¼ in. (31.1 cm)
HUCSM 22.21

LAVER
Maker: Carl August Setzer (active 1820–1835)
Heilbronn, Germany, ca. 1830
Pewter, cast
Basin: 9⅝ x 13 x 9⅝ in. (24.5 x 33.2 x 24.5 cm)
Cistern: 11¼ x 11 x 8½ in. (28.7 x 28 x 21.5 cm)
HUCSM 3.6 a/b

CUP AND SAUCER
Munich, late 18th century
Porcelain
2⅜ x 5 in. diameter (6.0 x 12.7 cm)
HUCSM 14.37 a/b

SALT CELLAR
Eger, Austrian Empire, 1793
Silver, repoussé, engraved and cast
3½ x 2¼ in. diameter (9.0 x 5.7 cm)
Gift of Charles A. Greenhall, in memory of A.
Frank Greenhall
HUCSM 14.319

Sabbath Afternoon (*Pl. 37*)
Moritz Oppenheim (1800–1882)
Frankfurt am Main, ca. 1866
Oil on canvas
19⅝ x 22⅝ in. (49.8 x 57.5 cm)
Gift of the Jewish Cultural Reconstruction, Inc.
HUCSM 41.135

Mizraḥ
Central Europe, 18th century
Watercolor, gold leaf and ink on paper
13⅞ x 16⅝ in. (35.2 x 42.2 cm)
Kirschstein Collection
HUCSM 39.12

Mizraḥ
Central Europe, 19th century
Cut-out and overlaid paper
14 x 15¾ in. (35.5 x 40.1 cm)
HUCSM 39.3

Spice Container
Maker: Friedrich August Ferdinand Eisolt
Berlin, 1854–1860
Silver, filigree, chased and die-stamped
8 in. (20.3 cm)
Gift of Mrs. Joseph Rauch
HUCSM 53.102

Kiddush Cup
Nuremberg, ca. 1804–1808
Silver, chased
2½ x 2¼ in. (6.2 x 5.7 cm)
Gift of Charles A. Greenhall, in memory of A.
Frank Greenhall
HUCSM 18.62

Hanukkah Lamp
Maker: Johann George Fournier II (active ca.
1810)
Berlin, 1804–1815
Silver, repoussé and cast
5 ⅜ x 5 ⅞ in. (13.6 x 15.0 cm)
Kirschstein Collection
HUCSM 27.37

Shofar
Europe, 18th–19th century
Ram's horn, carved
15¾ in. (40.1 cm)
Kirschstein Collection
HUCSM 52.13

Portrait of Frau Ottinger (*Pl. 41*)
Samuelssohn
Germany, 1838
Oil on canvas
25 x 20 in. (63.5 x 50.8 cm)
Kirschstein Collection
HUCSM 41.50

Havdalah Compendium
Germany, early 19th century
Silver
5⅝ x 2⅛ in. diameter (14.3 x 5.5 cm)
HUCSM 28.1

Etrog Container
Breslau, Silesia, ca. 1761–1776
Silver, repoussé
3¾ x 4 x 3¼ in. (9.5 x 10.1 x 8.3 cm)
HUCSM 21.3

Judenstern
Germany (?), 19th century
Brass, cast
21⅞ x 16 in. (55.5 x 40.5 cm)
Gift of Dr. Eric Werner
HUCSM 33.20

ROSH HASHANAH AND YOM KIPPUR

Shofar and Case (*Pl. 76*)
Maker: Marcus Jonas
Oakland, California, ca. 1870s
Wood and ram's horn
Case: 3¼ x 16½ in. (8.3 x 41.9 cm)
Gift of Mrs. Felix Jonas
HUCSM 52.36 a/b

Shofar
Central Europe (?), 19th century
Ram's horn
5 x 15½ in. (12.7 x 39.4 cm)
HUCSM 52.24

Shofar
Central Europe, 18th–19th century
Ram's horn, carved
5 x 18½ in. (12.7 x 46.9 cm)
HUCSM 52.15

Wall Decoration
Jerusalem, 1867
Perforated paper embroidered with wool
17¾ x 22½ in. (45.1 x 57.2 cm)
Gift of the Officers of the New York State
Federation of Temple Sisterhoods
HUCSM 39.16

Torah Mantle
Maker: Mary Ann Danin (b. 1928)
Los Angeles, 1995
Cotton velvet embroidered with metallic thread;
and gold and silver beads
33½ x 13¼ x 7 in. (84.5 x 33.7 x 17.8 cm)
Museum commission with funds provided by
The Estate of Fay Rossin Lewbin and Hyman
Lewbin in memory of their late son Morris
Rossin Lewbin
HUCSM 60.140

Torah Mantle
Alsace, 1926
Silk, embroidered with metallic thread
appliqués and metallic thread fringe
35½ x 18 in. (90.2 x 45.7 cm)
Gift of Robert Platzer
HUCSM 60.115

Apple and Honey Dish
Maker: Ori Resheff (b. 1955)
Israel, designed 1993
Pewter
2 x 8 x 10½ in. (5.1 x 20.3 x 26.7 cm)
Museum purchase in memory of Howard
Helfman with funds provided by his family and
friends
HUCSM 43.90

New Year's Greeting
United States, ca. 1920
Engraved shell
3½ x 2½ in. (8.9 x 6.3 cm)
HUCSM 38.116

New Year's Greeting
New York, early 20th century
Photograph and printed paper
9½ x 7 in. (24.1 x 17.7 cm)
Gift of Jeannette K. Multer
HUCSM 19.300

New Year's Greeting (*Pl. 91*)
Germany, early 20th century
Printed paper
11⅝ x 8¾ in. (29.5 x 22.2 cm)
Gift of Grace Cohen Grossman
HUCSM 19.178

Yom Kippur Belt Buckle
Central Europe, early 20th century
Silver, repoussé; and linen embroidered with
metallic thread
5¼ x 7 in. (13.4 x 17.8 cm)
Gift of the Jewish Cultural Reconstruction, Inc.
HUCSM 8.7

Prayers for the Day of Atonement
Editor: Dr. I. Mersbacher
New York, 1881
On loan from Hebrew Union College-Jewish
Institute of Religion, Francis-Henry Library, Los
Angeles

SUKKOT

Etrog Container
Makers: Tsirl Waletsky and David Nulman
New York, 1981
Glass; and tinned copper
3⅞ x 7⅝ x 5¼ in. (9.8 x 19.3 x 13.3 cm)
HUCSM 21.10

Etrog Container
Germany or Austria, late 19th-early 20th
century
Silver, repoussé
7¼ x 4 ⅜ x 3 ⅜ in. (18.5 x 11.2 x 8.7 cm)
Gift of the Jewish Cultural Reconstruction, Inc.
(No. 5937)
HUCSM 21.4

Etrog Container
Germany, 19th century
Silver, cast and engraved
5⅞ x 4½ in. (14.5 x 11.6 cm)
Gift of the Jewish Cultural Reconstruction, Inc.,
formerly Nauheim Collection
HUCSM 21.5

Etrog Container
Central Europe, late 18th–early 19th century
Silver, chased, engraved and parcel-gilt
5 x 6½ x 4⅝ in. (12.6 x 16.6 x 11.7 cm)
Museum purchase
HUCSM 21.8

Building Booths for Sukkot in Jerusalem
Augsburg, Germany, 18th century
Etching, hand-colored
13 x 17½ in. (33 x 44.5 cm)
HUCSM 66.1137

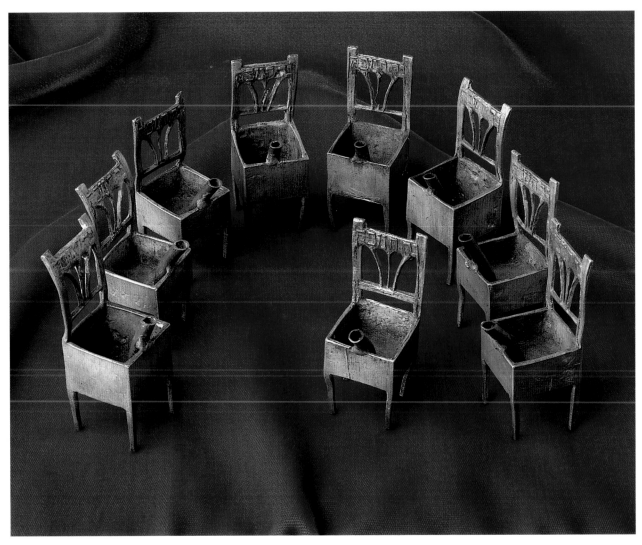

Plate 100. Miniature Chairs Hanukkah Lamp, late 19th-early 20th century

ETROG CONTAINER
Jerusalem, ca. 1915
Carved olivewood
3½ x 6 ⅜ x 4⅛ in. (8.8 x 16.1 x 10.4 cm)
Gift of Hester Harris Ehrlich
HUCSM 21.12

ETROG CONTAINER
Maker: H. Steiner
Central Europe, mid-19th century
Silver, cast and gilt
12 ⅜ x 6¾ in. (31.5 x 17.2 cm)
HUCSM 21.7

ETROG CONTAINER
Maker: Candace Knapp
Houston, 1986
Carved maple
6½ x 4 x 4 in. (16.5 x 10.2 x 10.2 cm)
HUCSM 21.11 a/b

RABBI SOLOMON ZALMAN LIPSCHITZ
IN THE SUKKAH
Warsaw, 19th century
Lithograph
16⅜ x 11⅞ in. (41.6 x 30.2)
HUCSM 66.1146

HANUKKAH

HANUKKAH LAMP
Germany, ca. 1900 (?)
Silver, die-stamped and engraved; and sheet iron
6¾ x 6¾ in. (17.1 x 17.1 cm)
Gift of the Jewish Cultural Reconstruction, Inc.
HUCSM 27.95

HANUKKAH LAMP
Germany, late 19th century
Pewter, cast and engraved
7⅞ x 9¼ x 3⅝ in. (20.0 x 23.5 x 9.2 cm)
Kirschstein Collection
HUCSM 27.49

HANUKKAH LAMP
Maker: Johann Jakob Leschhorn (active 1769–1787)
Frankfurt am Main, mid-18th century
Silver, repoussé and cast
6⅞ x 7 ⅜ x 3 in. (17.5 x 18.7 x 7.5 cm)
Gift of the Jewish Cultural Reconstruction, Inc.
HUCSM 27.94

HIRSCH HANUKKAH LAMP (PL. 18)
Germany, dated 1813/14
Silver, repoussé, pierced and cast
28 x 22¼ x 5½ in. (71.1 x 56.5 x 14 cm)
Museum purchase
HUCSM 27.70

HANUKKAH LAMP
Vienna, 1872–1922
Silver, die-stamped and cast
11½ x 11⅜ x 4 1/12 in. (29.1 x 28.8 x 11.3 cm)
Gift of the Jewish Cultural Reconstruction, Inc.
(No. 3296)
HUCSM 27.85

MINIATURE CHAIRS HANUKKAH LAMP *(PL. 100)*
Germany, late 19th–early 20th century
Pewter, cast; and brass
3 x 1¼ x 1⅜ in. (7.5 x 3.1 x 3.6 cm)
HUCSM 27.47

HANUKKAH LAMP
The Netherlands, early 20th century
Brass, cast and chased
11¾ x 9½ in. (30.0 x 24.0 cm)
Gift of Tilly Weil
HUCSM 27.173

HANUKKAH LAMP
Prague, 18th century
Brass, cast
7½ x 10⅛ x 3⅛ in. (18.9 x 25.8 x 8 cm)
Kirschstein Collection
HUCSM 27.4

OAK TREE HANUKKAH LAMP *(PL. 19)*
Lvov (?), Galicia, ca. 1800
Silver, repoussé, cast and parcel-gilt
23¼ x 26 ⅜ in. (59.1 x 67 cm)
HUCSM 27.100

BAAL SHEM TOV HANUKKAH LAMP
Germany (?), early 20th century
Silver, filigree, cast, die-stamped, engraved and
parcel-gilt
14 x 12⅞ x 5¼ in. (35.6 x 32.7 x 13.3 cm)
HUCSM 27.6

HANUKKAH LAMP
Moscow, 1836
Silver, cast, die-stamped, pierced and niello
12⅝ x 9 in. (32.0 x 22.8 cm)
Gift of Rabbi Ralph H. Blumenthal
HUCSM 27.123

STANDING HANUKKAH LAMP
Galicia, early 19th century
Brass, cast and turned
28⅛ x 25 ⅜ in. (71.5 x 64.5 cm)
HUCSM 27.5

HANUKKAH LAMP
Galicia or Ukraine, 19th century
Brass, cast and chased
10¾ x 9 ⅜ x 4⅛ in. (27.3 x 23.8 x 10.4 cm)
HUCSM 27.8

HANUKKAH LAMP
Italy, 17th-18th century
Bronze, cast
7¼ x 8¼ x 2⅝ in. (18.4 x 21.1 x 6.8 cm)
Kirschstein Collection
HUCSM 27.10

HANUKKAH LAMP
Italy, 19th century
Sheet iron, pierced; glass (mirror); pewter, cast;
and oil paints
13⅞ x 9⅝ x 2⅝ in. (35.2 x 24.4 x 6.8 cm)
Kirschstein Collection
HUCSM 27.56

HANUKKAH LAMP
Italy, 17th century
Brass, cast
4⅝ x 8¼ x 2 in. (11.6 x 21.0 x 5.0 cm)
Kirschstein Collection
HUCSM 27.22

HANUKKAH LAMP
Italy, late 17th–early 18th century
Brass, cast
11⅜ x 10⅞ x 3¼ in. (29.0 x 27.7 x 8.2 cm)
Kirschstein Collection
HUCSM 27.51

HANUKKAH LAMP
Siena (?), Italy, 17th century
Bronze, cast
8⅛ x 10⅝ in. (20.5 x 27 cm)
Gift of Dr. Lee M. Friedman
HUCSM 27.111

HANUKKAH LAMP
Italy, 17th–18th century
Brass, cast
7 x 10⅝ in. (17.9 x 27 cm)
Gift of Dr. Lee M. Friedman
HUCSM 27.114

HANUKKAH LAMP
Italy, 17th–18th century
Brass, cast
6¾ x 9¼ in. (17.0 x 23.6 cm)
Gift of Dr. Lee M. Friedman
HUCSM 27.110

HANUKKAH LAMP
Italy, 18th century
Bronze, cast
6 ⅜ x 8⅜ in. (16.2 x 21.2 cm)
Gift of Dr. Lee M. Friedman
HUCSM 27.112

HANUKKAH LAMP
Italy, 18th–19th century
Brass, cast
8 x 11⅝ x 3⅛ in. (20.4 x 29.4 x 8 cm)
Kirschstein Collection
HUCSM 27.45

HANUKKAH LAMP
Italy, 18th century
Brass, cast
9⅝ x 7 ⅜ in. (24.4 x 18.7 cm)
Kirschstein Collection
HUCSM 27.46

HANUKKAH LAMP
Jerusalem, 20th century
Brass, pierced, engraved, stamped and cast
12¼ x 10⅛ in. (31.2 x 25.8 cm)
HUCSM 27.41

HANUKKAH LAMP
Maker: Old Bezalel Workshops (active
1906–1932)
Jerusalem, ca. 1910–1914
Brass, repoussé and pierced; and carnelian
10 x 11¾ in. (25.3 x 29.8 cm)
HUCSM 27.25

HANUKKAH LAMP
Jerusalem, late 19th century
Olivewood
14½ x 16⅛ in. (36.8 x 40.9 cm)
Rabbi William M. Kramer Collection
HUCSM 27.184

MASADA HANUKKAH LAMP
Maker: Moshe Zabari (b. 1935)
New York, 1967
Silver, fabricated and embossed
6¾ x 11¾ in. (17.1 x 29.3 cm)
Gift of Mrs. John Hubbard, in honor of Jack
Skirball
HUCSM 27.121

HANUKKAH LAMP
Maker: Rod Kagan
Ketchum, Idaho, 1987
Bronze
10⅝ x 13⅛ x 3⅛ in. (27.0 x 33.4 x 7.9 cm)
Gift of Nathan and Marion Smooke
HUCSM 27.166

HANUKKAH LAMP *(PL. 36)*
Maker: Otto Natzler (b. 1908)
Los Angeles, 1988
Ceramic, olive and sang reduction glaze with
melt fissures and iridescences
8¾ x 13 x 5 in. (22.2 x 33.0 x 12.7 cm)
Museum purchase with funds provided by the
children, grandchildren and great-grandchildren
of Lee Kalsman in honor
of her eightieth birthday.
HUCSM 27.162

HANUKKAH LAMP *(PL. 30)*
Maker: Ludwig Y. Wolpert (1900–1982)
New York, ca. 1960
Silver
10⅞ x 11¼ x 4⅛ in. (27.5 x 28.5 x 10.5 cm)
Museum purchase with funds provided by the
Wilma and Howard Friedman Acquisition
Fund, in memory of Jeanette Sanditen Mann
HUCSM 27.131

HANUKKAH LAMP *(PL. 35)*
Maker: Richard Meier (b. 1935)
United States, 1990
Tin
12¼ x 13¾ x 2 in. (31.1 x 34.9 x 5.1 cm)
Museum purchase with funds provided by
Audrey and Arthur N. Greenberg
HUCSM 27.168

HANUKKAH LAMP
Maker: Hana Geber (1910–1990)
United States, ca. 1989
Bronze
13¾ x 13¼ x 11⅝ in. (35.0 x 33.5 x 29.5 cm)
Gift of the Estate of the Artist
HUCSM 27.180

HANUKKAH LAMP *(PL. 101)*
Maker: Peter Shire (b. 1947)
Los Angeles, 1986
Steel, painted, anodized and chrome-plated
21 x 24¼ in. (53.3 x 61.5 cm)
Museum commission with funds provided by
Marvin and Judy Zeidler
HUCSM 27.142

SYNAGOGUE HANUKKAH LAMP *(PL. 17)*
Aschaffenberg, Germany, dated 1706
Bronze, cast and engraved
37½ x 41¼ in. (95.3 x 104.8 cm)
HUCSM 27.73

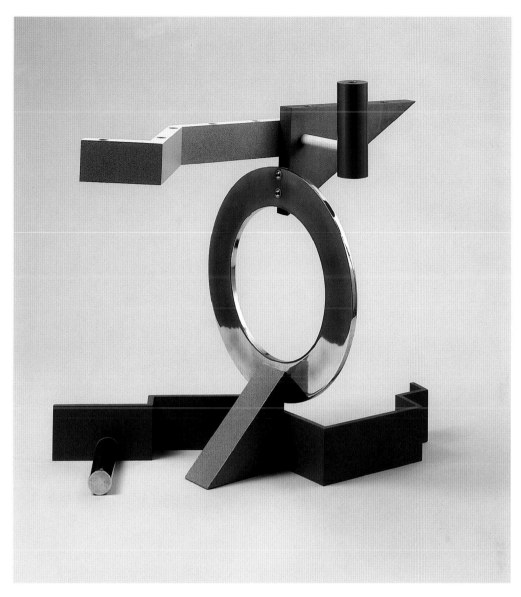

Plate 101. Hanukkah Lamp, Peter Shire, 1986

CANDELABRUM
Germany (?), late 19th–early 20th century
Bronze (?), cast and chased
11⅛ x 9¼ in. (28.3 x 23.5 cm)
Gift of Mr. Louis E. Shecter
HUCSM 11.22

DREIDELS
Germany, 18th–19th Century
Lead and wood
HUCSM 24.9

*KINDLING OF THE HANUKKAH LAMP IN A
POLISH-JEWISH HOME*
K. Felsenhardt
Poland, 1893
Colored chalk and gouache on paper
5⅞ x 9¾ in. (14.9 x 24.8 cm)
Kirschstein Collection
HUCSM 66.79

PURIM

SCROLL OF ESTHER AND CASE
Italy, 18th–19th century
Case: gold, filigree
Scroll: ink on parchment
Case: 1⅝ x ¾ in. diameter (4.0 x 2.0 cm)
HUCSM 22.11

SCROLL OF ESTHER (PL. 20)
Maker: Aryeh Loeb ben Daniel of Guria
Venice, 1748
Ink on parchment
9 in. (22.9 cm)
Kirschstein Collection, formerly Frauberger
Collection
HUCSM 22.12

SCROLL OF ESTHER (PL. 102)
Bohemia, ca. 1700
Ink and gouache on parchment
11 x 177½ in. (27.9 x 450.8 cm)
Gift of Felix and Evelyn E. Guggenheim,
formerly Kirschstein Collection
HUCSM 22.54

SCROLL OF ESTHER AND CASE
Turkey, late 19th–early 20th century
Case: silver, filigree and parcel-gilt; and coral
Scroll: ink on parchment
Case: 16½ x 1¾ in. (42 x 4.5 cm)
Scroll: 5½ in. (14.1 cm)
HUCSM 22.19

SCROLL OF ESTHER (PL. 103)
Maker: Aaron Wolf Herlingen of Gewitsch
Austria, mid-18th century
Ink and wash on parchment
10½ in. (26.7 cm)
HUCSM 22.48

Plate 102. Bohemian Scroll of Esther, ca. 1700

SCROLL OF ESTHER
Italy, ca. 1800
Ink on parchment
4⅝ in. (11.6 cm)
HUCSM 22.51

SCROLL OF ESTHER AND CASE
Italy, 18th century
Ink and gouache on vellum; and silver, chased
Case: 6⅝ x 1½ in. diameter (17.0 x 3.7 cm)
Scroll: 4⅛ in. (10.5 cm)
Kirschstein Collection
HUCSM 22.14

SCROLL OF ESTHER CASE
Makers: Lorelei (b. 1961) and
Alex Gruss (b. 1957)
New York, 1989
Padauk wood, purple heart and ebony inlaid
with ivory, silver, mother of pearl, abalone and
brass
20 x 4 in. diameter (50.8 x 10.2 cm)
Museum purchase with funds provided by
Leonard and Elaine Comess in memory of Elsie
Hackel
HUCSM 22.70

*MORDECAI OFFERED A HORSE BY THE KING
TO RIDE THROUGH THE STREETS* (PL. 38)
Lambert Lombard (1506–1566)
France, 16th century
Oil on wood panel
16½ x 11¾ in. (41.9 x 29.8 cm)
Kirschstein Collection
HUCSM 41.62

IT'S NOT ESTHER
Maker: Dina Dar (1939–1995)
Los Angeles, 1984
Watercolor on bark
23½ x 20 in. (59.7 x 50.8 cm)
Gift of the Artist
HUCSM 67.122

HAMAN FROM THE FIVE SCROLLS (PL. 64)
Leonard Baskin (b. 1922)
New York, 1980
Watercolor on paper
22 x 15⅛ in. (55.9 x 38.4 cm)
Museum purchase with funds provided by the
Gerald M. and Carolyn Z. Bronstein Acquisition
Fund for Project Americana
HUCSM 66.2651

THE WICKED HAMAN
Maryan (Pincas Burstein)
Paris (?), 1953
Oil on canvas
31¾ x 25⅝ in. (80.7 x 65.0 cm)
Gift of Mr. and Mrs. Louis Kaufman
HUCSM 41.274

PURIM GIFTS PLATES (PL. 21)
Amsterdam, dated 1785
Faience
9⅝ in. diameter (24.4 cm)
HUCSM 43.61-72

PURIM GIFTS PLATE
Germany, dated 1802
Pewter, engraved
9½ in. diameter (24.1 cm)
Kirschstein Collection
HUCSM 43.10

PURIM GIFTS PLATE
Germany (?), dated 1782
Pewter, engraved
8¼ in. diameter (20.9 cm)
Rabbi William M. Kramer Collection
HUCSM 43.86

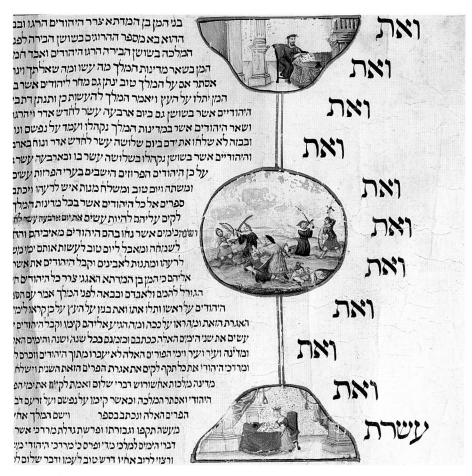

Plate 103. Scroll of Esther, Aaron Wolf Herlingen of Gewitsch, mid-18th century

SHALAḤ MANOT AND MATAN BESETER
TZEDAKAH PLATE (PL. 104)
Maker: Moshe Zabari (b. 1935)
Jerusalem, 1989
Silver
3½ x 11 in. diameter (8.9 x 28.0 cm)
Presented to the Hebrew Union College
   Skirball Museum in honor of the 40th
   Wedding Anniversary of Peachy and Mark
   Levy by their children and grandchildren
HUCSM 23.18

PURIM MOLD
Central Europe, 19th century
Wood, carved
3⅛ x 3 ⅜ x ½ in. (7.9 x 8.6 x 1.3 cm)
Kirschstein Collection
HUCSM 23.6

PURIM MOLD
Central Europe, 19th century
Wood, carved
3¼ x 1⅝ x⅝ in. (8.3 x 4.1 x 1.6 cm)
Kirschstein Collection
HUCSM 23.9

PURIM NOISEMAKER
Germany (?), 19th century
Silver
3¼ x 1¾ in. (8.1 x 4.3 cm)
Kirschstein Collection
HUCSM 23.10

PURIM NOISEMAKER (KLAPPER)
Maker: Max Sherman
United States, 1923
Wood
7½ x 5 ¾ x 2¼ in. (19.1 x 14.6 x 5.7 cm)
Gift of Mrs. Anna S. Vineburg
HUCSM 23.11

PURIM NOISEMAKER
Maker: Marnin Feinstein
Ranana, Israel,. ca. 1985
Wood, carved
9 x 8¾x 1½ in. (22.9 x 22.2 x 3.8 cm)
HUCSM 23.13

PURIM NOISEMAKER
Japan, 1960s
Metal; and plastic
5 x 2½ x 2 in. (12.7 x 6.4 x 5.1 cm)
Gift of Lynne Gilberg
HUCSM 23.14

PURIM NOISEMAKER
Maker: Edith Fishel
United States, 1982
Ceramic
4½ x 4½ in. (11.4 x 11.4 cm)
Museum purchase
HUCSM 23.12

HEBREW CHARITIES BALL INVITATION
New York, 1882
Chromolithograph
8¾ x 4¼ in. (22.2 x 10.8 cm)
Museum purchase with funds provided by
   the Lee Kalsman Project Americana
   Acquisition Fund
HUCSM 29.251

PURIM PROGRAM
San Luis Obispo, California, 1886
Printed paper
7⅞ x 4¾ in. (20.0 x 12.1 cm)
Anonymous Gift
HUCSM 13.35

Plate 104. Shalah Manot and Matan Beseter Tzedkah Plate, Moshe Zabari, 1989

PASSOVER

SEDER PLATE
Maker: Herend Workshop
Hungary, 19th century
Porcelain, hand-painted
14⅜ in. diameter (36.6 cm)
Gift of Ben Ari Arts, Ltd.
HUCSM 43.43

SEDER TOWEL
Turkey, 19th century
Linen embroidered with silk and metallic
thread
42 x 18½ in. (106.7 x 46.9 cm)
Gift of Mrs. Matilda Horn in memory of her
mother, Raina Levy Eskenazi and her sister,
Mary Eskenazi Caraco
HUCSM 50a.26

THE DROWNING OF THE EGYPTIANS IN
THE RED SEA
Harry Lieberman (1880–1983)
Los Angeles, 1964
Oil on canvas
30¾ x 41½ in. (78.2 x 105.4 cm)
Gift of Dr. and Mrs. Ronald Lawrence
HUCSM 41.276

TIERED SEDER PLATE
Maker: Moshe Zabari (b. 1935)
Jerusalem, 1987 (design 1961)
Silver and plexiglas
6⅛ x 10½ x 10½ in. (15.5 x 26.6 x 26.6 cm)
Museum purchase
HUCSM 50.19 a-k

KIDDUSH CUP
Moscow, 1872
Silver, engraved, and gilt
3½ x 2⅜ in. (8.8 x 6.0 cm)
Gift of Ida Renning and Frances Schiffler, in
memory of their parents, Anna and
Morris Ward
HUCSM 18.36

PASSOVER KIDDUSH CUP
Poland, late 19th century
Etched glass
3 x 2⅛ in. diameter (7.6 x 5.3 cm)
Gift of Vera Grossfield
HUCSM 18.48

AFIKOMEN BAG
Maker: Barbara Gordon
Los Angeles, 1984
Cotton
12½ x 12½ in. (31.8 x 31.8 cm)
Gift of the Artist
HUCSM 50a.59

MATZAH PERFORATOR
Germany, 18th–19th century
Wrought iron
6⅛ x 3⅞ in. (15.7 x 9.8 cm)
Kirschstein Collection
HUCSM 35.12

CANDLEHOLDER FOR SEARCHING FOR LEAVEN
Maker: Moshe Zabari (b. 1935)
Jerusalem, 1991 (design 1984)
Silver, fabricated and pierced
1⅞ x 7¾ in. (4.8 x 19.7 cm)
Museum purchase with funds provided by
Leonard and Elaine Comess in memory of
Harry Hackel
HUCSM 50.26 a/b

SEDER SHOW TOWEL (SEDERZWËHL) (PL. 23)
Alsace, 1821
Linen, embroidered with silk thread, and silk
ribbon
50 x 15½ in. (127.1 x 39.6 cm)
Gift of Rabbi Folkman
HUCSM 50a.36

SEDER SHOW TOWEL (SEDERZWËHL)
Germany, 1747
Linen, embroidered with silk and metallic
thread; silk velvet appliqué; and sequins
65 x 15½ in. (165.1 x 39.4 cm)
HUCSM 50a.4

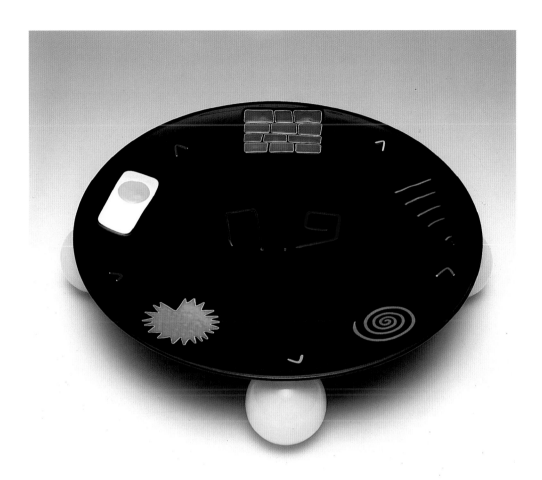

Plate 105. Seder Plate, Kerry Feldman, 1987

AFIKOMEN BAG
China, 19th century
Cotton and satin, embroidered with silk and metallic thread
5¾ in. diameter (14.6 cm)
HUCSM 50a.42

SEDER PLATE (PL. 105)
Kerry Feldman (b. 1953)
Los Angeles, 1987
Hand-blown colored glass
17 in. diameter (43.2 cm)
Museum purchase with funds provided by Jesse R. and Sylvia M. Gross in honor of their grandchildren
HUCSM 43.79

THE CHILDREN'S HAGGADAH
Editor: Dr. A. M. Silberman
Illustrator: Erwin Singer
Berlin, 1936
12¼ x 9¼ in. (31.1 x 23.5 cm)
Gift of Lloyd Cotsen
HUCSM 5.195

SEDER PLATE
Austria, dated 1776
Pewter, engraved
13⅛ in. diameter (33.4 cm)
HUCSM 43.1

TIERED SEDER PLATE (PL. 22)
Maker: Franz Strobl (?) (active 1811–1843)
Vienna, 1814
Silver, cast, pierced and engraved
14¾ x 16 in. diameter (37.5 x 40.6 cm)
HUCSM 50.12

PASSOVER PILLOW COVER
Germany, 18th century
Linen, embroidered with cotton thread
29½ x 29½ in. (74.93 x 74.93)
HUCSM 50a.1

PASSOVER PILLOW COVER
Germany, 18th century
Linen, embroidered with cotton thread
26½ x 31 in. (67.3 x 78.7 cm)
HUCSM 50a.2

MATZAH COVER
Jerusalem, early 20th century
Velvet, embroidered with silk and metallic thread; sequins; and fish-scales
24 in. diameter (61 cm)
HUCSM 50a.35

PASSOVER WINE CUP
Germany, 1824
Glass
5¼ x 3⅛ in. diameter (13.3 x 8 cm)
HUCSM 50.15

SEDER PLATE
Alsace, late 18th century
Pewter, later engraving
16⅞ in. diameter (42.8 cm)
Gift of Mr. and Mrs. Edward Adler
HUCSM 43.58

SEDER VESSEL
Maker: Bartolome May(e)rhofer (?)
Munich, 1820s; dated 1841
Silver, cast and die-stamped
3 x 3 in. diameter (7.7 x 7.7 cm)
HUCSM 50.1

SEDER VESSEL (FOR EGG)
Johann II Pfeffenhauser (active 1697–1754)
Augsburg, Germany, 1751–1753
Silver, chased and gilt
2⅛ x 1⅜ x 2⅛ in. (5.4 x 3.5 x 5.5 cm)
HUCSM 50.2

SEDER VESSEL
Germany, late 19th century
Silver, cast
1½ x 1⅝ x 5⅜ in. (3.8 x 4.0 x 13.5 cm)
HUCSM 50.3

SEDER VESSEL
Maker: Abraham Reiner (active 1851–1880)
Warsaw, 1873
Silver, repoussé and cast
6⅛ x 5⅜ x 2½ in. (16.0 x 13.5 x 6.5 cm)
Gift of Bernard and Sylvia Sayewitz
HUCSM 50.17

SEDER VESSEL
Warsaw, first half of 19th century
Silver, cast, die-stamped, and parcel-gilt
2⅝ x 3½ x 2⅜ in. (6.7 x 8.8 x 6.1 cm)
Gift of Bernard and Sylvia Sayewitz
HUCSM 50.18

SEDER PLATE
Cologne, dated 1779
Pewter, engraved
16¼ in. diameter (41.4 cm)
Kirschstein Collection
HUCSM 43.33

TIERED SEDER PLATE AND CUP OF ELIJAH
Maker: Friedrich Adler (1878–1942)
Hamburg, Germany, 1914
Pewter
11 x 19 in. diameter (28.0 x 48.3 cm)
On loan from the family descendants of Rabbi
    Jacob Sonderling: Fred and Helene Sonderling,
    Paul and Ruth Sonderling, Don Sonderling
    Family, Diane Sonderling Gray Family

SHAVUOT

CONFIRMATION CERTIFICATE
Demmin, Germany, 1869
Ink on paper
6⅞ x 8 in. (17.5 x 20.3 cm)
Gift of Herman and Polly Alevy
HUCSM 19a.46

CONFIRMATION CERTIFICATE
Printer: Bloch Publishing Co.
New York, 1911
Printed paper and ink
11⅞ x 14 ⅜ in. (30.2 x 37.8 cm)
Gift of Herman and Polly Alevy
HUCSM 19a.47

CONFIRMATION CERTIFICATE
New York, 1938
Printed paper and ink
7¾ x 9¾ in. (19.7 x 24.8 cm)
Gift of Herman and Polly Alevy
HUCSM 19a.48

CONFIRMATION CERTIFICATE
Long Beach, California, 1961
Printed paper and ink
7⅞ x 10⅞ in. (20 x 27.6 cm)
Gift of Herman and Polly Alevy
HUCSM 19a.49

CONFIRMATION CERTIFICATE
Long Beach, California 1966
Printed paper and ink
8½ x 11 in. (21.6 x 28 cm)
Gift of Herman and Polly Alevy
HUCSM 19a.50

MINIATURE TORAH SCROLL
Central Europe, dated 1869/70
Scroll: ink on parchment; and coconut shell
    rollers
Crown and pointer: silver, parcel-gilt pearls; and
    coral
Mantle: silk velvet, embroidered with silk and
    metallic thread; and sequins
3.7 x 3.2 in. (9.5 x 8.2 cm)
Gift of Mr. and Mrs. Max de Jong, Jr.
HUCSM 61.12

SHAVUOT PAPERCUT
Makers: Martin and Joan Benjamin-Farren
Cambridge, Massachusetts, 1978
Paper
11 x 8 in. (27.9 x 20.3 cm)
Gift of the Gang Family in honor of Martin
    Gang
HUCSM 66.2067

MIZRAH/OMER CALENDAR (PL. 74)
Printer: Moses H. Henry
Cincinnati, 1850
Ink on paper
25⅝ x 37½ in. (65.1 x 95.4 cm)
Gift of Mrs. Jacob Goldsmith
HUCSM 39.1

MIZRAH/OMER CALENDAR
Maker: Dov Margoliot, son of Asher Selig,
    Rabbi of Szezebrskyn, Poland
Germany, 1830
Ink on vellum
11⅜ x 12⅛ in. (29 x 30.8 cm)
HUCSM 39.37

OMER TABLET
Italy, 18th century
Ink on parchment
17¼ x 13 in. (43.8 x 33 cm)
HUCSM 40.2

DAILY PRAYERBOOK
Publisher: Star Hebrew Book Co.
Vienna, 1927
Printed paper; metal and enamel on velvet
4 ¾ x 3½ x 1⅛ in. (12.1 x 8.9 x 3.2 cm)
Gift of Joyce Pepper
HUCSM 5.166

SHAVUOT PAPERCUT
Maker: Y. Grossbard
Paper
9¼ x 7 in. (23.5 x 17.8 cm)
Gift of Mrs. Hyman Lewbin
HUCSM 66.2404

THE BOOK OF RUTH
Maker: Ze'ev Raban (1890–1970)
Jerusalem, 1930
12 x 9 in. (30.5 x 22.9 cm)
Gift of Arlene Appley in memory of Choya
    Wagner Applemen
HUCSM 5.9

Plate 106. Rondel's Haggadah, 15th century

LIFE CYCLE

FROM BIRTH TO CHILDHOOD,
from youth to old age, a person changes. Every human life is
shaped by a cycle, unique to each yet shared by all.

As Jews observe the patterns of time and season, so they also
mark the stages of life. Birth and growth,
love and loss — each moment of passage has its own rituals
and traditions. These connect the individual
to the family, the community, and all the generations
of the Jewish people.

When a Jew is born and when a Jew dies, there are
prayers of thanks for the gift of life. It is regarded by Jewish
tradition as sacred and supremely valuable.
"Just to be is a blessing," it has been taught.
"Just to live is holy."

Plate 107. Circumcision Cups and Case, Paul Solanier, 1695–1710

BIRTH

CIRCUMCISION KNIFE
Germany (?), 18th century
Silver, cast and chased; and steel
7¼ x ⅞ in. (18.3 x 2.3 cm)
HUCSM 15.1

CHAIR OF ELIJAH (PL. 25)
Rheda, Westphalia, 1803
Carved wood
53 x 52 x 20½ in. (134.6 x 132. x 52.1cm)
Kirschstein Collection
HUCSM 15.32

CIRCUMCISION CERTIFICATE
Maker: Meyer Sheinbaim
New Jersey, 1926
Ink and watercolor on paper
18¼ x 11⅝ in. (46.4 x 29.4 cm)
Gift of Ann and Seymour Kaplan
HUCSM 19a.83

CIRCUMCISION CUPS (WITH CASE)
Maker: Paul Solanier (1665–1724)
Augsburg, Germany,1695–1710
Cups: silver, engraved and gilt
Case: wood, leather
Cups: 1⅞ x 2½ in. diameter (4.7 x 6.4 cm)
Case: 2⅞ x 3⅛ in. diameter (7.3 x 7.9 cm)
Gift of Frank L. Weil
HUCSM 15.34 a-c

BABY CUP
United States, dated 1879
Silver, engraved
3½ x 2⅞ in. diameter (8.9 x 7.4 cm)
Gift of Walter S. Hilborn
HUCSM 14.57

TORAH SHIELD
Galicia, dated 1784/5
Silvered copper or silver, repoussé
5¾ x 6¼ in. (14.7 x 15.9 cm)
Gift of the Jewish Cultural Reconstruction, Inc.
HUCSM 7.7

ARBA KANFOT (PL. 109)
Maker: Anna Banks
Portsmouth, England, 1901
Crocheted cotton
36 x 8⅞ in. (91.4 x 22.5 cm)
Gift of Susan Moyse Richter in honor of the
Moyse family
HUCSM 46.65

ARBA KANFOT
Maker: Elkie Baker
Poland, ca. 1860
Crocheted linen
15 x 18 in. (38.1 x 45.7 cm)
Gift of Mrs. Anne Leader
HUCSM 46.43

MOHELET CERTIFICATE
Ruth Berman (b. 1947)
United States, 1985
Printed on paper
18 x 13 ¹⁵/₁₆ in. (45.7 x 35.5 cm)
Gift of the Brit Milah Board of Reform Judaism
through Dr. Lewis M. Barth
HUCSM 19a.22

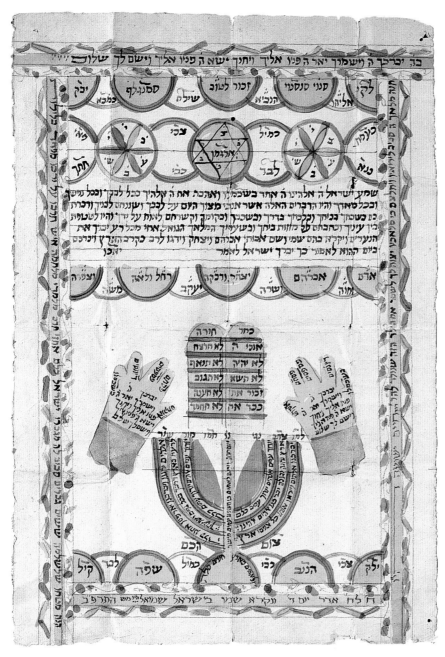

Plate 108. Amulet, ca. 1922

AMULET
Germany, 19th century
Ink on paper
7½ x 6¼ in. (19.1 x 15.9 cm)
Gift of Grete Benedix and Grete E. Benedix in
memory of Paul and Ernst Benedix
HUCSM 2.63

AMULET   (PL. 108)
New York, ca. 1922
Ink and watercolor on parchment
20 x 14 in. (50.8 x 35.6 cm)
Gift of Barbara Hade Kaplan
HUCSM 2.69

AMULET FOR NEW BEGINNINGS
Maker: Lila Wahrhaftig
Oakland, California, 1993
Handmade paper; bamboo; hand-spun yarns;
and foil
8⅜ x 4⅝ in. (22.3 x 11.7 cm)
HUCSM 2.70

AMULET
Italy, 19th century (?)
Silver, cast and gilt
4⅝ x 2¼ in. (11.8 x 5.7cm)
Kirschstein Collection
HUCSM 2.22

CIRCUMCISION CAP
Istanbul, 19th century
Silk, embroidered with metallic thread
4 x 7½ in. (10.2 x 19.1 cm)
Gift of Connie and Leonard Robin from the
Jack Eskenazi Family
HUCSM 15.55c

CIRCUMCISION CAP
Germany, ca. 1900
Crocheted cotton and silk
6 x 6 in. (15.2 x 15.2 cm)
Gift of Marianne Pinkus in memory of Fritz
Epstein
HUCSM 25.140

CIRCUMCISION DRESS
Maker: Flora Huniu Levy
Los Angeles, 1925
Linen; crocheted lace; and silk ribbon
24 in. (61 cm)
Gift of Myer A. Huniu
HUCSM 15.51

CIRCUMCISION DRESS
United States, late 19th–early 20th century
Cotton
29⅞ in. (76 cm)
Gift of Rabbi and Mrs. William M. Kramer
HUCSM 25.8

PLATE FOR THE REDEMPTION OF THE FIRST
BORN SON CEREMONY
Galicia, 19th century
Brass, repoussé
7½ x 10 in. (19 x 25.4 cm)
From the Collection of The Jewish Museum,
New York
HUCSM 15.36

THE REDEMPTION OF THE FIRST BORN SON
Bernard Picart (1673–1733)
France, 1722
Engraving
7⅞ x 9 1/8 in. (19.8 x 23.1 cm)
HUCSM 66.352

CIRCUMCISION SHIELD
Central Europe, 18th–19th century
Silver, engraved and gilt
3 x 1½ in. (7.7 x 3.7 cm)
HUCSM 15.19

CIRCUMCISION SHIELD
Central Europe, 18th–19th century
Silver
2¾ x 1⅝ in. (7.1 x 4.1 cm)
Gift of Rabbi Lou H. Silberman
HUCSM 15.30

AMULET
Persia, 19th–20th century
Silver, chased and filigree
6⅝ x 2⅛ in. (16.8 x 5.2 cm)
HUCSM 2.34

Plate 109. Arba Kanfot, Anna Banks, 1901

ולחופה

להורה

Plate 110. Torah Binder (detail), 1834

INVITATION TO REDEMPTION OF THE
FIRST BORN SON CEREMONY
Brooklyn, 1940
Engraving on paper
5½ x 4 in. (13.97 x 10.16 cm)
Gift of Henry Walter Weiss
HUCSM13.10 a-d

OUTFIT FOR REDEMPTION OF THE
FIRST BORN SON CEREMONY
New York, 1940
Silk; cotton; and wool
Robe: 21⅜ x 18⅜ in. (54.3 x 46.7 cm)
Gown: 16⅛ x 15⅜ in. (40.9 x 39.1 cm)
Scarf: 4¼ x 36⅞ in. (10.9 x 93.7 cm)
Gift of Henry Walter Weiss
HUCSM 15.48 a-c

PRINTING BLOCKS FOR WIMPELS
Germany, 19th century?
Wood and metal
2⅜ x 2⅝ in. (largest) (6 x 6.7 cm)
Kirschstein Collection
HUCSM 38.130

TORAH BINDER (PL. 110)
Germany, 1834
Linen, painted; and silk binding
7⅜ x 133 in. (18.7 x 337.8 cm)
Kirschstein Collection
HUCSM 56.341

TORAH BINDER
Mainz, Germany, 1845
Linen, painted
7¾ x 137 in. (19.7 x 348 cm)
Gift of Julia Scharvogel Fybel
HUCSM 56.599

TORAH BINDER
Germany, 1731
Undyed Linen, embroidered with silk thread
7½ x 123½ in. (19 x 313.7 cm)
HUCSM 56.1

TORAH BINDER (PL. 26)
Germany, 1733
Linen, embroidered with silk thread
7½ x 115 in. (19.1 x 292.1 cm)
HUCSM 56.5

TORAH BINDER
Germany, 1718
Linen, embroidered with silk thread
8 x 133 in. (337.8 cm)
HUCSM 56.474

TORAH BINDER
Germany, 1798
Linen, embroidered with silk thread
6½ x 129 in. (16.5 x 327.7 cm)
HUCSM 56.156

TORAH BINDER
Germany, 1792
Linen, painted
6 x 140 in. (15.2 x 355.6 cm)
HUCSM 56.475

TORAH BINDER (PL. 78)
Trinidad, Colorado, 1889
Linen, painted; and silk thread edging
9½ x 140 in. (24.1 x 358.1cm)
Gift of Gilbert Sanders
HUCSM 56.15

TORAH BINDER
Germany, 1777
Linen, embroidered with silk
6 x 142 in. (15.24 x 360.7 cm)
HUCSM 56.91

TORAH BINDER
Germany, 1837
Linen, painted; and silk edging
7½ x 131 in. (19.1 x 332.7 cm)
HUCSM 56.323

TORAH BINDER
Germany, 1743
Linen, printed linen lining, embroidered with
silk and metallic thread
5½ x 118 (14 x 299.8 cm)
HUCSM 56.444

TORAH BINDER
Germany, 1777
Linen, painted
7 x 119 in. (17.8 x 302.3 cm)
HUCSM 56.344

TORAH BINDER
Germany, 1726
Linen, embroidered with silk thread
7½ x 149 in. (19.1 x 378.5 cm)
HUCSM 56.58

TORAH BINDER
Germany, 1763
Linen, embroidered with silk thread
7 x 121 in. (17.8 x 307.3 xm)
HUCSM 56.486

TORAH BINDER
United States, 1942
Linen, painted
9 x 103 in. (22.9 x 261.6 cm)
Gift of Alison D. Bernhard
HUCSM 56.575

TORAH BINDER
Germany, 1778
Linen, embroidered with silk thread
7 x 118½ in. (17.8 x 301.0 cm)
HUCSM 56.29

TORAH BINDER
Germany, 1758
Linen, embroidered with silk and metallic
thread
7 x 143 in. (17.8 x 363.2 cm)
Kirschstein Collection
HUCSM 56.4

TORAH BINDER
France, 1945
Linen, painted
7½ x 9½ in. (19.1 x 224.9 cm)
On loan from the Neutrogena Corporation

BAR/BAT MITZVAH

TEFILLIN
Eastern Europe, early 20th century
Leather; and ink on parchment
1⅜ x 2 x 1½ in. (3.5 x 5.1 x 3.8 cm)
Gift of Gertrude Kallin
HUCSM 55.27 a/b

TORAH MANTLE
Germany, 1851
Velvet and velvet appliqués
37 x 19½ in. (93.9 x 49.5 cm)
HUCSM 60.46

KIPPAH FOR BAT MITZVAH
Los Angeles, 1985
Crocheted acrylic yarn and metallic thread
6½ in. diameter (16.5 cm)
Gift of Heidi and Stuart Laff
HUCSM 46.102

TALLIT
Makers: Laurie Gross (b.1952) with Jill Peek
Los Angeles, 1982
Cotton and wool
78 x 36 in. (198.1 x 91.4 cm)
Gift of Mr. and Mrs. Donald Glabman Purchase
Fund and Dr. Alfred Gottschalk Purchase Fund
in honor of Jack Skirball
HUCSM 46.74

TALLIT
Maker: Sharon Norry
Rochester, New York, 1980
Wool; silk; and metallic thread
77 x 37 in. (195.6 x 93.9 cm)
Gift of the Artist
HUCSM 46.69

TALLIT BAG
Maker: Bezalel Workshop
Jerusalem, early 20th century
Velvet, embroidered
11⅝ x 7⅞ in. (29.5 x 20.1 cm)
HUCSM 46.41

KIPPAH
Los Angeles, 1989
Cotton
4 x 8 in. diameter (12.1 x 20.3 cm)
Gift of Nancy M. Berman
HUCSM 46.130

TALLIT BAG
Maker: Barbara Gordon
Los Angeles, 1993
Velveteen, embroidered with cotton thread
11½ x 14 in. (29.2 x 35.6 cm)
Museum purchase with funds provided by the
Audrey and Arthur N. Greenberg Fund
HUCSM 46.134

TALLIT BAG
Algiers, 1880
Velvet, embroidered with metallic thread;
and silk
11½ x 9 in. (29.2 x 22.9 cm)
Museum purchase with funds provided by The
Maurice Amado Foundation
HUCSM 46.143

TEFILLIN CASE
Galicia, first half of 19th century
Silver, engraved
2¾ x 2⅛ x 1⅞ in. (7.0 x 5.3 x 4.7 cm)
Gift of the Jewish Cultural Reconstruction, Inc.
HUCSM 55.1

BAT MITZVAH INVITATION
Los Angeles, 1988
Printed paper
9¼ x 5¾ in. (23.5 x 14.61 cm)
Gift of Steven and Janet Scharf and Adina
Scharf
HUCSM 79.76

BAR MITZVAH INVITATION
Maker: Amy Goldenberg
Los Angeles, 1985
Printed on paper
8¼ x 5¼ in. (21 x 13.3 cm)
Gift of the Artist
HUCSM 79.90

BAR MITZVAH INVITATION
Los Angeles, 1977
Paper, engraved
6½ x 4½ in. (16.5 x 11.4 cm)
Gift of Bette Penzell
HUCSM 79.80 a-d

BAT MITZVAH FAVOR
Los Angeles, 1989
Glass, painted
6½ x 5½ x 2¾ in. (16.5 x 13.9 x 7.0 cm)
Gift of Nancy M. Berman
HUCSM 29.250

BAR MITZVAH BOOK
Yonah Weinrib
Chicago, 1992
Printed paper
8¾ x 11⅛ in. (22.4 x 28.2 cm)
Gift of Barbara and George Hanus and Family
HUCSM 79.9e

BAR MITZVAH CAKE DECORATION
United States, ca. 1915–1920
Bisque, painted; plaster; and cloth
9½ x 8 in. (24.1 x 20.3 cm)
Gift of the Estate of Mary Heller
HUCSM 14.203

MARRIAGE

WEDDING CUP AND SAUCER
Germany, mid-19th century
Porcelain
5 x 6 ¾ in. diameter (12.7 x 17.0 cm)
Kirschstein Collection
HUCSM 14.38 a/b

BRUSTTUCH
Poland, 18th century
Wool; and silk embroidered with metallic
thread
10 x 17½ in. (25.4 x 44.5 cm)
HUCSM 25.1

BRUSTTUCH
Poland, 18th–19th century
Silk and linen embroidered with metallic thread
9½ x 16 in. (24.1 x 40.6 cm)
HUCSM 25.4

GOLDEN WEDDING ANNIVERSARY CUP
Vienna, dated 1891
Silver, cast and engraved
10¼ x 3⅞ in. diameter (26 x 9.7 cm)
Gift of the Jewish Cultural Reconstruction, Inc.
(No. 258)
HUCSM 18.17

MARRIED WOMAN'S BONNET
Poland, 1810
Linen, embroidered with metallic thread
6 x 8½ x 7 in. (15.2 x 21.6 x 17.8 cm)
HUCSM 25.21

MARRIED WOMAN'S BONNET
Eastern Europe, early 20th century
Silk and crocheted cotton
5½ x 9 in. diameter (14 x 22.9 cm)
Gift of Lillian K. Stone
HUCSM 46.121

Plate 111. Venice Ketubbah, 1649

Plate 112. Corfu Ketubbah, 1781

Plate 113. Herat Ketubbah, 1895

158

WEDDING CAKE ORNAMENT
Japan, 1920
Porcelain, painted
5½ x 3½ in. (14 x 8.9 cm)
Gift of Mrs. Ida Kevitt
HUCSM 9.36

WEDDING RING
Italy, 18th century
Gold, filigree and engraved
⅜ x 1 in. diameter (1.0 x 2.6 cm)
Gift of Mrs. Otto V. Kohnstamm
HUCSM 9.8

WEDDING RING
Italy, 18th–19th century
Brass, cast, filigree, engraved and gilt
¾ x ⅞ in. diameter (1.8 x 2.3 cm)
HUCSM 9.7

WEDDING RING
Italy, 18th–19th century
Gold, filigree and engraved
⅝ x 1¼ in. diameter (1.6 x 3.2 cm)
HUCSM 9.6

MAZEL TOV BAG
Maker: Barbara Gordon
Los Angeles, 1992
Cotton and polyester
10⅛ x 8½ in. (25.7 x 21.6 cm)
Museum purchase with funds provided by the
   Audrey and Arthur N. Greenberg Fund
HUCSM 9.69

MARRIAGE BELT
Johann Conrad Freudenberger (active 1695–
   1732)
Frankfurt am Main, early 18th century
Silver, cast and chased
36 x 1⅛ in. (91.4 x 2.8 cm)
HUCSM 8.5

KETUBBAH (PL. 112)
Corfu, Greece, 1781
Ink, watercolor and gold paint on parchment
31 x 20⅝ in. (80.6 x 52.4 cm)
Kirschstein Collection
HUCSM 34.102

HET BAD DER HOOGDUITSCHE JOODEN,
TE AMSTERDAM (THE BATH OF THE HIGH
GERMAN JEWS OF AMSTERDAM)
P. Wagenaar and Caspar Jacobz Philips
Amsterdam, 1783
Engraving
11¼ x 13¼ in. (28.5 x 33.7 cm)
HUCSM 66.2301

MIKVEH CLOGS
Rhodes, 19th century
Wood, inlaid mother-of-pearl; and leather,
   embroidered with metallic thread
9⅜ x 3 x 2¼ in. (23.9 x 7.6 x 5.7 cm)
Gift of the family of Louis and Behora
   Benveniste
HUCSM 49.3 a/b

MIKVEH TOWEL
Rhodes, early 20th century
Linen, embroidered with silk and metallic
   thread
13 x 98 in. (33.0 x 248.9 cm)
Gift of Frances and Leon Franco
HUCSM 49.4

MIKVEH TOWEL BORDERS
Rhodes, early 20th century
Linen, embroidered with silk and metallic
   thread
a. 17 x 12⅞ in. (43.1 x 32.7 cm)
b. 17 x 14½ in. (43.1 x 36.8 cm)
Gift of Frances and Leon Franco
HUCSM 49.5 a/b

KITTEL AND KIPPAH
Maker: Leah Weselley
Warsaw, ca. 1880
Linen, with metallic thread work
kittel: 46 in. (116.8 cm)
kippah: 21 in. circumference (53.3 cm)
Gift of Ruth Terrace Hailparn
HUCSM 46.104, 46.105

KITTEL
United States, ca. 1942
Acetate satin
Gift of Anna W. Collons
HUSCM 46.118

DIVORCE DOCUMENT
Mantua, Italy, 1698
Ink on paper
21¼ x 15½ in. (54 x 39.37 cm)
HUCSM 19a.1

ḤALITZAH SHOE
Germany (?), 19th century
Leather
13 x 4¼ in. (33 x 10.9 cm)
HUCSM 12.1

KETUBBAH
Artist and Scribe: Judah Frances
Modena, Italy, 1657
Ink, watercolor and gold paint on parchment
23½ x 17¼ in. (59.7 x 43.8 cm)
Kirschstein Collection
HUCSM 34.66

KETUBBAH
Maker: N.D.M.
Livorno, Italy, 1782
Ink and watercolor on parchment
28½ x 19⅝ in. (72.4 x 49.8 cm)
Lipshutz Collection
HUCSM 34.57

KETUBBAH
Ragusa (Dubrovnik), Croatia, 1762
Ink and watercolor on parchment
29¼ x 19 in. (74. 3 x 50.2 cm)
Kirschstein Collection
HUCSM 34.60

KETUBBAH
Semlin (Zemun), Serbia, 1845
Ink, watercolor and gold paint on paper
24¼ x 18³/₁₆ in. (61.6 x 46.2 cm)
Kirschstein Collection
HUCSM 34.63

DRAFT OF A KETUBBAH
Scribe: Abraham Ḥayyim Nieto
San Francisco, 1894
Ink on parchment
14¹³/₁₆ x 10⅞ in. (37.6 x 27.6 cm)
HUCSM 34.116

KETUBBAH
Scribe: Abraham Ḥayyim Nieto
San Francisco, 1894
Ink on parchment
14⅜ x 10⅜ in. (36.6 x 26.4 cm)
Rabbi William M. Kramer Collection
HUCSM 34.381

KETUBBAH (PL. 81)
New York, 1819
Ink, pencil and watercolor on parchment
13⅞ x 14⅛ in. (35.2 x 35.9 cm)
Gift of Mr. and Mrs. William M. Daniel in
   honor of the 75th birthday of Mr. Bernard
   Gordon
HUCSM 34.304

KETUBBAH
Reggio, Italy, 1717
Ink, tempera and gold paint on parchment
26½ x 20⅛ in. (67.3 x 51.1 cm)
HUCSM 34.41

KETUBBAH
Spilimbergo, Italy, 1752
Ink, watercolor and gold paint on parchment
30 ¹¹/₁₆ x 21¹³/₁₆ in. (77.9 x 55.4 cm)
Kirschstein Collection
HUCSM 34.62

KETUBBAH
Rome, 1813
Ink and watercolor on parchment
35⅞ x 22 in. (91.1 x 57.8 cm)
Kirschstein Collection
HUCSM 34.99

KETUBBAH
Verona, Italy, 1686
Ink, watercolor and gold paint on parchment
30⅛ x 18½ in. (69.5 x 53.4 cm)
Kirschstein Collection
HUCSM 34.103

KETUBBAH
Ancona, Italy, 1723
Ink and watercolor on parchment
28 x 20 in. (73.0 x 52.7 cm)
Kirschstein Collection
HUCSM 34.119

KETUBBAH (PL. 28)
Pisa, Italy, 1790
Ink and watercolor on parchment
34⅞ x 22½ in. (88.6 x 57.2 cm)
Gift of the Berlin Jewish Museum
HUCSM 34.111

KETUBBAH
Scribe: Moses, son of Yeshu'ah
Isfahan, Persia, 1869
Ink and watercolor on paper
33⅜ x 26¾ in. (84.8 x 67.8 cm)
HUCSM 34.114

KETUBBAH
Artist and Scribe: Peretz Wolf-Prusan
San Bernardino, California, 1980
Silkscreen
26⅜ x 19⅜ in. (67.0 x 49.2 cm)
Gift of the Artist
HUCSM 34.216

Plate 114. Tzedakah Box, Tony Berlant, 1994

KETUBBAH
Artist and Scribe: Peretz Wolf-Prusan
California, 1979
Silkscreen
27½ x 21¹⁵/₁₆ in. (69.9 x 53.5 cm)
Gift of the Artist
HUCSM 34.217

KETUBBAH *(PL. 113)*
Herat, Afghanistan, 1895
Ink, watercolor and gold paint on paper
17½ x 13¹⁵/₁₆ in. (44.5 x 35.4 cm)
Museum purchase with funds provided by
Nancy F. and Herbert A. Bernhard
HUCSM 34.204

KETUBBAH *(PL. 111)*
Venice, 1649
Ink, tempera and gold paint on parchment
24¼ x 18½ in. (61.6 x 46.7 cm)
Kirschstein Collection
HUCSM 34.14

KETUBBAH
Busseto, Italy, text 1677, border 18th century
Ink, gouache and gold paint on parchment
26¼ x 19¼ in. (66.7 x 48.9 cm)
Kirschstein Collection
HUCSM 34.115

KETUBBAH
Conegliano, Italy, 1780
Ink, watercolor and gold paint on parchment
23⅞ x 16⅞ in. (60.6 x 42.9 cm)
Kirschstein Collection
HUCSM 34.77

FIRST WEDDING IN THE NEW LAND
MAMA, PAPA AND THE KIDS (PL. 80)
Marlene Zimmerman (b. 1933)
Los Angeles, 1972
Oil and wallpaper on canvas
24 x 30 in. (60.9 x 76.2 cm)
Donated in loving memory of Rose Merkin
Kabrins by her children, Sondra K. Bayley,
Ronald M. Kabrins and Howdy S. Kabrins
HUCSM 41.396

WEDDING GOWN *(PL. 89)*
Philadelphia, 1907
Satin; cotton net; sequins; glass beads; and
pearls
53½ in. (135.9 cm)
Gift of Florence R. Robins; Conservation funds
donated by Dr. and Mrs. William M. Gray
HUCSM 9.19

WEDDING PORTRAIT OF
JANET CHOYNSKI FLEISHHACKER
San Francisco, 1928
Photograph
14 x 11 in. (35.6 x 28 cm)
Gift of Delia Ehrlich, and Mortimer and
 David Fleishhacker
HUCSM 68.284

GOWN OF JANET CHOYNSKI FLEISHHACKER
San Francisco, 1928
Satin and lace
51 in. (129.5 cm)
Gift of Delia Ehrlich, and Mortimer and David
Fleishhacker
HUCSM 9.67 a-g

BRIDE AND GROOM CLOTHING AND JEWELRY
Djerba, Tunisia, 19th–20th century
On loan from the Keren T. Friedman Collection

MA'ASIM TORIM (GOOD DEEDS)

GREETING CARD
Brooklyn, ca. 1970
Multicolor ink on paper
17½ x 23⅛ in. (44.5 x 58.7 cm)
Gift of Muriel and David Rothenberg
HUCSM 19.225

ALMS BOX
Maker: Joseph Teschlag (active 1851– after
1868)
Budapest, 1865
Silver, repoussé and engraved
7¼ x 7 x 9 in. (18.5 x 17.6 x 22.8 cm)
Gift of the Jewish Cultural Reconstruction, Inc.
HUCSM 1.5

INFANTS' HOME GAVEL
New York, 1929
Coin silver
9¼ x 3¼ in. (23.5 x 8.3 cm)
Gift of Herman and Polly Alevy
HUCSM 29.170

BEAKER OF THE HOLY SOCIETY FOR VISITING
THE SICK *(PL. 29)*
Maker: Daniel Matignon (active 1763–1791)
Berlin, 1779
Silver, chased and engraved
14⅝ x 5½ in. diameter (37.1 x 14 cm)
Gift of the Jewish Cultural Reconstruction, Inc.
HUCSM 29.19

BURIAL SOCIETY PLATE
Neumark, Germany, 1839
Faience
9 in. diameter (24.8 cm)
Kirschstein Collection
HUCSM 43.60

BURIAL SOCIETY CUP
Germany (?), 19th century
Pewter, engraved
3⅞ x 3½ in. diameter (9.9 x 9.0 cm)
HUCSM 18.10

ALMS BOX
Budapest, late 19th–early 20th century
White metal; and brass, stamped
9 x 7 x 5⅛ in. diameter (24.8 x 17.8 x 13.2 cm)
Gift of Mrs. Ellen Addelson
HUCSM 1.9

ALMS BOX
Maker: Hana Geber (1910–1990)
New York, 1986
Bronze, cast
6 x 4 x 3⅜ in. (15.3 x 12.0 x 8.4 cm)
Museum purchase
HUCSM 1.13 a/b

ALMS PLATE
Frankfurt am Oder, dated 1738/39
Silver, cast and engraved
5⅝ in. diameter (14.4 cm)
Kirschstein Collection
HUCSM 1.4

ALMS PLATE
Maker: J.C. Prevot
Frankfurt am Oder, 1789/90
Silver, chased
5 ½ in. diameter (14.1 cm)
Kirschstein Collection
HUCSM 1.2

TZEDAKAH BOX *(PL. 114)*
Maker: Tony Berlant (b. 1941)
Los Angeles, 1994
Found tin collage over plywood with steel brads
8¼ x 8¼ x 6 in. (21 x 21 x 17.1 cm)
Museum commission with funds provided by
the Museum Membership, Purim 1994
HUCSM 1.33

DEATH

MEMORIAL LAMP
Maker: Moshe Zabari (b. 1935)
New York, 1974
Silver, hammered and welded; and glass
8 x 6 in. (20.3 x 15.2 cm)
Gift of Pnina and Moshe Zabari, in memory of
Amikam Dvir, Yigal Japko, and Ya'acov
Kamersky who fell in the Yom Kippur War,
October 1973
HUCSM 64.2a/b

BURIAL DRESS
Germany, ca. 1915–1930
Cotton; lace; and silk
46 in. length (116.8 cm)
Gift of Kurt and Lois Rollman
HUCSM 63.5 a-h

KADDISH CONTRACT
Jerusalem, 1892
Ink and gold leaf on parchment
17 x 22 in. (43.1 x 55.9 cm)
HUCSM 64.1

YAHRZEIT LAMP
Makers: Gertrud and Otto Natzler
Los Angeles, ca. 1958
Ceramic, patina mat glaze
3½ x 4 in. diameter (9.0 x 10.2 cm)
Gift of Ruth and Don Salk
HUCSM 64.25

MEMORIAL PLAQUE
Morocco, early 20th century
Silver, engraved, die-stamped and pierced
21 x 10⅞ in. (53.3 x 27.6 cm)
Anonymous Purchase Fund
HUCSM 64.10

MOURNING, ILLUSTRATION TO STORY
BY SALOMON HERMANN MOSENTHAL
(1821–1877) (PL. 42)
Moritz Oppenheim (1800–1882)
Germany, 1876–1877
Oil on canvas
10 x 13⅛ in. (27.3 x 33.6 cm)
Kirschstein Collection
HUCSM 41.106

MEMORIAL PAPERCUT *(PL. 83)*
Scranton, Pennsylvania, 1901
Ink, tempera and gold leaf on craft paper
20 x 24 in. (50.8 x 61.0 cm)
Gift of Rebecca and Leo Weinberger
HUCSM 64.17

MEMORIAL LAMP
Tunisia, dated 1935
Silver, chased; and wood
22 x 11½ in. (55.9 x 29.3 cm)
Museum purchase with funds provided by
Nancy F. and Herbert A. Bernhard
HUCSM 64.26

TOMBSTONE FRAGMENTS
Cairo, 19th century
Limestone
Gift of Uri and Myna Herscher
HUCSM 63.34a-d

SACRED SPACE

IN THE JEWISH RELIGION,
there are sacred spaces as well as sacred times. Wherever
Jews have dwelled, they have set aside holy places
for the worship of God.

When the early Israelites crossed the desert, they
reserved a place in their midst for a shrine to God, the
tabernacle. In the days of King Solomon, they built a Temple
in Jerusalem. After it was destroyed by conquerors, they created a new kind of sacred space: the synagogue.

The holy places of the Jews mirror their history.
Both their ancestral traditions and their encounters with
different cultures are reflected in the changing
architecture of the synagogue.

Plate 115. Romberg-Glass Torah Ark Curtain and Valance, 1785

Plate 116. *Is There Any Number to His Legions?* Neil Folberg, 1993

TORAH CURTAIN AND VALANCE *(PL. 115)*
Menden, Germany, 1785
Silk damask embroidered with metallic and silk
thread; and silk velvet appliqués
67 x 55 in. (170.2 x 139.7 cm)
Gift of John and Thomas Glass and Family
in memory of Margarete Romberg Glass,
Paul and Richard Glass
HUCSM 59.88

SYNAGOGUE LAMP
Naples, 1832–1872
Silver, cast and repoussé
27⅛ x 6¾ in. diameter (69.0 x 17.0 cm)
Gift of Mr. and Mrs. Isadore Schagrin,
Wilmington, Delaware, in memory of their
fathers, Mr. Charles W. Schagrin and
Mr. Isaac Starr
HUCSM 33.19

TORAH SHIELD
Maker: Joseph and Horace Savory
London, 1888
Silver, repoussé, engraved, and parcel-gilt; semi-
precious stones; and glass
13⅝ x 13½ in. (34.7 x 34.2 cm)
Museum purchase with funds provided by
Gerald and Carolyn Bronstein, Lee and Irving
Kalsman, and Peachy and Mark Levy
HUCSM 7.28

TORAH SHIELD
Maker: Carl Vogel
Berlin, ca. 1845–1818
Silver, chased and cast
13⅝ x 10 in. (34.5 x 25.5 cm)
HUCSM 7.2

SYNAGOGUE PEW
Merano, Italy, late 19th century
Wood
44 x 45 x 24 in. (111.8 x 114.3 x 60.9 cm)
Museum purchase
HUCSM 73.8

ALL THE WORLD IS FULL OF HIS GLORY
Photographer: Neil Folberg
Prague, 1993
EverColor print
24 x 20 in.
HUCSM 68.744

VIEW TO TEVA, SPANISH-PORTUGUESE
SYNAGOGUE
Photographer: Neil Folberg
Amsterdam, 1993
EverColor print
20 x 24 in.
HUCSM 68.745

VIEW FROM HEICHAL
Photographer: Neil Folberg
Florence, 1994
EverColor print
24 x 20 in.
HUCSM 68.746

SEFER TORAH, SADOUN SYNAGOGUE
Photographer: Neil Folberg
Fez, Morocco, 1993
EverColor print
24 x 20 in.
HUCSM 68.747

IS THERE ANY NUMBER TO HIS LEGIONS? *(PL. 116)*
Photographer: Neil Folberg
Szeged, Hungary, 1993
EverColor print
20 x 24 in.
HUCSM 68.748

TEMPLE GEMILUTH CHESED
Photographer: Neil Folberg
Port Gibson, Mississippi, 1994
EverColor print
20 x 24 in.
HUCSM 68.749

SYNAGOGUE

ASYNAGOGUE IS A BUILDING
or room for Jewish prayer, study, and meeting. For two thousand
years, the synagogue has preserved Jewish religious
beliefs and spiritual ideals.

While outward forms vary, all synagogues contain a
Torah scroll, the first five books of the Bible handwritten in
Hebrew. The Torah is housed in a special cabinet called an ark
and is read aloud from a raised platform. Also found in the
synagogue are symbols recalling the biblical priesthood and the
ancient Temple in Jerusalem.

In Jewish tradition, both prayer and study are forms of
worship. But nothing is more holy than a life of good deeds.

ASHKENAZ

TORAH FINIALS
Galicia (?), 18th century (?)
Silver, chased
7¼ x 2⅝ in. diameter (18.4 x 6.6 cm)
Kirschstein Collection
HUCSM 47.1 a/b

TORAH FINIALS
Germany, 19th century
Silver, cast and die-stamped
9⅜ x 4 in. diameter (23.7 x 10.3 cm)
HUCSM 47.15 a/b

TORAH FINIALS
Maker: Rötger Herfurt (active 1748–1776)
Frankfurt am Main, 1748–1750
Silver, chased, pierced, cast and parcel-gilt
8½ x 4¼ in. (21.4 x 10.7 cm)
Gift of the Jewish Cultural Reconstruction, Inc.
(No. 7a-b)
HUCSM 47.25 a/b

TORAH FINIALS (PL. 7)
Maker: Johann Jacob Leschhorn (active 1769–1787)
Frankfurt am Main, 1769–1787
Silver, cast, chased and parcel-gilt
12⅞ x 5¼ in. (32.7 x 13.2 cm)
Gift of the Jewish Cultural Reconstruction, Inc.
HUCSM 47.24 a/b

TORAH FINIALS
Germany, late 19th century
Silver, repoussé and gilt; and glass
12⅝ x 5 in. diameter (32.0 x 12.8 cm)
Gift of the Jewish Cultural Reconstruction, Inc.
HUCSM 47.26 a/b

TORAH MANTLE
Germany, 1840s
Cotton and satin ribbon
21 x 13 in. (53.3 x 33.0 cm)
HUCSM 60.21

TORAH SHIELD (PL. 9)
Nürnberg (?), ca. 1720
Silver, cast and parcel-gilt; and glass stones
9 x 7¼ in. (22.8 x 18.4 cm)
HUCSM 7.21

TORAH SHIELD
Maker: Hans Philipp Stenglin (active 1661–1706)
Germany, 19th century
Silver, repoussé, cast and engraved
7⅜ x 5¾ in. (18.7 x 14.6 cm)
Gift of the Jewish Cultural Reconstruction, Inc.
("I/9, No. 26")
HUCSM 7.22

TORAH CROWN (PL. 10)
Germany, dated 1771
Silver, repoussé and gilt
8¼ x 8⅛ in. diameter (28.0 X 26.5 cm)
HUCSM 58.11

TORAH SHIELD
Maker: Jeremias Zobel (active 1701–1741)
Frankfurt am Main (?), 18th century
Silver, repoussé and engraved
9¾ x 7⅛ in. (24.8 x 18.1 cm)
Gift of the Jewish Cultural Reconstruction, Inc.
HUCSM 7.18

TORAH POINTER
Germany, dated 1715
Silver, cast and engraved
17⅜ in. (44.1 cm)
HUCSM 44.4

TORAH POINTER
Galicia, late 18th–early 19th century
Silver, cast, chased, engraved and pierced
8½ x ¾ in. diameter (21.6 x 2.0 cm)
HUCSM 44.12

TORAH POINTER
Maker: Franz Zeitler (active 1848–after 1866)
Vienna, 1854
Silver, cast, chased and engraved
12¼ x 1¼ in. diameter (31 x 3.0 cm)
Gift of the Jewish Cultural Reconstruction, Inc.
(No. 5687)
HUCSM 44.30

TORAH SHIELD
Germany, dated 1711
Silver, cast
7 x 7⅝ in. (17.8 x 19.5 cm)
HUCSM 7.1

TORAH MANTLE
Germany, 19th century
Satin embroidered with satin and ribbon appliqué
21½ x 13 in. (54.6 x 33.0 cm)
HUCSM 60.111

TORAH BINDER
Germany, 19th century
Silk, embroidered with silk and metallic thread
5¾ x 55 in. (14.6 x 139.7 cm)
HUCSM 56.511

TORAH MANTLE
Germany, 1813
Velvet, embroidered and appliquéd with metallic thread
30 x 16 in. (76.2 x 40.6 cm)
HUCSM 60.7

TORAH MANTLE
Germany, 1789
Velvet, embroidered and appliquéd with silk and metallic thread
32 x 16 in. (81.5 x 40.75 cm)
HUCSM 60.8

TORAH ARK VALANCE (PL. 14)
Prague, 1724
Silk damask embroidered with silk and metallic thread and appliques; metallic thread fringe: colored and foil-backed glass
33½ x 77½ in. (84.9 x 196.8 cm)
HUCSM 59.59

SEPHARD / EDOT MIZRACH

TORAH FINIALS
Persia, late 19th–early 20th century
Silver, chased
11¼ x 3⅜ in. diameter (28.5 x 8.5 cm)
HUCSM 47.29 a/b

TORAH MANTLE
Ottoman Empire, early 18th century
Silk, embroidered gauze, embroidered with silk and silk fringe
25 x 12 in. (63.5 x 30.5 cm)
Kirschstein Collection
HUCSM 60.4

TORAH FINIALS
Turkey, late 18th–early 19th century
Silver, repoussé and cast
14¾ x 3⅞ in. (37.5 x 10.0 cm)
HUCSM 47.36 a/b

TORAH CASE (PL. 4)
India, late 19th–early 20th century
Silver, chased, die-stamped; and wood, painted
Finials: silver, chased and parcel-gilt
Pointer: silver
Case: 33½ x 10 in. diameter (85.1 x 25.4 cm)
Finials: 7⅞ x 2½ in. diameter (20 x 6.6 cm)
Pointer: 12⅝ in. (32.1 cm)
Museum purchase with funds provided by
The Maurice Amado Foundation at the behest
of the Tarica Family
HUCSM 57.6; 47.35 a/b; 44.54

TORAH FINIALS (PL. 117)
Morocco, ca. 1906
Silver, cast and engraved
16⅝ x 4⅜ in. diameter (42.2 x 11 cm)
Museum purchase with funds provided by The
Maurice Amado Foundation at the behest of the
Tarica Family
HUCSM 47.37 a/b

PARADESI SYNAGOGUE
Jay A. Waronker
Atlanta, 1993
Watercolor and ink on paper
11 x 14⅞ in. (27.9 x 37.8 cm)
HUCSM 41.836

TORAH MANTLE
Morocco, 1916
Velvet, embroidered with metallic thread
Museum purchase with funds provided by
The Maurice Amado Foundation
HUCSM 60.140

TORAH MANTLE
Morocco, early 20th century
26 in. (66.0 cm)
Velvet, embroidered with metallic thread
Museum purchase with funds provided by
The Maurice Amado Foundation
HUCSM 60.139

TORAH POINTER
Morocco, ca.1906
Silver, cast, engraved and die-stamped
9⅝ in. (24.3 cm)
Museum purchase with funds provided by The
Maurice Amado Foundation at the behest of the
Tarica Family
HUCSM 44.55

TORAH ARK

TORAH CURTAIN (PL. 13)
Bohemia, 1697
Satin velvet embroidered with metallic thread;
and metallic appliqués
87 x 53 in. (221 x 134.6 cm)
Kirschstein Collection
HUCSM 59.41

TORAH ARK CURTAIN AND VALANCE
Germany, 18th century
Quilted taffeta, embroidered with silk thread
and bugel beads
Valence: 18½ x 40 in. (47 x 101 cm)
Curtain: 60 x 40½ in (152.2 x 102.9 cm)
HUCSM 59.78; 59.79

< Plate 117. Torah Finials, ca. 1906

ASHKENAZI TORAH

Torah Finials
Maker: János Lehman (?) (active 1856–1868)
Budapest, late 19th century
Silver, chased, cast and gilt
16¼ x 6⅜ in. diameter (41.2 x 16.8 cm)
Gift of the Jewish Cultural Reconstruction, Inc.
(No. 4441/4597)
HUCSM 47.20 a/b

Torah Shield
Maker: János Lehman (?) (active 1856–1868)
Budapest, late 19th century
Silver, repoussé, cast and parcel-gilt
17 ½ x 11⅜ in. (44.5 x 29 cm)
Gift of the Jewish Cultural Reconstruction, Inc.
(No. 4441/4597)
HUCSM 7.15

Torah Mantle
Germany, 1863
Velvet, embroidered with metallic thread
35½ x 18 in. (90.2 x 45.7)
HUCSM 60.6

Torah Mantle
Germany, 18th century
Silk brocade on figured taffeta, embroidered with
metallic thead
34 x 20 in. (86.3 x 50.8 cm)
HUCSM 60.25

Torah Mantle
Germany, 1868
Velvet, embroidered with metallic thead; metallic
appliqués; and sequins
31½ x 18½ in. (80.0 x 47 cm)
HUCSM 60.14

ITALIAN TORAH

Torah Finials
Venice, 18th century
Silver, chased and cast
22 x 4¾ in. diameter (56 x 12 cm)
HUCSM 47.13 a/b

Torah Crown (Pl. 11)
Venice, 1758–1802
Silver, repoussé, cast and pierced
7 x 9½ in. diameter (17.9 x 24 cm)
HUCSM 58.12

Torah Mantle
Italy, 17th–18th century
Satin embroidered with metallic thread
28 x 10 x 10 in. (71.1 x 25.4 x 25.4 cm)
HUCSM 60.2

Memorial Plaque
Italy (?), 1804 or after
Silver, engraved
8⅛ x 6 in. (20.6 x 15.2 cm)
HUCSM 33.52

Torah Shield
Italy, late 18th century
Silver, repoussé and engraved
6¼ x 10⅜ in. (16 x 26.5 cm)
HUCSM 7.24

AMERICAN TORAH CASE

Torah Mantle
Maker: Eva Robbins
Los Angeles, 1988
Velvet; silk charmuse appliqués, embroidered
with silk thread; and brass
26 x 13 in. (66 x 33 cm)
Gift of Arnold L. Gilberg, M.D., Ph.D., Suzanne
and Jonathan
HUCSM 60.135

Torah Mantle (Pl. 121)
Maker: Peachy Levy
Santa Monica, 1991
Wool, embroidered and appliquéd with cotton
and metallic thread
28 x 13 ½ x 8⅛ in. (71.1 x 33.3 x 20.6 cm)
Museum commission
HUCSM 60.138

Torah Crown (Pl. 118)
Maker: Bernard Bernstein (b. 1928)
New York, 1969
Silver, parcel-gilt
9 x 9 x 2 ½ in. (22.9 x 22.9 x 6.4 cm)
Museum purchase with funds provided by the
estate of Tutty Lowens and the estate of Fay
Rossin Lewbin and Hyman Lewbin
HUCSM 58.13

Torah Crown (Pl. 32)
Maker: Moshe Zabari (b. 1935)
New York, design 1968
Silver, fabricated, forged; and pearls
16 x 14⅜ x 8 ½ in. (40.6 x 37.1 x 21.6 cm)
Museum purchase with funds provided by the
Ada Brown Trust
HUCSM 58.14

Plate 118. Torah Crown, Bernard Bernstein, 1969

Plate 119. Hanukkah Menorah, Shabbat Menorah and Tefillin Box from the "Tree of Life Shtender," David Moss and Noah Greenberg, 1990s

THE TREE OF LIFE SHTENDER
David Moss and Noah Greenberg
Design: Israel, 1990s
Cabinet: Walnut
Objects: Walnut; ebony; silver; ink on
  parchment; leather; printed paper and glass
Overall: 43 x 16 x 14 in. (109 x 40.6 x 35.6 cm)
Gift of Lee and Irving Kalsman in honor of
  their daughter Peachy Levy
HUCSM 73.10

PASSAGE TO AMERICA

Immigration is a leap into the unknown. To take leave of old ties and familiar sights, to cross an ocean to a strange land, is an enormous challenge.

For the Jewish people, immigration was an old story. But the promise of the American republic was new: freedom, equality, and opportunity. As life in Europe became harder and more dangerous for many Jews, they looked across the ocean toward a land where they could have the same chance as everyone else.

Once an outpost at the edge of Jewish life, the United States became the largest center of Jewish population in the world. Millions of Jews found in America a *goldene medineh* — a golden land.

STATUE OF LIBERTY HANUKKAH LAMP
(PL. 120, COVER)
Maker: Manfred Anson (b,1922)
New Jersey, 1985
Brass, cast
23 x 16½ in. (58.4 x 41.9 cm)
Museum purchase with Project Americana
funds provided by Peachy and Mark Levy
HUCSM 27.154

PORTRAIT OF BILHAH ABIGAIL LEVY FRANKS
(MRS. JACOB FRANKS) (1696–1756)
Attributed to Gerardus Duyckinck
New York, ca. 1735
Oil on canvas
44 x 35 in. (111.76 x 88.9 cm)
On loan from the American Jewish Historical
Society, Waltham, Massachusetts. Gift of
Captain N. Taylor Phillips.

PORTRAIT OF JACOB FRANKS (1688–1769)
Attributed to Gerardus Duyckinck
New York, ca. 1735
Oil on canvas
45 x 35 in. (114.3 x 88.9 cm)
On loan from the American Jewish Historical
Society, Waltham, Massachusetts. Gift of
Captain N. Taylor Phillips.

PORTRAIT OF MOSES [RAPHAEL] LEVY
Attributed to Gerardus Duyckinck
New York, ca. 1735
Oil on canvas
45 x 36 in. (114.3 x 91.4 cm)
On loan from the American Jewish Historical
Society, Waltham, Massachusetts. Gift of
Captain N. Taylor Phillips.

Plate 120. Statue of Liberty Hanukkah Lamp, Manfred Anson, 1985 >

THE PURSUIT OF LIBERTY

THE DECLARATION OF Independence in 1776 promised every person a right to "life, liberty, and the pursuit of happiness." Soon after, New York adopted a constitution granting Jews political equality. But a hundred years would pass before these rights were granted to Jews in every one of the original thirteen states.

Other minorities have also struggled for their rights in America. For example, Catholic immigrants were denied equality in New York until the early 1800s. African Americans waged a century-long struggle for civil equality. Japanese Americans interned during World War II waited forty years for the government to apologize.

Jews too have learned that, even in America, liberty and equality can never be taken for granted.

LINCOLN LETTERS

ABRAHAM LINCOLN, AUTOGRAPH LETTER
Signed A. Lincoln, to A. Jonas Esq. Sending
  Regrets that He Cannot Keep an Appointment
Urbana, Illinois, October 21, 1856
7¼ x 4⅞ in. (18.4 x 12.4 cm)
On loan from The David Shapell and Benjamin
  Shapell Family Collection of Judaica

ABRAHAM LINCOLN, AUTOGRAPH LETTER
Signed A. Lincoln, to Edwin M. Stanton, His
  Secretary of War, Regarding the Appointment
  of Colonel Frederick Salomon to the Post of
  Brigadier General Volunteers
Executive Mansion, Washington, D.C.,
May 17, 1862
8 x 5 in. (20.3 x 12.7 cm)
On loan from The David Shapell and Benjamin
  Shapell Family Collection of Judaica

ABRAHAM LINCOLN, AUTOGRAPH MEDICAL
ENDORSEMENT
Signed A. Lincoln, Regarding His Treatment by
  a Medical Practitioner, Dr. I. Zacharie
September 20, 1862
5¼ x 5¼ in. (13.3 x 13.3 cm)
On loan from The David Shapell and Benjamin
  Shapell Family Collection of Judaica

ABRAHAM LINCOLN, AUTOGRAPH LETTER
Signed A. Lincoln, to Secretary of War,
  Regarding the Appointment of [Ch ?] Levy to
  Assistant Quarter Master with the Rank of
  Captain
Executive Mansion, Washington, D.C.,
November 4, 1862
8 x 5 in. (20.32 x 12.7 cm)
On loan from The David Shapell and Benjamin
  Shapell Family Collection of Judaica

ABRAHAM LINCOLN, PRINTED COPY OF THE
EMANCIPATION PROCLAMATION
Signed Abraham Lincoln, One of Forty-eight
  Original Copies
8 x 5 in. (20.32 x 12.7 cm)
On loan from The David Shapell and Benjamin
  Shapell Family Collection of Judaica

ABRAHAM LINCOLN, AUTOGRAPH MANUSCRIPT
Signed Abraham Lincoln, the Concluding
  Paragraph of His Second Inaugural Address
  "With Malice Toward None" Written One
  Month Before His Death
No date, probably March, 1865
Single side: 9 x 5¾, spine: ¾ in.
  (22.9 x 14.6, 1.9 cm)
On loan from The David Shapell and Benjamin
  Shapell Family Collection of Judaica

PORTRAIT OF ABRAHAM LINCOLN
Photographer: Matthew Brady
3⅝ x 2¼ in. (9.2 x 5.7 cm)
On loan from the David Shapell and Benjamin
  Shapell Family Collection of Judaica

LIFE MASK OF ABRAHAM LINCOLN
Leonard Volk
Springfield, IL, 1860
Plaster
11½ x 8¾ x 6½ in. (36.7 x 22.2 x 16.5 cm)
Anonymous loan

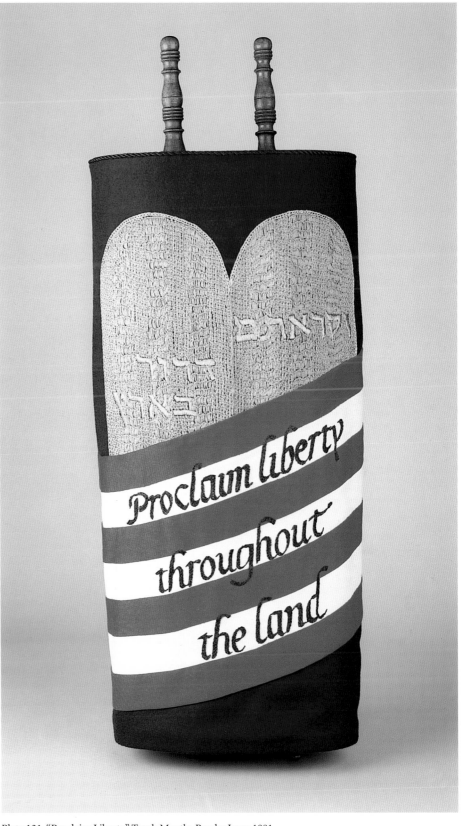

Plate 121. "Proclaim Liberty" Torah Mantle, Peachy Levy, 1991

A Nation of Immigrants

Except for the native American peoples, every American is an immigrant or the descendant of immigrants. The ideals that led them here, the cultures they brought with them, the opportunities they discovered — these have given America its dynamic character.

Not all immigrants came here willingly. Many, particularly from Africa and East Asia, were brought to these shores by force. Yet they too found their future in America.

Most immigrants came in search of economic opportunity. For the Jews, America meant this and more: a haven from persecution. Between 1880 and 1920, one-third of all the Jews in eastern Europe migrated to America. Here they created the most populous, vibrant Jewish community in the world.

Plate 122. *Food Will Win the War*, Charles Edward Chambers, ca. 1918

IMMIGRATION

FOOD WILL WIN THE WAR
Charles Edward Chambers (1883–1941)
United States, ca. 1918
Color lithograph
30 x 20 in. (76.2 x 50.8 cm)
Museum purchase with funds provided by
the Lee Kalsman Project Americana
Acquisition Fund
HUCSM 66.2729

FOOD WILL WIN THE WAR (YIDDISH) *(PL. 122)*
Charles Edward Chambers (1883–1941)
United States, ca. 1918
Color lithograph
30 x 20 in. (76.2 x 50.8 cm)
Gift of Dr. and Mrs. Boris Catz
HUCSM 66a.106

FOOD WILL WIN THE WAR (ITALIAN)
Charles Edward Chambers (1883–1941)
United States, ca. 1918
Color lithograph
30 x 20 in. (76.2 x 50.8 cm)
Museum purchase with funds provided by
the Lee Kalsman Project Americana
Acquisition Fund
HUCSM 66.2769

CENTRAL EUROPE

TRUNK
Germany, 18th century
Wood and brass
25 x 48⅛ x 22½ in. (63.5 x 122.2 x 57.2 cm)
Gift of Alice Gumprich Steinberg
HUCSM 31.189

SEDER PLATE
Alsace (?), 19th century
Pewter, engraved
1¼ x 13⅛ in. diameter (3.2 x 33.4 cm)
Gift of Mr. and Mrs. Edward Adler
HUCSM 43.59

JUDENSTERN
Germany, 19th century
16 in. (40.6 cm)
Brass
Gift of the children of Alfred and Emily
Seasongood
HUCSM 33.16

PORTRAIT OF ABRAHAM GREENHALL
(1838–1898)
United States, late 19th century
28¼ x 24¼ in. (71.7 x 61.6 cm)
Gift of Charles A. Greenhall in memory of
Frank Greenhall
HUCSM 68.333 0

SHOFAR
Germany, 19th century
Ram's horn, carved
16 in. (40.6 cm)
Gift of the children of Alfred and
Emily Seasongood
HUCSM 52.26

SHAWL
Austria, 1850
Silk
23 x 96 in. (58.4 x 243.84 cm)
Gift of Rae Greenwald Weil
HUCSM 25.20

RUMANIA

TRUNK
Rumania, ca. 1890
21 x 30 x 19 in. (53.3 x 76.2 x 48.3 cm)
Gift of Brenda Grossman Spivack
HUCSM 31.194

BOY'S VEST
Rumania, ca. 1900
Wool felt; metal braid; metal disks; seed beads
16 x 14½ in. (40.6 x 36.8 cm)
Gift of Harold Brill and Regina Starr Brill
HUCSM 25.178

BOY'S TUNIC
Rumania, ca. 1900
Linen embroidered with wool and cotton
    thread
32½ x 17 in. (82.6 x 43.2 cm)
Gift of Harold Brill and Regina Starr Brill
HUCSM 25.180 a

BOY'S TROUSERS
Rumania, ca. 1900
Linen embroidered with wool and cotton
    thread
25¾ in. (65.4 cm)
Gift of Harold Brill and Regina Starr Brill
HUCSM 25.180 b

TALLIT KATAN
Rumania, ca. 1900
Cotton embroidered with cotton thread; wool;
    and mother-of-pearl button
9 x 11½ in. (22.9 x 29.2 cm)
Gift of Harold Brill and Regina Starr Brill
HUCSM 46.144

BEDSPREAD
Rumania, ca. 1900
Cotton; and linen
74 x 72 in. (188 x 182.9 cm)
Gift of Harold Brill and Regina Starr Brill
HUCSM 14.353

WOMAN'S SKIRT
Rumania, ca. 1900
Linen embroidered with wool thread; and
    cotton edging
31½ x 54 in. (80.1 x 137.2 cm)
Gift of Harold Brill and Regina Starr Brill
HUCSM 25.181

EMBROIDERED SLEEVE FRAGMENTS
Rumania, ca. 1900
Linen embroidered with wool and cotton
    thread; metal disks; and seed beads
25 x 14 in. each (63.5 x 35.6 cm)
Gift of Harold Brill and Regina Starr Brill
HUCSM 25.175 a/b

EMBROIDERED SLEEVE FRAGMENTS
Rumania, ca. 1900
Linen embroidered with wool and cotton
    thread; metal disks; and seed beads
a. 15 x 32 (38.1 x 81.3 cm)
 b. 17 x 24 (43.2 x 60.9 cm)
Gift of Harold Brill and Regina Starr Brill
HUCSM 25.176 a/b

WOMAN'S HEADCOVERING
Rumania, ca. 1900
Cotton ?
93 x 18 in. (236.2 x 45.7 cm)
Gift of Harold Brill and Regina Starr Brill
HUCSM 25.182

HAND TOWELS
Rumania, ca. 1900
Cotton embroidered with cotton thread
a. 42½ x 20¼ in. (107.9 x 51.4 cm)
 b. 14¼ x 17½ in. (36.2 x 44.4 cm)
Gift of Harold Brill and Regina Starr Brill
HUCSM 14.354 a/b

DECORATIVE TEXTILE
Rumania, ca. 1900
Linen?
63¾ x 17½ in. (161.9 x 44.4 cm)
Gift of Harold Brill and Regina Starr Brill
HUCSM 14.355

TABLE RUNNER
Rumania, ca. 1900
Linen embroidered with cotton? thread
72¼ x 20 in. (183.5 x 50.8 cm)
Gift of Harold Brill and Regina Starr Brill
HUCSM 14.356

EASTERN EUROPE

TRUNK
Moscow, ca. 1900
24 x 32 x 24 in. (60.9 x 81.3 x 60.9 cm)
Gift of Alvin and Irene Saltzman
HUCSM 31.190

CANDLESTICKS
Poland, early 20th century
Brass, silver-plated
12 x 5 in. (30.5 x 12.7 cm)
Gift of Regina Kirman Sidler
HUCSM 11.38 a/b

HANUKKAH LAMP
Warsaw, late 19th century
Brass, die-stamped, cast, silver-plated
11⅜ x 9⅜ in. (29.0 x 24.0 cm)
Gift of Vera S. Hoffman Grossfield
HUCSM 27.149

SAMOVAR (PL. 86)
St. Petersburg, 1847
Brass; and wood
28½ x 11½ x 13½ in. (72.4 x 29.2 x 34.3 cm)
Gift of Kate Gordon Shapiro in loving memory
of her mother, Dena Rose Geller Gordon
HUCSM 14.51

WEDDING SUIT
Ukraine, ca. 1900
Wool; cotton; and metal buttons
47 x 23 in. (119.4 x 58.4 cm)
Gift of Thelma Geller
HUCSM 9.21

BEDSPREAD
Odessa, ca. 1900 or earlier
91 x 63 in. (231.1 x 160.0 cm)
Gift of Rose and Leon Mend
HUCSM 14.150

WOMAN'S SHAWL
Lithuania, 1872
Wool
63 x 59 in. (160 x 149.8 cm)
Gift of Anna Shewach
HUCSM 25.19

PILLOWCASES
Maker: Sarah Shapiro Glober
Minsk, Russia, late 19th century
Cotton, embroidered with cotton thread
33 x 30 in. (83.8 x 76.2 cm)
Gift of Betty G. Miller
HUCSM 14.182–3

TABLECLOTH
Eastern Europe, late 19th – early 20th century
Linen, embroidered with cotton thread
76 x 65 in. (193 x 165.1 cm)
Gift of Arthur M. Feldman
HUCSM 14.366

PRE-WORLD WAR II

SUITCASES
Germany, 1920s–1930s
Metal; wood; leather; cloth; and paper
17 x 29 ¾ x 9 in. (43.2 x 75.6 x 22.9 cm)
Gift of Marion Stiebel Siciliano
HUCSM 31.97, 31.99

TENNIS RACKET AND PRESS
Germany, 1930s
Wood; gut; and metal
Gift of Marion Stiebel Siciliano
HUCSM 31.53

TYPEWRITER
Dresden, 1930
Metal; rubber; roller; black paint; wood; and
cloth
5½ x 12 x 12 in. (13.9 x 30.5 x 30.5 cm)
Gift of Marion Stiebel Siciliano
HUCSM 31.54

HAND HARMONICA AND CASE
Germany, ca. 1935
Plastic; wood; metal; leather; coated fabric;
fabric screen; and lacquer
5 ¾ x 10 ¾ x 9¼ in. (14.6 x 27.3 x 23.5 cm)
Gift of Marion Stiebel Siciliano
HUCSM 31.93

SUITCASE
Poland, 1930s
Leather; and brass
9½ x 29 x 16½ in. (24.1 x 73.6 x 41.9 cm)
Gift of Allison and Abby Lauterbach
HUCSM 31.187

HATBOX
Czechoslovakia, 1930s
8½ x 16 in. diameter (21.6 x 40.6 cm)
Gift of Betty and Charles Ullman
HUCSM 31.160

STRUGGLE AND OPPORTUNITY

IN THE LATE NINETEENTH century, America's expanding industries created millions of new jobs. Earlier Jewish immigrants from central Europe were mostly peddlers and shopkeepers; by 1900, half of all immigrant Jews labored in the tenement sweatshops of the garment industry.

Although few immigrant Jews were well educated, they came from a culture that had revered learning for centuries. The respect and drive for education were vital to the success that Jews achieved in America.

Building on the skills and values they brought with them, American Jews eventually earned a major role in the nation's economic and cultural life.

LEVI STRAUSS

Los Pantalones Overalls con Remaches de Cobre
PARA HOMBRES Y MUCHACHOS
Han Demostrado Su Excelencia por Mas de Cincuenta Años, Siendo los Favoritos de los Vaqueros

¶ Sin duda, la prueba mas dificil a que se pueden someter las calidades de Pantalones Overalls es el uso diario de ellos por los vaqueros. Estos jinetes exigen que VENGAN BIEN y que RESISTAN USO DURO y que no-obstante queden en buena condición.

¶ Una investigación esmerada entre los jinetes campeones en los Rodeos de Prescott, Cheyenne, Pendleton, Winnemucca, Salinas y otros semejantes nos han demostrado que el cien por ciento de los participantes en esos concursos usan los Overalls de Levi.

¶ No solamente los usan para los concursos sinó tambien para todos los dias de trabajo.

¶ Esta fotografía es de Lawton Champie, Campeon Mundial del jineteo montado en el caballo Firebug Fits, en el Concurso de Prescott Frontier Days, el 4 de Julio de 1926.

Lawton Champie montado en el caballo Firebug Fits, en Prescott Frontier Days

Los fabricantes recibieron el siguiente telegrama relativo a la victoria:

"*Prescott, Arizona, 9 de Julio de 1926.*

Lawton Champie, victorioso en el Campeonato Mundial de Ginetes de Prescott Frontier Days, en Prescott, Arizona, no solo usó los Overalls de Levi durante todo el concurso sino tambien los usa para todos los dias en su trabajo.

Prescott Frontier Days.

G. M. SPARKS, Secretario."

El mismo Campeon, Lawton Champie, dice en una de sus cartas escrita en Crown King, Arizona:

"*Desde mi infancia siempre he usado los Overalls de Levi Strauss. Ahora tengo mas de veintitres años. La ropa de Levi Strauss es la unica que resiste con exito el uso y abuso continuo del trabajo cotidiano del vaquero, ademas se ven muy bien.*"

Los Overalls sin Pechera con Remaches de Cobre vienen solamente en Mezclilla Azul, Chaquetas Cerradas y Abiertas, Blusas Plegadas de la misma clase.

[Los Overalls sin Pechera con Remaches de Cobre de Levi Strauss han sido el modelo universal por mas de 50 años y en la tienda donde los compre le diran que nuestra garantia "*Un Par Nuevo* GRATIS *si Se Descosen*" significa lo que implican esas palabras y nada mas.]

De Venta Por

GOLDBERG BROS.
Phoenix, Arizona

Plate 123. Levi Strauss & Co. Advertisement, 1920s

ADVERTISEMENTS

HEBREW BOOK STORE SIGN
New York, ca. 1960
Painted tin
76 x 16 in. (193 x 40.6 cm)
Museum purchase with funds provided by the
Lee Kalsman Project Americana Acquisition Fund
HUCSM 69.175

WOLF CLOTH CUTTERS CLOCK
United States, 1930s-1940s
Metal; glass; and paint
18 x 18 x 6 in. (45.7 x 45.7 x 15.2 cm)
Museum purchase with funds provided by the
Lee Kalsman Project Americana Acquisition Fund
HUCSM 69.251

HENDLER'S ICE CREAM SIGN
Baltimore, ca. 1940s
Painted tin
31½ x 51¾ in. (80 x 131.5 cm)
Museum purchase with funds provided by the
Peachy and Mark Levy Project Americana
Acquisition Fund
HUCSM 69.258

LEVI STRAUSS

**ADVERTISEMENT IN SPANISH FOR
LEVI STRAUSS & CO.** (PL. 123)
San Francisco, 1920s
Printed paper
10⅞ x 8 in. (27.6 x 20.3 cm)
Gift of Levi Strauss & Co. Archives, San
Francisco
HUCSM 69.354

LEVI STRAUSS & CO. REPRODUCTION JEANS
San Francisco, 1990s
Cotton duck
43½ in. (110.5 cm)
Gift of Levi Strauss & Co. Archives, San
Francisco
HUCSM 69.356

**ADVERTISEMENT FOR LEVI STRAUSS & CO. FROM
THE PANAMA-PACIFIC EXPOSITION**
San Francisco, 1915
Printed on paper
7 ¾ x 3 ¾ in. (19.7 x 9.5 cm)
Gift of Levi Strauss & Co. Archives, San
Francisco
HUCSM 69.355

DIE CUT STAMP FOR LEATHER PATCH
San Francisco, 1940s
On loan from Levi Strauss & Co. Archives, San
Francisco

LILLIAN WALD KITCHEN

(ALL PL. 88)

APPLE PEELER
United States, 1920s - 1930s
Wood; and steel, painted
6½ x ⅞ in. diameter (16.5 x 2.2 cm)
Gift of Joseph and Fannie Mann Farkas
HUCSM 14.114

BAUER BOWL
Los Angeles, ca. 1930
Glazed pottery
4 x 8½ in. (10.2 x 21.6 cm)
Gift of Jacqueline Levy Fuhrman and Millicent
Levy Small
HUCSM 14.225

BENSINGER OUTFITTING CO. ICEBOX
Louisville, Kentucky, ca. 1900
Oak; and metal
41 x 24 x 26 in. (10.4 x 61 x 66 cm)
Gift of Lynn and Leonard Goddy
HUCSM 73.7 a/b

BLOCH AND GUGGENHEIMER CROCK
New York, ca. 1900
Glazed earthenware
10 x 8½ in. (25.4 x 21 cm)
Museum purchase with funds provided by the
Lee Kalsman Project Americana Acquisition Fund
HUCSM 69.95

BOWL
United States, 1920s
Glass
10 in. diameter (25.4 cm)
Gift of Bertha Kretzer Tuttelman
HUCSM 14.173

CANDLESTICKS
England, ca. 1880
Brass
9¾ in. (24.8 cm)
Gift of Mrs. Ben Isaacson
HUCSM 11.35 a/b

CARVING KNIFE
New York, 1920s
Steel; wood; and brass
12¼ in. (31.1 cm)
Gift of Mrs. Harold J. Siegel
HUCSM 14.157

CHOPPER
Russia, late 19th century
Steel; and wood
5 x 7 in. (12.7 x 17.8 cm)
Gift of Mrs. Harold J. Siegel
HUCSM 14.156

COFFEE GRINDER
United States, ca. 1912
Wood; iron; and paper
4¾ x 9¾ x 9 in. (12.1 x 24.8 x 22.9 cm)
Gift of Sidney and Mary B. Green
HUCSM 14.134

COFFEE POT
Cleveland, ca. 1920
Enameled aluminum; and glass
9 x 8 in. (22.9 x 20.3 cm)
Gift of Bertha Bolnick
HUCSM 14.212 a-d

COLANDER
Philadelphia, ca. 1900
Tin
3 ⅜ x 9⅞ in. (8.6 x 25.1 cm)
Gift of Bella Root
HUCSM 14.140

COLANDER
United States, 1900-1915
Enameled metal
3⅞ x 12¼ in. (9.8 x 31.1 cm)
Gift of Betty and Charles K. Ullman
HUCSM 14.228

COOKING POT
Lithuania, before 1890
Copper
5 ⅜ x 10⅞ x 9¼ in. (13.6 x 27.6 x 23.5 cm)
Gift of Marcia Cohn Spiegel
HUCSM 14.104

CUP FOR RITUAL WASHING
Russia, ca. 1870-1880
Brass
7¼ x 5¼ in. (18.4 x 13.3 cm)
Gift of Leona G. Rubin in memory of Simon
Rubin
HUCSM 14.199

DEPRESSION GLASS DISHES
United States, 1920s
Gift of Tobey B. Gitelle and Shoshana B. Tancer
from the Estate of Salo W. Baron
HUCSM 14.358

DISHCLOTH
Cotton
46½ in. (118 cm)
Gift of Joseph and Fannie Mann Farkas
HUCSM 14.121

DISKIN SOCIETY TZEDAKAH BOX
New York, pre-1948
Painted tin
3 x 3⅜ x ¾ in. (7.6 x 8.6 x 1.9 cm)
Gift of the Estate of Mary Heller
HUCSM 1.23

DOLLS
Provenance unknown, ca. 1890
Bisque
16 x 7 x 4 in. (40.7 x 17.8 x 10.2 cm)
Gift of Louis and Ida Stamler
HUCSM 24.27; 24.28

DOLL BUGGY
United States, ca. 1900
Wicker; painted metal; wood; and rubber
26¾ x 14 x 28 in. (68 x 35.6 x 71.1 cm)
Gift of Mrs. Ralph Mills
HUCSM 24.49

EGG BEATER
United States, Patent 1923
Steel; and wood, painted
10½ x 4⅝ in. (26.7 x 11.7 cm)
Gift of Bertha Bolnick
HUCSM 14.213

ENAMEL KITCHENWARE SET
United States, ca. 1940
Enamelled metal
4¼ x 8¼ in. (largest) (10.8 x 21 cm)
Gift of Selma A. Largeman and Lila L. Gable
HUCSM 14.191 a-e

ENAMEL POT
United States, 1920s
Enameled metal
7 x 10¼ in. diameter (17.8 x 26 cm)
Gift of Leba Kramer
HUCSM 14.171 a/b

FISH SCRAPER
New York, ca. 1920s
Wood; and metal
9½ x 1½ in. (24.1 x 3.8 cm)
Gift of Bess and Herbert Paper
HUCSM 14.237

GEFILTE FISH POT
Poland, ca. 1900
Copper; and tin
5 x 19 x 8⅛ in. diameter (12.7 x 48.3 x 20.6 cm)
Gift of Alter and Rose Rosenblum
HUCSM 14.179 a/b

GRATER
United States, 1920s
Stainless steel
7¼ x 3¾ x 2¾ in. (18.4 x 9.5 x 7.0 cm)
Gift of Bertha Kretzer Tuttelman
HUCSM 14.176

HALLAH KNIFE
United States, ca. 1930
Wood; and steel
12½ in. (31.8 cm)
Gift of Ruth Feuer Kornfield
HUCSM 14.185

ICE SCRAPER
New York, ca. 1920's
Steel
2 x 5½ x 2 in. (5.1 x 14.0 x 5.1 cm)
Gift of Bess and Herbert Paper
HUCSM 14.238

JELLY PAN
Mayarupel, Russia, ca. 1895
Brass
4 x 16 in. (10.2 x 40.6 cm)
Gift of Olga Klanno Slone
HUCSM 14.207

KOSHERING BOARD
Maker: Ben Silvers
Russia or United States, early 20th century
Wood
13⅛ x 22½ in. (33.3 x 55.2 cm)
Gift of Lauretta and Charles Witzman
HUCSM 14.201

KUGEL PAN
Maker: Berel Baril
Los Angeles, 1931
Copper; and tin
1⅝ x 7 x 10¼ in. (4.1 x 17.8 x 26.0 cm)
Gift of Norma Michelson Arbit and
Betty Pilson Goldwater
HUCSM 14.226

LADLE
United States, ca. 1920s
Enameled metal
10 x 4 in. (25.4 x 10.2 cm)
Gift of Leba Kramer
HUCSM 14.170

MEAT GRINDER
United States, ca. 1930s
Steel; and wood
10 x 7 in. (25.4 x 17.8 cm)
Gift of Ruby and Gerald B. Bubis
HUCSM 14.172

MORTAR AND PESTLE
Russia, 19th century
Brass
mortar: 3⅜ x 5¼ x 4¼ in. diameter
(8.6 x 13.3 x 10.8 cm)
pestle: 1⅜ x 7½ x 1½ in. diameter
(3.5 x 19.1 x 3.8 cm)
Gift of Bernard and Sylvia Sayewitz
HUCSM 14.128a/b

NOODLE BOARD AND ROLLING PIN
Maker: Samuel Pine
Chicago, ca. 1905-1923
Wood
31 x 20½ x 1½ in. (78.8 x 52.1 x 3.8 cm)
Gift of Evelyn Pine Brodie
HUCSM 14.216 a/b

NOODLE CUTTER
Germany, ca. 1900
Cast iron; wood; and enamel
7 ⅜ x 12½ x 6¾ in. (18.7 x 31.8 x 17.2 cm)
Gift of Gustine and John Weber
HUCSM 14.209

NUTMEG GRATER
United States, ca. 1900
Tin
5⅛ x 2 x 1 in. (13.3 x 5.1 x 2.5 cm)
Gift of Myra Schwager Sharken
HUCSM 14.162

OCTAGON CLEANSER
Jersey City, 1928-29
Tin; and printed paper
5 x 3⅛ in. (12.7 x 7.9 cm)
Gift of the Kate Simon Family
HUCSM 14.155

PASSOVER COOKING POT
Russia, 1885
Copper
8 x 9½ in. diameter (20.3 x 24.1 cm)
Gift of Janet Hecker
HUCSM 50.21

POTATO MASHER
Philadelphia, ca. 1895-1900
Wood
10¾ x 2⅝ in. (27.3 x 6.7 cm)
Gift of Bella Root
HUCSM 14.138

ROSENBAUM MANUFACTURING CO. IRON REST
New York, ca. 1895
Iron
3 x 1⅜ x 6¾ in. (7.6 x 3.5 x 15.9 cm)
Gift of Lillian Kahan
HUCSM 70.79

RUG BEATER
Minneapolis, 1920s
Steel; and wood
22⅛ x 5½ in. (56.2 x 14 cm)
Gift of Lauretta and Charles Witzman
HUCSM 14.211

SALT AND PEPPER SHAKERS
United States, early 20th century
Glass; and pewter
⅜ x ⅝ in. (6.0 x 4.1 cm)
Gift of Bella Root
HUCSM 14.142 a/b

SAUCEPOT
Latvia, 1890-1900
Copper; and brass
3¾ x 5⅝ in. diameter (9.5 x 14.3 cm)
Gift of Dora R. Kohn
HUCSM 14.194

SAUCEPOT
Russia, ca. 1870-1880
Copper; and brass
3¾ x 14½ in. (9.5 x 36.8 cm)
Gift of Leona G. Rubin in memory of
Simon Rubin
HUCSM 14.192

SELTZER BOTTLE
New York, ca. 1950
Glass, etched; and metal, embossed
11 x 3½ in. diameter (27.9 x 8.9 cm)
Gift of Lauretta and Charles Witzman
HUCSM 69.86

SIFTER
United States, 1920s
Enamelled tin
5 ⅜ x 5 in. diameter (13.6 x 12.7 cm)
Gift of Bertha Kretzer Tuttelman
HUCSM 14.174

SPICES
United States, ca. 1920
Painted tin
3¼ x 2¼ x 1⅛ in. (8.2 x 5.7 x 2.8 cm)
Gift of Betty and Charles K. Ullman
HUCSM 14.231; 14.232

TABLE AND CHAIR
Gift of Leah and Nathan Selk

TABLECLOTH
Eastern Europe, late 19th - early 20th century
Linen, embroidered with cotton thread
76 x 79 in. (193 x 200.7 cm)
Gift of Arthur M. Feldman
HUCSM 14.367

W. WISSOTSKY & CO FINE TEA
New York, 1950s
Tin, enamelled
2¼ x 2 x 3¼ in. (5.7 x 5.1 x 8.3 cm)
Gift of Sandra and Merrill Bonar
HUCSM 69.33

TEA KETTLE
United States, ca. 1860
Copper
10 x 14½ in. (25.4 x 36.8 cm)
Gift of Mrs. Harold J. Siegel
HUCSM 14.158

"TEMPTING KOSHER DISHES" RECIPE BOOK
B. Manischewitz Co.
Cincinnati, 1930
Paper, printed; cloth and paper binding
7¾ x 5¾ x ⅝ in. (19.7 x 13.3 x 1.6 cm)
Gift of Peachy and Mark Levy
HUCSM 5.261

TRIVET
Maker: Johanna Zimmerman
Los Angeles, 1930s
Cotton; and bottle caps
12½ x 7½ in. (31.8 x 19.1 cm)
Gift of Anna Tenn Parker
HUCSM 14.187

VASE
Minneapolis, ca. 1912
Glass
4⅞ x 6¾ x 4½ in. (12.4 x 17.2 x 11.4 cm)
Gift of Sidney and Mary B. Green
HUCSM 14.136

WASHBOARDS AND LAUNDRY STICK
Lithuania, ca. 1880
Wood
20⅞ x 5¼ x 3¾ in. (53 x 13.3 x 9.5 cm)
Gift of Dr. Joseph and Charlotte Eiser
HUCSM 14.184 a-c

WOODEN BOWL AND CHOPPER
Philadelphia, early 20th century
Wood; and steel
6½ x 12¾ in. diameter (16.5 x 32.4 cm)
Gift of Morton and Sue Richter
HUCSM 14.101 a/b

MORTON'S KOSHER SALT
Gift of Gloria Stone

MARCUS C. ILLIONS

SYNAGOGUE LIONS (PL. 82)
Maker: Marcus Charles Illions (1865-1949)
Brooklyn, early 20th century
Wood, carved and painted; and glass
20 x 26½ x 3¾ in. (50.8 x 67.3 x 9.5 cm)
Museum purchase with Project Americana
Acquisition Funds provided by Irving and Lee
Kalsman, Peachy and Mark Levy, and Gerald M.
and Carolyn Z. Bronstein
HUCSM 30.13 a/b

CAROUSEL HORSE
Maker: Marcus Charles Illions (1865-1949)
Brooklyn, ca. 1903
Wood, carved and painted; and glass
57⅛ x 59 x 13 in. (145 x 150 x 33 cm)
On loan from the Smithsonian Institution, Washington, D.C. Gift of Dr. Roland and Jo Summit

ISAAC MAYER WISE

SHIVITI (PL. 70)
Maker: Phillip Cohen
United States, 1861
Paper cut; and ink
25¼ x 19⅜ in. (64.1 x 49.2 cm)
HUCSM.39.17

PLUM STREET TEMPLE (PL. 1)
Henry Mosler (1841-1920)
Cincinnati, ca. 1866
Oil on canvas
29½ x 24⅝ in. (75 x 62.5 cm)
Gift of The Skirball Foundation
HUCSM 41.259

ISAAAC MAYER WISE
Moses Jacob Ezekiel (1844-1917)
Cincinnati, 1899
Bronze
25 in. (63 cm)
HUCSM 67.45

MINHAG AMERICA PRAYER BOOK
Bloch & Co. Publishers
Cincinnati, 1862
On loan from Hebrew Union College-Jewish
Institute of Religion Frances-Henry Library, Los
Angeles

Plate 124. *Portrait of Albert Einstein*, Hermann Struck, 1921

ISAAC MAYER WISE TORAH
SHIELD (PL. 75) AND FINIALS
Cincinnati, 1899
Silver; and semi-precious stones
Shield: 10½ x 6¼ in. (26.7 x 15.9 cm)
Finials: 13 in. (33 cm)
HUCSM.7.4: 47.10 a/b

JOURNALISM

HEBREW/ENGLISH TYPEWRITER
New York, 1920
Wood; and metal
8 x 15 x 13½ in. (20.3 x 38.1 x 34.3 cm)
From Hebrew Union College-Jewish Institute of
Religion, Cincinnati
HUCSM 31.59

JEWISH DAILY FORWARD CALENDAR
New York, 1917
Painted tin; and glass
3⅞ in. diameter (9.8 cm)
Gift of Peachy and Mark Levy
HUCSM 69.2

ALBERT EINSTEIN

PORTRAIT OF ALBERT EINSTEIN (PL. 124)
Hermann Struck (1876-1943)
Germany, 1921
Oil on canvas
34 x 23 ¾ in. (86.4 x 60.3 cm)
Gift of Mr. Ben Selling
HUCSM.41.37a

ALBERT EINSTEIN, AUTOGRAPH LETTER
Signed A. Einstein, to Nat Levin
June 10, 1939
11 X 8½ in. (27.9 x 21.6 cm)
On loan from The David Shapell and Benjamin
Shapell Family Collection of Judaica

ALBERT EINSTEIN, PHOTOGRAPH WITH
AUTOGRAPH QUOTATION
Signed A. Einstein, in German, "No Human
Society Can Stay Healthy Without a Common
Goal. This Must Be Taken Into Consideration in
Order to Understand the Supreme Importance
of Palestine for All Jews..."
1924
13½ x 10 in. (34.3 x 25.4 cm)
On loan from The David Shapell and Benjamin
Shapell Family Collection of Judaica

The Holocaust

The Holocaust is the most tragic experience of Jewish history and of modern times. The systematic murder of six million European Jews, carried out by the German state under Adolph Hitler during World War II (1939–1945), was shocking in its savagery and scope. Rarely before had one people set out to destroy another as the fulfillment of an ideology.

In the ghettos and death camps of eastern Europe, the thousand-year-old culture of European Jewry came to a sudden end. The effect on world Jewry was catastrophic: one out of every three Jews perished.

The process of genocide began with the rousing of historic hatreds. It involved the cooperation of many people. But it depended on the indifference of many more.

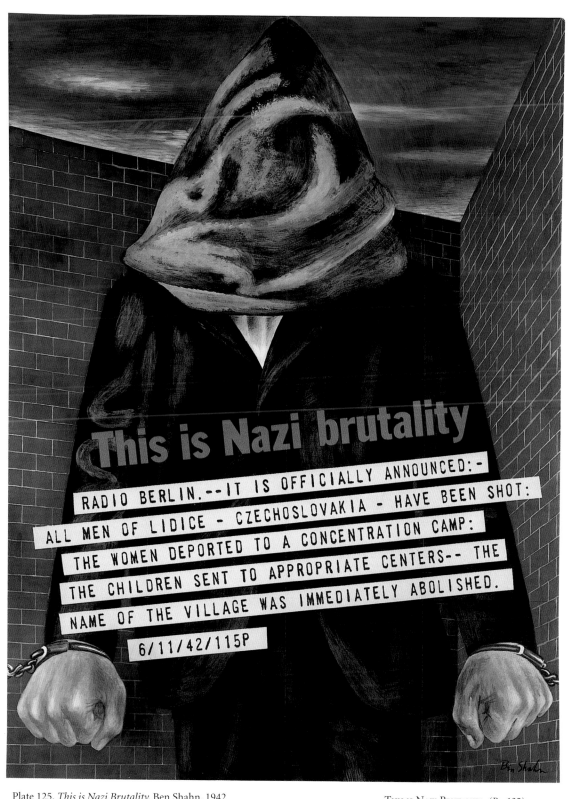

This is Nazi brutality

RADIO BERLIN.--IT IS OFFICIALLY ANNOUNCED:--
ALL MEN OF LIDICE - CZECHOSLOVAKIA - HAVE BEEN SHOT:
THE WOMEN DEPORTED TO A CONCENTRATION CAMP:
THE CHILDREN SENT TO APPROPRIATE CENTERS-- THE
NAME OF THE VILLAGE WAS IMMEDIATELY ABOLISHED.
6/11/42/115P

Plate 125. *This is Nazi Brutality*, Ben Shahn, 1942

THIS IS NAZI BRUTALITY (PL. 125)
Ben Shahn (1898–1969)
Washington, D.C., 1942
Color lithograph
38 x 28 in. (96.5 x 71.1 cm)
Gift of Dana Asbury and Richard K. Levy,
Alexandra and Kate Levy
HUCSM 66.2728

Israel

THE CAUSE OF NATIONAL Jewish rebirth in the Land of Israel took on new urgency after the Holocaust. Zionism, the movement to re-establish a Jewish state, gained in strength as it won support in other nations, especially in America.

The creation of the State of Israel in 1948 set in motion a large migration of Jews to the new nation. It also awakened feelings of pride and solidarity among Jews throughout the world.

Despite several wars with neighboring Arab states and unrest within its own Arab population, Israel has established a stable democracy. It has also absorbed several million immigrants, expanded its economy and technology, and developed a dynamic cultural life.

ZIONISM: HERZL/WEIZMANN

PORTRAIT OF THEODOR HERZL
Hermann Struck (1876-1944)
Germany
Reproduction of etching
8⅛ x 5¾ in. (20.6 x 14.6 cm)
Kirschstein Collection
HUCSM 66a.78

CHAIM WEIZMANN, LETTER
London, July 14, 1916
8⅞ x 7 in. (22.5 x 17.8 cm)
On loan from The David Shapell and Benjamin
Shapell Family Collection of Judaica

DER JUDENSTAAT
Author: Theodor Herzl
publisher: M. Breitenstein
Leipzig, Vienna, 1896
On loan from Hebrew Union College-Jewish
Institute of Religion Frances-Henry Library,
Los Angeles

THEODOR HERZL, AUTOGRAPH LETTER
Signed Th Herzl
Vienna, May 8, 1896
8⅞ x 11½ in. slightly irregular (22.5 x 29.2 cm)
On loan from The David Shapell and Benjamin
Shapell Family Collection of Judaica

ZIONISM: SZOLD/WISE

STEPHEN WISE, LETTER
Unsigned, to Felix M. Warburg
New York, April 30, 1937
8½ x 11 in. (21.6 x 27.9 cm)
On loan from the American Jewish Archives

AMERICAN ZIONIST RIBBON: DELEGATE,
MIDWEST REGIONAL CONFERENCE PIONEER
WOMEN'S ORGANISATION FOR PALESTINE
St. Louis, June 17-18, 1944
Silk; and tin
5⅞ x 1⅝ in. (14.9 x 4.1 cm)
Museum purchase
HUCSM 29.548

HENRIETTA SZOLD DANCING THE HORA *(PL. 126)*
Photographer: Nachum Tim Gidal
Jordan Valley, 1937
9 x 6½ in. (22.9 x 16.5 cm)
Museum purchase
HUCSM 68.743

AMERICAN ZIONIST RIBBONS: DELEGATE,
TWENTIETH ANNIVERSARY CONVENTION N.L.C.
FOR PALESTINE HISTADRUT
New York, November 27–28, 1943
Museum purchase
HUCSM 29.549, 29.550

AMERICA/ISRAEL

LOUIS D. BRANDEIS, LETTER
Signed Louis D. Brandeis, from Brandeis to
President Franklin Delano Roosevelt, From
Correspondence Regarding Jewish
Colonization in Palestine, Leading to the
Formation of the State of Israel in 1948
December 4, 1939
8 x 6⅜ in. (20.3 x 16.2 cm)
On loan from The David Shapell and Benjamin
Shapell Family Collection of Judaica

Plate 126. *Henrietta Szold Dancing the Hora,* Nachum Tim Gidal, 1937

HARRY S. TRUMAN AUTOGRAPH DRAFT
STATEMENT OF POLICY ON ISRAEL
Notes on United Nations Partition Vote
September, 1948
10½ x 8 in. (26.7 x 20.3 cm)
On loan from The David Shapell and Benjamin
Shapell Family Collection of Judaica

JOHN F. KENNEDY AUTOGRAPH NOTES ON
THE CREATION OF ISRAEL
Boston, April 3 or 4, 1948
6⅞ x 10¾ in. open (17.4 x 27.3 cm)
On loan from The David Shapell and Benjamin
Shapell Family Collection of Judaica

GREAT IS PEACE, COPY OF BOOK
PRESENTED TO MENACHEM BEGIN
Publisher: Masada Press and Golden Pages.
Editor: Daniel Sperber
Jerusalem, 1979
Printed and silkscreened on paper; bound in
leather
16 x 10 x ⅞ in. (40.6 x 25.4 x 2.2 cm)
Gift of Metuka Benjamin
HUCSM 5.270a

At Home in America

S INCE 1945, AMERICAN JEWRY has flourished. The generation that came of age in these decades prospered in an expanding economy. American Jews stood in the forefront of the civil rights movement and have played a major role in the nation's intellectual life.

In contemporary American culture, the impact of Jews has been striking. However their Jewish identity is defined — as religious or cultural, ethnic or ancestral — its vitality is reflected in literature, film, music, drama, education, science, commerce, and technology.

Yet if Jews are now at home in America, their success has generated new challenges. Having entered the mainstream, how will they maintain their spiritual, cultural, and ethnic identity? What forms of Jewish expression will survive? What does it mean to be a Jew today?

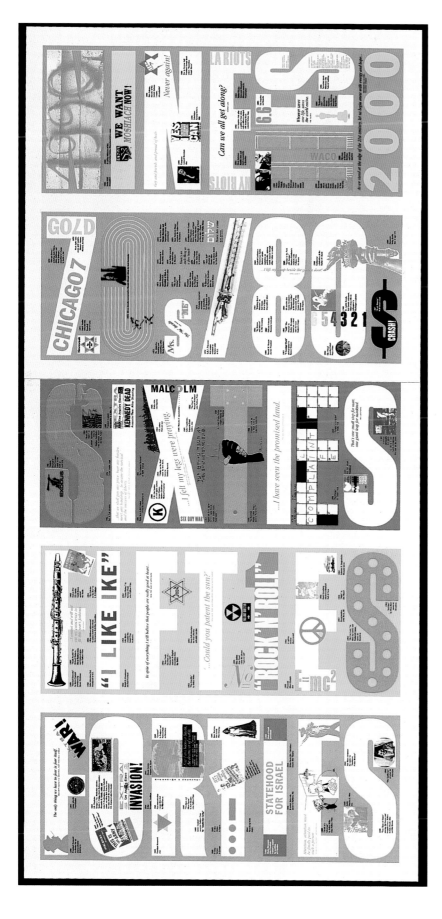

Plate 127. *Time Capsule*
Designer: Arnold Schwartzman
Los Angeles, 1995

HIDDEN HISTORY

WELCOME TO THE DISCOVERY Center. Archaeologists are explorers, historians, and scientists. To learn about past human history, they search for artifacts—things that people made and used. Archaeologists in Israel are looking for the hidden history of the peoples of the ancient Near East, including the Jewish people.

Pretend that you are an archaeologist of the ancient world. Practice the how-to's of digging in an interactive computer experience. Explore an ancient burial cave to discover treasures left behind with the dead. Handle the tools of the archaeologist. Guess what types of materials will survive over long periods of time. Learn how the people of biblical lands lived, prayed, worked, and communicated.

WHAT TOMBS TELL US

JUGLET
Khirbet el Qom
Iron IIA-B, 1000–800 BCE
Clay, burnished, fired
5¹/₁₆ x 2⅞ in. diameter (12.7 x 7.3 cm)
HUCSM A209

JUGLET
Khirbet el Qom
Iron IIA-B, 1000–800 BCE
Clay, slipped, fired
5½ x 3½ in. diameter (14.0 x 8.9 cm)
HUCSM A216

JUGLET
Khirbet el Qom
Iron IIC, 800–586 BCE
Clay, slipped, fired
3 x 10⅞ in. diameter (9.5 x 27.6 cm)
HUCSM A232

JUGLET
Israel, provenance unknown
Iron II, 1000–586 BCE
Clay, burnished, fired
3½ x 2⅜ in. diameter (8.9 x 6.0 cm)
HUCSM A237

COMBINATION PILGRIM FLASK AND
BLACK JUGLET
Israel, provenance unknown
Iron IIB-C, 900–586 BCE
Clay, slipped, burnished, fired
4¼ x 2⅞ in. diameter (10.8 x 7.3 cm)
HUCSM A239

SPOUTED JUGLET
Israel, provenance unknown
Iron IIB-C, 1000–586 BCE
Clay, fired
5⅜ x 2⅞ in. diameter (13.6 x 7.3 cm)
HUCSM A299

BEER JUG
Khirbet el Qom
Iron I, 1200–1000 BCE
Clay, slipped, perforated, incised, fired
6 x 3¾ in. diameter (15.2 x 9.5 cm)
HUCSM A306

PYXIS
Khirbet el Qom
Iron IIA-B, 1000–900 BCE
Clay, slipped, fired
3⅝ x 3⅝ in. diameter (9.2 x 9.2 cm)
HUCSM A307

JUG
Khirbet el Qom
Iron IIB-C, 900–586 BCE
Clay, slipped, burnished, fired
7 x 4 in. diameter (17.8 x 10.2 cm)
HUCSM A336

COOKPOT
Khirbet el Qom
Iron IIB-C, 900–586 BCE
Clay, fired
7⅛ x 6½ in. diameter (18.1 x 16.5 cm)
HUCSM A353

CHALICE
Khirbet el Qom
Iron, 1200–586 BCE
Clay, slipped, fired
5¾ x 7¾ in. diameter (14.6 x 19.7 cm)
HUCSM A463

JUG
Israel, provenance unknown
Iron IIB-C, 900–586 BCE
Clay, slipped, burnished, painted, fired
8½ x 5⅜ in. diameter (21.6 x 13.6 cm)
HUCSM A688

DECANTER-TYPE JUG
Khirbet el Qom
Iron IIB-C, 900–586 BCE
Clay, slipped, burnished, fired
10 x 5⅝ in. diameter (25.4 x 14.3 cm)
HUCSM A690

DECANTER-TYPE JUG
Khirbet el Qom
Iron II B-C, 900–586 BCE
Clay, slipped, burnished, fired
6⅝ x 5 in. diameter (15.8 x 12.7 cm)
HUCSM A691

BRACELET/ ANKLET
Israel, provenance unknown
Middle Bronze - Iron, 2000–586 BCE
Bronze, cast
3¼ in. diameter (8.3 cm)
HUCSM A808

BOWL
Tel Eitun
Iron IIA-B, 1000–800 BCE
Clay, slipped, burnished, fired
3½ x 2⅞ in. diameter (8.9 x 7.3 cm)
HUCSM A83

BOWL
Khirbet el Qom
Iron IIC, 800–586 BCE
Clay, slipped, burnished, fired
1⅝ x 2⅜ in. diameter (4.1 x 6.0 cm)
HUCSM A85

BOWL
Khirbet el Qom
Iron II, 1000–586 BCE
Clay
1¾ x 2½ in. diameter (4.5 x 6.4 cm)
HUCSM A125

OIL LAMP
Israel, provenance unknown
Iron IIA-B, 1000–800 BCE
Clay, fired
1⅞ x 5⅞ in. diameter (4.8 x 14.9 cm)
HUCSM A721

ANCIENT POTS AND PANS

JUGLET
Israel, provenance unknown
Middle Bronze II - Late Bronze, 1750–1400 BCE
Clay, slipped, burnished on neck, fired
8¼ x 2⅞ in. diameter (20.9 x 7.3 cm)
HUCSM A177

JUGLET
Israel, provenance unknown
Middle Bronze IIB-C, 1750–1500 BCE
Clay, slipped, burnished, fired
5⅛ x 4¼ in. diameter (13.0 x 10.8 cm)
HUCSM A189

BEER JUG
Israel, provenance unknown
Iron I, 1200–1000 BCE
Clay, slipped, perforated, fired
8 x 6¼ in. diameter (20.3 x 16.5 cm)
HUCSM A344

JUG
Israel, provenance unknown
Iron II, 1000 - 586 BCE
Clay, ribbed, fired
5 x 4½ in. diameter (12.7 x 11.4 cm)
Gift of Mr. Jack Skirball
HUCSM A441

JAR
Israel, provenance unknown
Iron IIA-B, 1000–800 BCE
Clay, slipped, burnished, fired
16 x 11 in. diameter (40.6 x 28.0)
HUCSM A471

STORE JAR
Israel, provenance unknown
Middle Bronze IIB-C, 1750–1500 BCE
Clay, fired
26¼ x 14⅝ in. diameter (66.7 x 37.1 cm)
HUCSM A483

JAR
Israel, provenance unknown
Byzantine, 324-640 CE
Clay, ribbed, fired
8½ x 9½ in. diameter (21.6 x 24.1 cm)
HUCSM A490

GRINDING BOWL
Hebron
Chalcolithic, 3800–3400 BCE
Basalt, carved
3½ x 11 in. rim diameter (8.9 x 27.9 cm)
HUCSM A500

JUG
Israel, provenance unknown
Early Bronze I, 3400–3100 BCE
Clay, slipped, burnished, fired
5¼ x 2⅞ in. diameter (13.3 x 7.3 cm)
HUCSM A512

STORE JAR
Hebron
Middle Bronze I , 2000–1750 BCE
Clay, fired
14 x 10⅛ in. diameter (35.6 x 25.7 cm)
HUCSM A552

STORE JAR
Israel, provenance unknown
Early Bronze IV, 2300–2000 BCE
Clay
18⅞ x 11⅜ in. diameter (47.9 x 28.9 cm)
HUCSM A558

Plate 128. Cypriot Milk Bowl, Late Bronze I, 1500–1400 BCE

JAR
Israel, provenance unknown
Early Bronze IV-Middle Bronze I,
2300–1750 BCE
Clay, fired
13 x 11½ in. diameter (33.0 x 29.2 cm)
HUCSM A559

BOWL
Ain Samiyeh
Late Bronze II, 1400–1200 BCE
Clay, slipped, fired
7½ rim x 2⅝ in. base diameter (19.0 x 6.6 cm)
HUCSM A567

KRATER
Israel, provenance unknown
Middle Bronze II B-C, 1750–1500 BCE
Clay, slipped, fired
12¾ x 13¼ in. diameter (32.4 x 33.7 cm)
HUCSM A569

JUG
Ain Samiyeh
Late Bronze I, 1500–1400 BCE
Clay, slipped, painted, fired
9⅞ x 8¼ in. diameter (25.1 x 21.0 cm)
HUCSM A572

AMPHORA
Ain Samiyeh
Late Bronze II, 1400–1200 BCE
Clay, slipped, painted, fired
11¼ x 7⅝ in. diameter (28.6 x 19.4 cm)
HUCSM A576

BOWL
Ain Samiyeh
Middle Bronze IIB, 1750–1650 BCE
Clay, fired
3⅛ x 7⅜ in. rim diameter (7.9 x 18.7 cm)
HUCSM A583

JUGLET
Tel el Yehudiah
Middle Bronze IIB, 1750–1650 BCE
Clay, slipped, burnished, incised, fired
5⅜ x 3¾ in. base diameter (13.6 x 9.5 cm)
HUCSM 604

COOKPOT
Israel, provenance unknown
Iron IIB-C, 900–586 BCE
Clay, fired
3⅜ x 6⅞ in. handle to handle (8.6 x 17.4 cm)
Gift of Mr. Jack Skirball
HUCSM A623

BOWL
Khirbet el Qom
Iron II B-C, 900–586 BCE
Clay, slipped, burnished, fired
4½ x 6 in. rim diameter (11.4 x 17.2 cm)
HUCSM A674

STRAINER CUP
Israel, provenance unknown
Iron II 1000–586 BCE
Clay, perforated, fired
3 x 3⅞ in. rim diameter (7.6 x 9.8 cm)
HUCSM A703

KRATER
Israel, provenance unknown
Late Bronze IIB-Iron I, 1300–1000 BCE
Clay, slipped, burnished, fired
9½ x 8¼ in. diameter (24.1 x 21.0 cm)
HUCSM A750

JUGLET
Israel, provenance unknown
Middle Bronze IIA, 2000–1750 BCE
Clay, slipped, burnished, fired
5½ x 7½ in. diameter (14.0 x 19.0 cm)
Gift of Bella Newman Sang
HUCSM A1336

JUGLET
Israel, provenance unknown
Iron IIA, 1000–900 BCE
Clay, slipped, burnished, painted, fired
3½ x 4 in. diameter (8.9 x 10.2 cm)
Gift of Bella Newman Sang
HUCSM A1339

JAR
Khirbet el Kirmil
Early Bronze I, 3400–3100 BCE
Clay, slipped, incised, fired
5⅜ x 4¾ in. diameter (13.6 x 12.1 cm)
HUCSM A509

BOWL
Israel, provenance unknown
Middle Bronze IIB-C, 1750–1500 BCE
Clay, fired
2¼ x 7½ in. diameter (5.7 x 19.0 cm)
HUCSM A33

BOWL
Tel Eitun
Iron IIA-B, 1000–800 BCE
Clay, burnished, fired
2⅝ x 8¼ in. diameter (6.6 x 20.9 cm)
HUCSM A102

BOWL
Tel Eitun
Iron IIB-C, 900–586 BCE
Clay, slipped, burnished, fired
2⅛ x 7⅝ in. diameter (5.4 x 19.4 cm)
HUCSM A128

BOWL
Tel Eitun
Iron IIA-B, 1000–800 BCE
Clay, slipped, burnished, fired
1⅝ x 5¼ in. diameter (4.1 x 10.8 cm)
HUCSM A126

JUGLET
Khirbet el Qom
Iron IIA-B, 1000–800 BCE
Clay, slipped, burnished, fired
4⅛ x 2⅞ in. diameter (10.5 x 7.3 cm)
HUCSM A224

JUGLET
Khirbet el Qom
Iron IIB-C, 900–586 BCE
Clay, slipped, burnished, fired
5½ x 2⅞ in. diameter (14.0 x 7.3 cm)
HUCSM A267

JUGLET
Israel, provenance unknown
Iron II, 1000–586 BCE
Clay, slipped, burnished, fired
5¹/₁₆ x 3 in. diameter (13.0 x 7.6 cm)
HUCSM A301

JAR
Israel, provenance unknown
Early Bronze I, 3400–3100 BCE
Clay, fired
6¼ x 3½ in. base diameter (15.9 x 8.9 cm)
HUCSM A508

BOWL
Ain Samiyeh
Middle Bronze IIB-C, 1750–1500 BCE
Clay, fired
3⅛ x 7¼ in. rim diameter (7.9 x 18.4 cm)
HUCSM A580

JUG
Khirbet el Qom
Late Bronze, 1500–1200 BCE
Clay, slipped, burnished, fired
4⅞ x 3½ in. diameter (12.4 x 8.9 cm)
HUCSM A637

PITCHER
Israel, provenance unknown
Middle Bronze IIA, 2000–1750 BCE
Clay, slipped, burnished, fired
10 x 6¼ in. diameter (25.4 x 15.9 cm)
HUCSM A587

STORE JAR
Israel, provenance unknown
Iron IIC, 900–586 BCE
Clay
19¾ x 12 in. diameter (50.2 x 30.5 cm)
HUCSM A851

JUGLET
Ain Samiyeh
Late Bronze IIA-B, 1400–1200 BCE
Clay, fired
5¾ in. (14.6 cm)
HUCSM A181

BOWL
Israel, provenance unknown
Middle Bronze- Late Bronze, 2000–1200 BCE
Clay, slipped, incised, fired
2¼ x 8¼ in. rim diameter (5.7 x 21.0 cm)
HUCSM A493

JUGLET
Israel, provenance unknown
Early Bronze III, 2650–2300 BCE
Clay, slipped, burnished, fired
3⅞ x 2¾ in. diameter (9.8 x 7.0 cm)
HUCSM A518

EXACTING EXCAVATIONS

BOWL
Ain Samiyeh
Late Bronze II, 1400–1200 BCE
Clay
3⅜ x 8⅛ x 8⅛ in. rim diameter
  (8.6 x 20.6 x 20.6 cm)
HUCSM A564

GRINDING STONE, TOP
Israel, provenance unknown
Date unknown
Stone
3 x 18 x 6 in. (7.6 x 45.7 x 15.2 cm)
HUCSM A1345 a

GRINDING STONE, BOTTOM
Israel, provenance unknown
Date unknown
Stone
4 x 12½ x 13½ in. (10.2 x 31.8 x 34.3 cm)
HUCSM A1345 b

LIGHTING THE WAY
FROM THE PAST TO TODAY

OIL LAMP
Israel, provenance unknown
Early Bronze, 3400–2000 BCE
Clay
1¼ x 4½ in. (3.2 x 11.4 cm)
HUCSM A1341

OIL LAMP
Israel, provenance unknown
Persian, 586-332 BCE
Clay
5⅜ x 5⅛ x 1⅛ in. (13.5 x 13.0 cm x 3.0 cm)
HUCSM A1342

OIL LAMP
Israel, provenance unknown
Byzantine, 324 -640 CE
Clay
¹⁵/₁₆ x 2⅜ x 3⅝ in. (2.5 x 6.0 x 9.2 cm)
HUCSM A534

OIL LAMP
Israel, provenance unknown
Early Bronze, 3400–2000 BCE
Clay
1⅜ x 4⅛ in. diameter (3.5 x 10.5 cm)
HUCSM A537

OIL LAMP
Israel, provenance unknown
Roman, 40 BCE-324 CE
Clay
2¼ x 2⅞ in. diameter (5.7 x 7.3 cm)
HUCSM A538

OIL LAMP
Ain Samiyeh
Middle Bronze, 2000–1500 BCE
Clay
5¾ in. (14.6 cm)
HUCSM A542

OIL LAMP
Tel el Ful
Middle Bronze I, 2000–1750 BCE
Clay
1⅞ x 3⅝ in. diameter (4.8 x 9.2 cm)
HUCSM A555

OIL LAMP
Israel, provenance unknown
Late Bronze IIC, 1300–1200 BCE
Clay
2⅜ x 6¼ in. diameter (6.0 x 15.9 cm)
HUCSM A560

OIL LAMP
Tel Eitun
Middle Bronze II-Late Bronze I, 1750–1400 BCE
Clay
1¾ x 5⅜ in. diameter (4.4 x 13.6 cm)
HUCSM A612

OIL LAMP
Israel, provenance unknown
Iron IIB-C, 900–586 BCE
Clay
1⅞ x 4½ x 4⅜ in. (4.8 x 11.4 x 11.1 cm)
HUCSM A643

OIL LAMP
Israel, provenance unknown
Iron IIA-B, 1000–800 BCE
Clay
1⅜ in. (3.5 cm)
HUCSM A644

OIL LAMP
Israel, provenance unknown
Late Bronze II, 1400–1200 BCE
Clay
1½ x 5½ x 5¼ in. rim diameter
  (3.7 x 13.4 x 13.9 cm)
HUCSM A718

OIL LAMP
Israel, provenance unknown
Iron I, 1200–1000 BCE
Clay
1¾ x 4¾ (4.4 x 12.1 cm)
HUCSM A720

OIL LAMP
Jebel Qa'aqir
Middle Bronze I - Late Bronze I, 2000–1400 BCE
Clay
1⅞ x 5⅛ x 4⅝ in. (4.8 x 13.0 x 12.1 cm)
HUCSM A734

OIL LAMP
Khirbet el Qom
Hellenistic II, 167-40 BCE
Clay
1³/₁₆ x 4¾ x 2⅝ in. (3.2 x 12.1 x 6.6 cm)
HUCSM A744

OIL LAMP
Israel, provenance unknown
Iron I, 1200–1000 BCE
Clay
3⅛ x 5⅝ in. diameter (7.9 x 14.3 cm)
HUCSM A719

OIL LAMP
Khirbet el Qom
Byzantine, 324–640 CE
Clay
1½ x 1½ x 3 in. (3.8 x 3.8 x 7.7 cm)
HUCSM A745

OIL LAMP
Israel, provenance unknown
Byzantine, 324-640 CE
Clay
1⅝ x 1⅞ x 3 in. (4.1 x 4.8 x 9.5 cm)
HUCSM A747

OIL LAMP
Israel, provenance unknown
Hellenistic II-Early Roman, 167 BCE-70 CE
Soapstone or diorite
1 x 2⅛ x 4 in. (2.5 x 5.4 x 10.2 cm)
HUCSM A782

OIL LAMP
Israel, provenance unknown
Hellenistic, 332-40 BCE
Clay
¾ x 2⅝ x 4 in. (1.9 x 6.6 x 10.2 cm)
HUCSM A785

OIL LAMP
Israel, provenance unknown
Late Roman, 70–324 CE
Clay
1¼ x 2⅜ x 3¼ in. (3.2 x 6.1 x 8.3 cm)
HUCSM A866

SABBATH LAMP
Europe, provenance unknown
19th century
Pewter
8½ x 4 in. diameter (21.6 x 12.1 cm)
Rosa F. Sachs Collection
HUCSM 33.8

WRITING: PICTURE
TO SYMBOL TO SOUND

MESOPOTAMIAN CUNEIFORM TABLET
Drehem, Southern Iraq
2250–2000 BCE
Clay
¾ x 4 x 2½ in. (1.9 x 1.6 x 6.4 cm)
HUCSM A901

MESOPOTAMIAN CUNEIFORM TABLET
Drehem, Southern Iraq
2250–2000 BCE
Clay
⅝ x 2⅜ x 1 in. (1.6 x 6.0 x 4.4 cm)
HUCSM A903

MESOPOTAMIAN CUNEIFORM TABLET
Umma, Southern Iraq
2250–2000 BCE
Clay
1½ x 1¾ x ½ in. (3.8 x 4.4 x 1.3 cm)
HUCSM A906

MESOPOTAMIAN CYLINDER SEAL
Israel, provenance unknown
Neo-Assyrian, 1000–612 BCE
Black limestone, hand-carved
1½ x ½ in. (3.8 x 1.3 cm)
Anonymous donation
HUCSM A1089

LIMESTONE RELIEF, FRAGMENT
Egypt
Date unknown
Limestone, hand-carved, painted
9½ x 10½ x 1 in. (24.1 x 26.7 x 2.5 cm)
Gift of Dr. Julius Winer
HUCSM A1006

Plate 129. Amphoriskos, Hellenistic II, 2nd-1st century BCE

USHABTI
Egypt
New Kingdom, 19th Dynasty (1300–1200 BCE)
Clay, polychrome, painted, fired
6¾ in. (17.2 cm)
Gift of Dr. David Garner
HUCSM A976

RING
Egypt
New Kingdom, 18th Dynasty (1570–1085 BCE)
Copper and ivory
⅜ in. scarab (1.0 cm) ¾ in. diameter (2.0 cm)
Anonymous donation
HUCSM A1110

PTAH-SEKER-OSIRIS FIGURE
Egypt, Akhmin?
Late Period, 26th Dynasty (656–332 BCE)
Wood, gesso, paint
6½ in. (16.5 cm)
Anonymous donation
HUCSM A963

BAR KOKHBA COIN
Israel, provenance unknown
Roman, 132-135 CE
Bronze, cast, stamped
⅝ in. diameter (1.7 cm)
HUCSM 65.2

BAR KOKHBA COIN
Israel, provenance unknown
Roman, 132-135 CE
Ferrous metal, worked
¾ in. diameter (1.9 cm)
HUCSM 65.13

BAR KOKHBA COIN
Israel, provenance unknown
Roman, 132-135 CE
Bronze, cast, stamped
⅞ in. diameter (2.3 cm)
HUCSM 65.19

COIN OF THE JEWISH WAR
Israel, provenance unknown
Roman, 66-70 CE
Silver?
1½ in. diameter (2.9 cm)
HUCSM 65.47

ARAMAIC AMULET
Provenance unknown
Roman, 40 BCE-324 CE
Hammered foil, incised
4 x 3½ in. (10.2 x 8.9 cm)
Gift of Ira M. Goldberg
HUCSM A943

CUNEIFORM TABLET
Sen Kereh (Larsa)
First Babylonian Dynasty
Clay
3 x 1⅞ x 1⅜ in. (7.6 x 4.8 x 3.5 cm)
HUCSM A911

JAR HANDLE WITH ROYAL SEAL IMPRESSION
Tel ed-Duweir (Lachish)
Iron IIC, 800–586 BCE
Clay
4⅝ x 2 in. (11.7 x 5.0 cm)
On loan from The Jewish Museum, New York,
Archaeology Acquisition Fund

LAYERS OF LIFE IN THE TEL

LADLE
Israel, provenance unknown
Chalcolithic, 3800–3400 BCE
Clay, fired
5¾ x 2½ in. (14.6 x 6.3 cm)
HUCSM A539

BILBIL
Ain Samiyeh
Late Bronze IIA, 1400–1300 BCE
Clay, fired, painted
10 x 5⅜ in. diameter (25.4 x 13.6 cm)
3¼ base diameter (8.3 cm)
HUCSM A634

BOWL
Ain Samiyeh
Middle Bronze II, 1750–1650 BCE
Clay
2⅞ x 9 in. rim x 2⅝ base diameter
(7.3 x 22.9 x 6.6 cm)
HUCSM A45

BOWL
Israel, provenance unknown
Early Bronze I, 3400–3100 BCE
Basalt, hand-carved
4¼ x 6 in. rim x 5¼ base diameter
(10.8 x 15.2 x 13.3 cm)
Gift of Helen I. Glueck
HUCSM A521

CYPRIOT MILK BOWL
Israel, provenance unknown
Late Bronze I, 1500–1400 BCE
Clay, slipped, painted, fired
4⅜ x 9 x 6⅞ in. diameter (11.0 x 23.0 x 17.5 cm)
Gift of Helen I. Glueck
HUCSM A1008

AX HEAD
Israel, provenance unknown
Middle Bronze IIA, 2000–1750 BCE
Bronze, cast
6⅛ in. (15.5 cm)
Gift of Helen I. Glueck
HUCSM A827

KERNOS
Israel, provenance unknown
Early Bronze, 3400–2000 BCE
Clay, hand-molded, fired
3⅞ x 6 in. rim diameter (9.8 x 15.2 cm)
HUCSM A533

PILLAR FIGURINE
Israel, provenance unknown
Iron II, 1000–586 BCE
Clay, molded, fired
6 x 3½ x 1½ in. (15.2 x 8.9 x 3.8 cm)
HUCSM A455

NETZEF WEIGHT
Israel, provenance unknown
Iron II, 1000–586 BCE
1⅜ x 1⅜ in. (3.5 x 3.5 cm)
Henry Kaner Memorial Purchase Fund
HUCSM A997

COIN OF THE JEWISH WAR
Israel, provenance unknown
Early Roman, 66–70 CE
Bronze, cast, stamped
⅝ in. diameter (1.5 cm)
HUCSM 65.53

COIN OF THE JEWISH WAR
Israel, provenance unknown
Early Roman, 66–70 CE
¾ in. diameter (1.96 cm)
HUCSM 65.48

BAR KOKHBA COIN
Israel, provenance unknown
Roman, 132–135 CE
Bronze, cast, stamped
1¼ in. diameter (3.3 cm)
HUCSM 65.32

BAR KOKHBA COIN
Israel, provenance unknown
Roman, 132–135 CE
Bronze, cast, stamped
¾ in. diameter (1.9 cm)
HUCSM 65.33

BAR KOKHBA COIN
Israel, provenance unknown
Roman, 132–135 CE
Bronze, cast, stamped
¾ in. diameter (1.9 cm)
HUCSM 65.34

ROMAN COIN
Israel, provenance unknown
Roman, 67 BCE - 325 CE
Bronze, cast, stamped
⅝ in. diameter (1.7 cm)
HUCSM 65.116a

ROMAN COIN
Israel, provenance unknown
Early Roman, 26-36 CE
Bronze, cast, stamped
½ in. diameter (1.3 cm)
HUCSM 65.130a

EIGHT-SHEKEL WEIGHT
Tel ed Duweir (Lachish)
Iron II, 1000–586 BCE
Limestone, hand-carved
¾ x ¾ in. (1.9 x 1.9 cm)
Henry Kaner Memorial Purchase Fund
HUCSM A994

OSSUARY DOOR FRAGMENT
Azor
Chalcolithic, 3800–3400 BCE
Clay, hand molded, painted, fired
8¼ x 7⅞ in. (21.0 x 20.0 cm)
On loan from Israel Antiquities Authority

CYLINDER SEAL
Hazor
Late Bronze I, 1500–1400 BCE
Faience, hand-carved
1 x ½ in. (2.5 x 1.2 cm)
On loan from Israel Antiquities Authority

Copper Ore
Khirbet Matar
Chalcolithic, 3800–3400 BCE
Copper
3⅞ x 2⅜ in. (10.0 x 6.0 cm)
On loan from Israel Antiquities Authority

Stamped Jar Handle
Be'er Sheva
Iron, 1200–586 BCE
Clay, molded, fired
4⅜ x ⅜ x 1⅜ in. (4.0 x 1.0 x 11.0 cm)
On loan from Israel Antiquities Authority

Phoenician Red Ware
Akhziv, Port
Iron II, 1000–586 BCE
Clay
7⅞ x 5½ in. (20.0 x 14.0 cm)
On loan from Israel Antiquities Authority

Arrowhead
Tel Mikhal
Persian, 586-332 BCE
Bronze, cast
1⅝ x ⅜ in. (4.0 x 1.0 cm)
On loan from Israel Antiquities Authority

Phoenician Red Ware
Akhziv, Port
Iron II, 1000–586 BCE
Clay, painted, fired
8⅝ x 5⅞ in. (22.0 x 15.0 cm)
On loan from Israel Antiquities Authority

Plow Tip
Tel Yinam
Iron II, 1000–586 BCE
Iron
6½ x 1⅝ in. (16.5 x 4.0 cm)
On loan from Israel Antiquities Authority

Lead from Sarcophagus
Israel, provenance unknown
Byzantine, 324–640 CE
Lead, cast
9½ x 10¼ in. (24.0 x 26.0 cm)
On loan from Israel Antiquities Authority

Box and Lid
Naveh Yam
Roman, 40–324 CE
Lead, molded
7⅛ x 1¾ in. (18.0 x 4.5 cm)
On loan from Israel Antiquities Authority

Juglet
Tel Anafa
Hellenistic, 332–40 BCE
Lead, cast
¾ x ¾ in. (1.9 x 1.9 cm)
On loan from Israel Antiquities Authority

Violin-shaped Figurine
Shiqmim
Chalcolithic, 3800–3400 BCE
Limestone, hand-carved
2⅞ x 1⅝ in. (7.3 x 4.2 cm)
On loan from Israel Antiquities Authority

Blade
Gilat
Chalcolithic, 3800–3400 BCE
Obsidian, worked
1 x ⅛ in. (2.5 x 0.3 cm)
On loan from Israel Antiquities Authority

Ossuary Front Fragment
Azor
Chalcolithic, 3800–3400 BCE
Clay, hand molded, painted, fired
15¾ x 11 in. (40.0 x 28.0 cm)
On loan from Israel Antiquities Authority

Nile Valley Shell
Shiqmim
Chalcolithic, 3800–3400 BCE
Aspatharia (Spathopsis) rubens
3⅜ x 2⅜ x ⅛ in. thick (8.5 x 6.0 x 0.4 cm)
On loan from Israel Antiquities Authority

Macehead
Judean desert
Chalcolithic, 3800–3400 BCE
Copper, smelted to mold
1½ x 1⅜ in. (3.9 x 3.6 cm)
On loan from Israel Antiquities Authority

Ax
Shiqmim
Chalcolithic, 3800–3400 BCE
Copper, cast
4⅛ x 1⅛ in. (10.5 x 3.0 cm)
On loan from Israel Antiquites Authority

War Ax
Bet Yerah
Early Bronze I, 3400–3100 BCE
Bronze, cast
2½ x 6⅛ x ¼ in. (6.5 x 15.7 x 0.7 cm)
On loan from Israel Antiquities Authority

Copper Ore
Khirbet Matar
Chalcolithic, 3800–3400 BCE
Copper slag
5⅞ x 3⅛ in. (15.0 x 8.0 cm)
On loan from Israel Antiquities Authority

Scarab
Tel el Ajjul
Middle Bronze IIA-B, 1900–1700 BCE
Steatite
⅜ x ⅞ x ⅝ in. diameter (0.9 x 2.4 x 1.7 cm)
On loan from The Jewish Museum, New York, Archaeology Acquisition Fund

Crucible
Tel Dan
Iron, 1200–1000 BCE
Stone, hand-carved
11⅞ x 11⅞ in. (30.0 x 30.0 cm)
On loan from Hebrew Union College, Jerusalem, Nelson Glueck School of Biblical Archaeology

Tin Ore
Bolivia
Cassiterite
3½ x 2⅝ x 2⅝ in. (9.0 x 6.8 x 6.8 cm)
On loan from the Natural History Museum of Los Angeles County

Iron Ore
England
Hematite
3½ x 3⅛ x 1⅝ in. (9.0 x 7.9 x 4.2 cm)
On loan from the Natural History Museum of Los Angeles County

Lead Ore
Peru
Galena
3 x 2 x 1⅜ in. (7.5 x 5.0 x 3.4 cm)
On loan from the Natural History Museum of Los Angeles County

GLEAMING, GLOWING, GLIMMERING, GLORIOUS GLASS

Square Bottle
Israel, provenance unknown
Roman, 1st–4th century CE
Glass, mold-blown
6⅞ x 3 x 2¾ in. (17.5x 7.6 x 6.9 cm)
Anonymous donation
HUCSM A1034

Bottle
Northern Israel
Late Roman, 2nd - 3rd century CE
Glass, blown
5¾ x 2 in. base diameter (14.6 x 5.1 cm)
Gift of the Ziffren Family
HUCSM A1355

Globular Bottle
Eastern Mediterranean Late Roman, Late 3rd–4th century CE
Glass, blown
5⅜ x 3 x 1⅜ in. base diameter (13.5 x 9.5 x 3.5 cm)
Gift of the Ziffren Family
HUCSM A1358

Cosmetic Tube with Base
Israel, provenance unknown
Late Roman, 4-5th century CE
Glass, blown, threaded
4⅜ x 2⅝ x 1¼ in. base diameter (11.0 x 6.5 x 3.0 cm)
Gift of the Ziffren Family
HUCSM A1359

Flask
Israel, provenance unknown
Late Roman, Late 3rd century CE
Glass, molded
3 x 1¾ x 1 in. base diameter (7.5 x 4.5 x 2.5 cm)
Gift of the Ziffren Family
HUCSM A1372

Amphoriskos
Eastern Mediterranean
Hellenistic II, 2nd-1st century BCE
Glass, core-formed, applied decorative threading
5½ in. (14 cm)
Gift of Lois and Richard Gunther
HUCSM A1373

AMPHORISKOS
Eastern Mediterranean
Hellenistic II, 2nd-1st century BCE
Glass, core-formed, applied decorative
threading
5⅞ x ½ in. base diameter (15.0 x 1.5 cm)
Gift of Lois and Richard Gunther
HUCSM A1374

ALABASTRON
Eastern Mediterranean
Persian, 5th century BCE
Glass, core-formed, applied decorative
threading
3⅞ x ⅝ in. base diameter (10.0 x 2.0 cm)
Gift of Lois and Richard Gunther
HUCSM A1375

AMPHORISKOS
Eastern Mediterranean
Hellenistic II, 2nd-1st century BCE
Glass, core-formed, applied decorative
threading
5⅛ x ¼ in. base diameter (13.0 x 0.5 cm)
Gift of Lois and Richard Gunther
HUCSM A1376

ALABASTRON
Eastern Mediterranean, probably Asia Minor
Persian, Late 6th-5th century BCE
Glass, core-formed, applied decorative
threading
3½ x ⅜ in. base diameter (9.0 x 1.0 cm)
Gift of Lois and Richard Gunther
HUCSM A1377

AMPHORISKOS
Eastern Mediterranean, probably Phoenician
Persian, late 6th-5th century BCE
Glass, core-formed, applied decorative
threading
2⅞ x ⅜ in. base diameter (7.5 x 1.0 cm)
Gift of Lois and Richard Gunther
HUCSM A1378

DOUBLE-HEAD FLASK
Eastern Mediterranean, probably Syria
Early Roman, 1st century CE
Glass, mold-blown
2 x 1⅛ in. base diameter (7.0 x 3.0 cm)
Gift of Lois and Richard Gunther
HUCSM A1379

AMPHORA BOTTLE
Eastern Mediterranean, probably Syria
Early Roman, 1st century CE
Glass, mold-blown
2⅞ x ¼ in. base diameter (7.5 x 0.5 cm)
Gift of Lois and Richard Gunther
HUCSM A1380

HEXAGONAL BOTTLE
Eastern Mediterranean
Early Roman, 1st century CE
Glass, mold-blown
3½ x 1¼ in. base diameter (9.0 x 3.0 cm)
Gift of Lois and Richard Gunther
HUCSM A1381

BOTTLE
Eastern Mediterranean
Early Roman, 1st century CE
Glass, mold-blown
2⅞ x 1 in. base diameter (7.5 x 2.0 cm)
Gift of Lois and Richard Gunther
HUCSM A1382

PITCHER
Eastern Mediterranean
Roman, 1st-2nd century CE
Glass, mold-blown
2⅞ x ¾ in. base diameter (7.5 x 2.5 cm)
Gift of Lois and Richard Gunther
HUCSM A1383

COSMETIC TUBE
Eastern Mediterranean
Late Roman, Late 3rd-4th century CE
Glass, blown
2⅞ x 1 in. base diameter (11.0 x 4.0 cm)
Gift of Lois and Richard Gunther
HUCSM A1384

"DATE" FLASK
Eastern Mediterranean
Roman, 1st-2nd century CE
Glass, mold-blown
3⅛ x ¼ in. base diameter (8.0 x 0.5 cm)
Gift of Lois and Richard Gunther
HUCSM A1385

"MILLEFIORI" BOWL
Eastern Mediterranean
Early Roman, 1st century CE
Glass, cut and fused on molded form
1⅝ x ¼ in. base diameter (4.0 x 0.5 cm)
Gift of Lois and Richard Gunther
HUCSM A1386

SQUAT GLOBULAR VASE
Probably Syria or Egypt
Islamic, 9th-12th century CE
Glass, mold-blown, threaded
2¾ x 1¾ in. base diameter (7.0 x 4.5 cm)
Gift of Lois and Richard Gunther
HUCSM A1387

FLAT FLASK
Eastern Mediterranean, probably Northern
Israel or Syria
Late Roman, 3rd-4th century CE
Glass, blown, added threading
5⅛ x ¾ in. base diameter (13.0 x 2.0 cm)
Gift of Lois and Richard Gunther
HUCSM A1388

BOTTLE
Eastern Mediterranean, probably Syria
Late Roman, 1st-early 2nd century CE
Glass, blown, marbled
3⅛ x 1⅛ in. base diameter (8.0 x 3.0 cm)
Gift of Lois and Richard Gunther
HUCSM A1389

COSMETIC STIRRER / APPLICATOR
Phoenician, found in Egypt
Iron, 1200–586 BCE
Glass, blown
7⅜ in. (18.8 cm)
HUCSM A853

TWO-HANDLED COSMETIC FLASK
Eastern Mediterranean
Late Roman, Second half, 4th century CE
Glass, fluted, mold-blown
4½ x 2⅜ x 1⅜ in. base diameter
(11.3 x 6.0 x 3.5 cm)
Gift of the Ziffren Family
HUCSM A1362

UNGUENTARIAN DOUBLE COSMETIC TUBE
Israel
Byzantine, 4th-5th century CE
Glass, blown
5⅞ x 3⅛ x 1⅜ in. base diameter
(15.0 x 8.0 x 3.5 cm)
Gift of the Ziffren Family
HUCSM A1363

SPOOL-SHAPED UNGUENTARIUM
Eastern Mediterranean
Late Roman, 3rd century CE
Glass, blown
4⅛ x 3⅜ x 4⅜ in. base diameter
(10.5 x 8.5 x 11.0 cm)
Gift of the Ziffren Family
HUCSM A1366

WHAT SURVIVES OVER TIME

MINIATURE COOKPOT
Israel, provenance unknown
Iron II, 1000–586 BCE
Clay
2⅝ x 4 in. diameter (6.6 x 10.2 cm)
HUCSM A329

BOWL/ MORTAR
Israel, provenance unknown
Chalcolithic, 3800–3400 BCE
Basalt, hand-carved
3¾ x 10 in. diameter (9.5 x 25.4 cm)
HUCSM A502

HYKSOS DAGGER
Ain Samiyeh (?)
Middle Bronze I, 2000–1750 BCE
Bronze, cast
8 in. (20.3 cm)
Gfit of Helen I. Glueck
HUCSM A846

FIGURINE
Syria
Hellenistic, 2nd century BCE
Clay, slipped, burnished, fired
3½ in. (8.9 cm)
Gift of Mr. and Mrs. Marshall Goldberg
HUCSM A1229

POTTERY PUZZLE

RECONSTRUCTED POT
Israel, provenance unknown
Clay
4 x 2 in. base diameter (10.2 x 5.1 cm)
HUCSM A1393

WORKS ILLUSTRATED BUT NOT IN EXHIBITION

JUDAICA

RONDEL'S HAGGADAH (PL. 106)
Italy, 15th century
Watercolor, ink and gold leaf on parchment
Each rondel: 1½ in. diameter (3.8 cm)
Gift of Mr. and Mrs. Felix Guggenheim
HUCSM 5.1

LAVER (PL. 31)
Maker: Zelig Segal (b. 1933)
Jerusalem, ca. 1980
Silver
7⅛ x 6⅝ x 5½ in. (18.1 x 16.8 x 14,0 cm)
Museum Purchase with Funds Provided by
   Audrey and Arthur N. Greenberg
HUCSM 14.80

FINE ARTS

VANITAS STILL LIFE (PL. 39)
Evert Collier (Dutch, d. ca. 1702)
Leyden, 1696
Oil on canvas
39½ x 48¼ in. (100.3 x 122.6 cm)
Gift of The David B. Goldstein and Edward C.
   Goodstein Foundation
HUCSM 41.320

WOMEN AT PRAYER IN SYNAGOGUE (PL. 43)
K. Felsenhardt (active 1890s)
Poland, 1893
Gouache on paper
8 x 7¾ in. (20. 3 x 19.7 cm)
Kirschstein Collection
HUCSM 41.98

MEN AT PRAYER IN SYNAGOGUE (PL. 44)
K. Felsenhardt (active 1890s)
Poland, 1893
Gouache on paper
8 x 7¾ in. (20. 3 x 19.7 cm)
Kirschstein Collection
HUCSM 41.99

CANTOR AND CHOIR IN THE SYNAGOGUE (PL. 45)
Edouard Moyse (b. 1827, a. 1850–1881)
Paris, ca. 1860
Oil on canvas
28½ x 19 in. (72.4 x 48.3 cm)
Gift of Mr. Jack Cottin
HUCSM 41.153

WOMAN SEATED AT TABLE BY WINDOW (PL. 46)
Joseph Israels (1828–1911)
Holland, late 19th century
Oil on canvas
15½ x 12¾ in. (39.4 x 32.9 cm)
Gift of Alice and Sidney Eisenshtat
HUCSM 41.326

YOUNG WOMAN, 1889 (PL. 47)
Simeon Solomon (1834–1905)
London, 1899
Red crayon drawing
15 x 13 in. (38.1 x 33.0 cm)
Gift of The Union of American Hebrew
   Congregations
HUCSM 66.1125

VIKI (PL. 49)
Oto Gutfreund (1889–1927)
London, from an edition cast in the 1960s of a
   1913 sculpture
13 in. (33.0 cm)
Gift of Reinhard and Selma Lesser
HUCSM 67.176

KADDISH (PL. 30)
Joseph Budko (1880–1940)
Germany, 1930
Oil on canvas
25⅜ x 20¼ in. (64.5 x 51.4 cm)
Gift of the Jewish Restitution Successor
   Organization
HUCSM 41.132

GIRL IN BOOTS (PL. 51)
Jules Pascin (1885–1930)
France, ca. 1927
Oil on canvas
35 x 27½ in. (88.9 x 69.9 cm)
Gift of Jane K. Ransohoff and S.J. Freiberg
HUCSM 41.20

STILL LIFE OF FISH AND FRUIT (PL. 52)
Pinchus Krémègne (1890–1981)
Paris, ca. 1928
Oil on canvas
32 x 27½ in. (81.3 x 69.9 cm)
Gift of Louis and Annette Kaufman
HUCSM 41.419

PORTRAIT OF BIALIK (1873–1934) (PL. 53)
Chana Orloff (1881–1968)
Paris, 1926
Bronze
21 x 20 in. (53.3 x 50.8 cm)
HUCSM 67.47

JACOB AND THE ANGEL (PL. 54)
Jacques Lipchitz (1891–1973)
France, 1931
Plaster
8¾ in. (22.2 cm)
Gift of The Jacques and Yulla
   Lipchitz Foundation
HUCSM 67.159

BUST OF JACOB KRAMER (PL. 55)
Jacob Epstein (1880–1959)
London, ca. 1920
Bronze
26 x 20 in. (66.0 x 50.8 cm)
HUCSM 67.46

KAPPAROT (PL. 57)
Maryan [Pincas Burstein] (1927–1977)
Paris, 1952
Oil on canvas
32 x 25½ in. (81.3 x 27.9 cm)
Gift of Louis and Annette Kaufman
HUCSM 41.322

THE DRILLERS (PL. 56)
Aaron Goodleman (1890–1978)
New York, 1933
Bronze
12¼ x 11 in. (31.1 x 64.8 cm)
Gift of Sarah and Aaron Goodleman
HUCSM 67.82

THE WANDERERS (PL. 58)
Peter Krasnow
Los Angeles, 1927
Oil on canvas
49½ x 32¼ in. (125.7 x 81.9 cm)
Gift of Mr. and Mrs. Peter Krasnow
HUCSM 41.289

SCISSORS SHOP (PL. 59)
Godfrey Frankel (b. 1920)
New York, 1946
Silver gelatin print
10 x 8 in.(25.4 x 20.3 cm)
Museum purchase with funds provided by
   The Roth Family Foundation
HUCSM 68.313

JUDEAN HILLS (PL. 60)
Anna Ticho (1894–1980)
Jerusalem, ca. 1970
Pencil drawing
27 x 21½ in. (68.6 x 54.6 cm)
Gift of Janet and George Jaffin
HUCSM 66.1148

LITTLE ANGELS (PL. 61)
Moshe Gershuni (b. 1936)
Tel Aviv, 1987
Mixed media on paper
59½ x 83 in. (151.1 x 210.8 cm)
Museum purchase
HUCSM 41.380

SHIMSHON (PL. 62)
Gabi Klasmer (b. 1950)
Jerusalem, 1982
Superlac on chromo paper
27⅜ x 78⅜ in. (69.6 x 199.1 cm)
Museum purchase with funds provided by
   Lydia and Bernie Kukoff in memory of
   Celia and Arthur Kukoff
HUCSM 41.338

ELEMENT C-15 (PL. 63)
Zvi Goldstein (b.1947)
Israel, 1985
Paint on metal
68 x 217 x 20 in. (172.8 x 551.2 x 50.8 cm)
Gift of Frederick R. Weisman Art Foundation
HUCSM 41.408

WESTERN WALL AT NIGHT (PL. 69)
Harry Zeitlin (b. 1952)
Israel, 1982
Photograph
16 x 20 in. (40.6 x 50.8 cm)
Museum purchase
HUCSM 68.297

COLLAGE (PL. 66)
Hannelore Baron (1926–1987)
New York, 1981
Cloth, paper, ink
5 x 19 in. (12.7 x 48.3 cm)
Museum purchase
HUCSM 41.837

Plate 130. *Generations,* Malcah Zeldis

JOSEPH'S COAT OF FATE (PL. 6)
Dina Dar (1939–1995)
Los Angeles, 1990
Electrography on paper
69½ x 82¼ in. (176.5 x 208.9 cm)
Museum purchase with funds provided by the
  Neutrogena Corporation and Audrey and
  Arthur N. Greenberg
HUCSM 41.439

*THE PAST: THE GREAT SYNAGOGUE
OF DANZIG (PL. 65)*
Ruth Weisberg (b. 1942)
Los Angeles, 1983
Oil on canvas
84 x 60 in. (213.4 x 152.4 cm)
Gift of Sandy Miller in honor of John and
  Idelle Levey
HUCSM 41.343

HOLY, HOLY, HOLY IS THE LORD OF HOSTS (PL. 67)
Laurie Gross (b. 1952)
Los Angeles, 1984
Linen
34 x 28 in. (86.4 x 71.1 cm)
Anonymous donor
HUCSM 67.143

AMERICANA

BERNARD GRATZ (PL. 71)
Charles Peale Polk (1767–1822)
Baltimore (?), ca. 1792
Watercolor on ivory
1⅞ x 1½ in. (4.7 x 3.8 cm)
HUCSM 45.26

JUDAH P. BENJAMIN (1811–1884) (PL. 72)
United States, 1854
Oil on canvas
42 x 33 in. (106.7 x 83.8 cm.)
Gift of Col. Lionel L. Layden
HUCSM 41.166

WATER SERVICE (PL. 73)
United States, inscribed 1878
Pewter
Tray: 13½ x 19½ in. (34.3 x 49.5 cm)
Gift of Martha Sarner Levy
HUCSM 14.30-14.32 a/b

*CHARTER OF THE SOUTHERN CALIFORNIA
BROTHERHOOD ASSOCIATION (PL. 77)*
Los Angeles, 1936
Ink and watercolor on paper
34½ in. x 26½ in.
Gift of Joseph and Doris Winton in memory of
  Frank and Becky Weinstein
HUCSM 199.29

ZION BOX (PL. 79)
Chicago, early 20th century
Leaded glass
5⅜ x 10¼ x 5 in. (13.6 x 26.0 x 12.7 cm)
Gift of the Robert and Joseph Hirsch Families
HUCSM 14.108

"BRIVELE DEM TATEN" SHEET MUSIC (PL. 84)
Publisher: Hebrew Publishing Co.
New York, 1911
13¼ x 10⅜ in. (33.7 x 26.3 cm)
Gift of the Kluger Family
HUCSM 70.164

MOGEN DAVID CHERRY WINE
ADVERTISEMENT *(PL. 85)*
New York, 1970s
Printed on paper
25¼ x 17½ in. (63.1 x 44.4 cm)
Gift of Grace Cohen Grossman
HUCSM 69.70

MRS. KAPLAN'S BUTTER CROCK *(PL. 90)*
Missouri Valley, Iowa, late 1920s
Ceramic
5½ x 6 in. diameter (13.9 x 15.2 cm)
Gift of Mr. and Mrs. Martin Ricks and Family
HUCSM 69.13

ROKEACH SCOURING POWDER *(PL. 90)*
Brooklyn, 1912
Tin; and printed paper
5⅞ x 3¼ in. diameter (14.9 x 18.3 cm)
Gift of Peachy and Mark Levy
HUCSM 69.7

ELKAY RED RASPERRIES *(PL. 90)*
Chicago, ca. 1920s
TIn; and printed paper
4 x 3⅜ in. diameter (10.2 x 8.6 cm)
Gift of Lynne Gilberg
HUCSM 69.93

KASHA ALA KING *(PL. 90)*
Chicago, ca. 1939
Printed paper
4⅞ x 3 x 1½ in. (12.4 x 7.6 x 3.8 cm)
Museum purchase with funds provided by the Lee
 Kalsman Project Americana Acquisition Fund
HUCSM 14.297

GOTTSCHALK'S METAL SPONGE *(PL. 90)*
Philadelphia, ca. 1931
Box: Printed paper
5 x 5 x 2 in. (12.70 x 12.7 x 5.1 cm)
Museum purchase with funds provided by
 the Lee Kalsman Project Americana
 Acquisition Fund
HUCSM 14.296

VICTORY PRAYER *(PL. 87)*
United States, 1941-1945
Rayon; and wood
13 x 8⅞ in. (33.0 x 22.5 cm)
Gift of Rabbi and Mrs. Alfred Wolf
HUCSM 45a. 24

BOMBER JACKET *(PL. 87)*
Chicago, 1941-1945
Leather, painted; cotton; and metal fittings
Gift of Earl B. Gross
HUCSM 71.41

MILITARY ORDER OF THE PURPLE HEART *(PL. 87)*
Awarded to Samuel Cohen
United States, ca. 1918
Enamelled bronze; and silk ribbon
3 x 1½ in. (7.6 x 3.8 cm)
Gift of Willyne Bower and Saretta Berkson
 Cohen
HUCSM 71.57

WACS JACKET *(PL. 87)*
United States, 1941-1945
Wool; rayon; and metal fittings
Gift of Tonie Keller
HUCSM 71.5a

GENERATIONS
Malcah Zeldis (b. 1931)
New York, 1985
Oil on masonite
35 x 40 in. (88.9 x 122.0 cm)
Gift of Marian and Don DeWitt
HUCSM 41.432

TAILOR SHOP
(ALL PL. 89)

BLOTTER
Denver, ca. 1930
Paper, printed; and blue ink blotter
5⅜ x 8¾ in. (13.6 x 22.2 cm)
Gift of Mr. and Mrs. Norbert Weber
HUCSM 69.56

HARRY SCHWARTZ YARNS ADVERTISING
THERMOMETER
Corona, California,1930s–1940s
Wood; glass; and mercury
8½ x 3 in. (21.6 x 7.6 cm)
Gift of Peachy and Mark Levy
HUCSM 69.34

COLLARS AND SLEEVE TRIM
Maker: Gertrude Baum
Fayetteville, Arkansas, 1900
Silk
11¾ x 13½ in. (29.8 x 33.7 cm)
Gift of Gustine and John Weber
HUCSM 25.118 a-c

IRON
Geneva, Illinois, early 20th century
Iron; and wood
5 x 6¼ x 3¼ in. (12.7 x 15.9 x 8.3 cm)
Gift of Ruth and Ed Krischer
HUCSM 14.102

SINGER SEWING MACHINE
United States, ca. 1915–1920
Oak; and metal
38 x 50½ x 18 in. (96.5 x 128.3 x 45.8 cm)
Gift of Alter and Rose Rosenblum
HUCSM 70.27

TAILOR'S WEIGHT
Chicago, 1910
Iron
2¾ x 5½ in. (7 x 14 cm)
Gift of Charlotte M. and George J. Weiss
HUCSM 70.9

TAILOR'S SHEARS
Newark, NJ, early 20th century
12½ in. (31.8 cm)
Gift of Judith Rutenberg Wunch
HUCSM 70.1

TAILOR'S SQUARE
United States, early 20th century
Wood; and brass, printed and embossed
12 x 6 in. (30.5 x 15.2 cm)
Gift of Annabelle and Arthur Sandler in
memory of Maurice Marks
HUCSM 70.74

WORK PERMIT
Poland, 1870 - 1880
Paper; cloth; and leather
8 x 5 in. (20.3 x 12.7 cm)
Gift of Alan Seth Markell
HUCSM 31.85 a/b

SLEEVE PADS
United States or Russia 1900
Wool felt
5½ x 12½ in. (14 x 31.8 cm)
Gift of Lauretta and Charles Witzman
HUCSM 70.63

PRESSBOARD
United States, ca. 1900
Wood; cotton; and cotton batting
8¼ x 10 x 26½ in. (21 x 25.4 x 67.3 cm)
Gift of Dr. and Mrs. Eugene Kompaniez
HUCSM 70.35

OFFICIAL DUES CARD ILGWU
New York, 1943
Printed paper and ink /:k
5½ x 4¾ (open) in. (14 x 12.1 cm)
Gift of Gladys Fox
HUCSM 70.6

THIMBLE
1920s
Metal
¾ in. (1.9 cm)
Gift of Bertha Kretzer Tuttelman
HUCSM 70.22

TAILOR'S SHEARS
Newark, ca. 1914
Forged steel
11½ x 3½ in. (29.2 x 8.9 cm)
Gift of Mr. and Mrs. Norbert Weber
HUCSM 70.28a

TAILOR'S WAX
New York, 1915–1920
Beeswax
½ x 1¾ in. (1.3 x 4.5 cm)
Gift of Mr. and Mrs. Norbert Weber
HUCSM 70.32

PATTERN CUTTING WHEEL
United States, ca. 1910
Wood; and metal
4 ⅝ x 1⅜ in. diameter (11.7 x 3.5 cm)
Gift of Dr. and Mrs. Eugene Kompaniez
HUCSM 70.36

ZAYDE'S NEEDLES
Oakville, CT, 1900-20
Cloth; paper; and metal
Gift of Dr. and Mrs. Eugene Kompaniez
HUCSM 70.39 a-p

PENCIL
United States, ca. 1950
Wood; paint; and graphite
8⅞ in. (22.5 cm)
Gift of Annabelle and Arthur Sandler in
memory of Maurice Marks
HUCSM 70.78

SINGER SEWING MACHINE SIGN
Italy (?), 1929
Painted tin
38½ x 28 in. (97.79 x 71.12 cm)
Museum Purchase with funds provided by
 the Lee Kalsman Project Americana
 Acquistion Fund
HUCSM 69.174

Contributors

Uri D. Herscher, President, Skirball Cultural Center

Alfred Gottschalk, Chancellor, Hebrew Union College-Jewish Institute of Religion

Nancy M. Berman, Director, Skirball Museum

Joseph Gutmann, Professor Emeritus of Art History, Wayne State Universityvista

Barbara C. Gilbert, Curator, Skirball Museum

Grace Cohen Grossman, Curator, Skirball Museum

Stanley F. Chyet, Professor of Jewish History, Hebrew Union College-Jewish Institute of Religion

Robert Kirschner, Program Director, Skirball Cultural Center

Adele Lander Burke, Director of Museum Education, Skirball Museum

VISIONS AND VALUES:

JEWISH LIFE FROM ANTIQUITY TO AMERICA

Core Exhibition of the Skirball Cultural Center and Museum

CONCEPT DEVELOPMENT
Uri D. Herscher, President; Nancy M. Berman, Museum Director;
Stanley F. Chyet, Professor of American Jewish History, HUC-JIR;
Sara S. Lee, Director of the Rhea Hirsch School of Education, HUC-JIR;
Robert Kirschner, Program Director; Grace Cohen Grossman, Senior Curator;
Adele Lander Burke, Museum Education Director

EXHIBITION DIRECTOR
Robert Kirschner

EXHIBITION CURATORS
Grace Cohen Grossman
Adele Lander Burke
Barbara Gilbert

PROJECT HISTORIAN
Stanley F. Chyet

EXHIBITION COORDINATION
Michal S. Friedlander
Amina Sánchez

CONTENT CONSULTANTS
Isa Aron
Ran Boytner
Susan Braunstein
William G. Dever
Rafi Grafman
Thomas E. Levy
Jonathan Sarna
Harold Schulweis

PLANNING CONSULTANTS
Avraham Biran
Walt Disney Imagineering
Barbara Kirschenblatt Gimblett
Elaine Heumann Gurian
E. Verner Johnson and Associates
Barbara Meyerhoff
Jeshayahu Weinberg

CURATORIAL ASSISTANCE
Rachel V. Benjamin
Susan Doniger
Michal S. Friedlander
Lynne Gilberg
Ellen D. Kaplan
Nina Spiegel

RESEARCH
Robin Beningson
Elizabeth Kessin Berman
Samuel Cohon
Esti Duenyas
Herschel Fox
William Fulco
Sharon Gillerman
Nancy Klein
Sandra Malamed
Yaffa Weisman
Jay Weissberg

CONSERVATION
Anna M. Fine
Lisa Courtney Forman
Rosa Lowinger
Linda Shaffer
Sharon Shore
Nancy Kent Turner
Donna Williams

CONSERVATION TECHNICIANS
Ruth Askren
Linda Lyons
Margot Mentley
Jim Neal
Kristina Seyferth
Rosemary Shambaris
John Williams
Erica Yao

PHOTOGRAPHY
Susanne Kester
Lelo Carter
Susan Einstein
Marvin Rand

REGISTRATION
Jacqueline Frager
Vicki Gambill
Monique Maas
Joellyn Wallen

EXHIBIT PREPARATION
Debbie Ball
Dorothy Clark

MUSEUM SUPPORT
Monica Billet
Peggy Kayser
Nadine McLaren
Julie Rona
Gabrielle Tsabag
Hana Vamos

DESIGN

EXHIBITION DESIGN
Jean Jacques André Consultants Ltd.
Jean Jacques André, Chief Designer
Rennie Knowlton, Senior Designer
Ken Johnson, Coordinator/Designer
John Robertson, Design
Yvette André-Lemke, Fabrication Supervision
Bianca Message, Interpretive Planning
Joan André, Planning
Nick Fenger, Electrical and Lighting Engineer

ARCHITECTS
Moshe Safdie and Associates
Moshe Safdie, Design Advisor
James B. Herold, Coordinator

MULTIMEDIA
Paul Heller Productions

CREATIVE CONSULTANTS:
Gregg Alpert
Arthur Barron
Adam Coleite
Michael Connell
Johanna Cooper
Gerald Fried
David Inocencio/Minette Siegel
Cy Poole
Rusty Russell
Andrea Scharf
Arnold Schwartzman

FABRICATION

FABRICATORS
Maltbie Associates
The Larson Company
James Dow Design
Avant-Garde Studios
Artkraft
Center for Restoration of the Israel Museum

CONTRACTORS
C.J. Peck Jones

INSTALLATION
Benchmark
Lee Abrahmov
Robert Espinoza

Special thanks to the faculty and staff of the Hebrew Union College-Jewish Institute of
Religion, its Libraries and Museums, and the American Jewish Archives.

Pl. 131. Skirball Cultural Center, Moshe Safdie and Associates, Architects.
View from the southeast showing the Museum and Discovery Center

Photograph Credits

Bill Aron: Plate 68

Gray Crawford: Plate 63

Susan Einstein: Front cover, Plates 5, 6, 10, 14, 21, 26, 29, 30, 31, 32, 33, 34, 35, 36, 40, 41, 42, 43, 44, 46, 47, 48, 49, 50, 51, 52, 53, 54, 55, 56, 57, 58, 59, 60, 61, 62, 64, 66, 69, 71, 72, 73, 77, 84, 85, 86, 91, 93, 97, 98, 99, 101, 103, 104, 105, 107, 108, 109, 114, 117, 118, 120, 123, 124, 125, 129

Neil Folberg: Plate 116

John Reed Forsman: Plates 1, 2, 4, 8, 9, 12, 15, 16, 17, 18, 19, 20, 22, 23, 24, 25, 38, 45, 70, 75, 76, 78, 79, 80, 81, 82, 83, 92, 94, 95, 96, 100, 102, 106, 121, 122, 128

John Reed Forsman: Courtesy Home Savings of America, Plates 87, 88, 89,90

Nachum Tim Gidal: Plate 126

Erich Hockley: Plate 110

David Moss and Noah Greenberg: Plate 119

Marvin Rand: Back cover, Plates 3, 7, 11, 13, 27, 28, 37, 65, 67, 74, 111, 112, 113, 115, endsheet

Arnold Schwartzman: Plate 127

NEW BEGINNINGS
The Skirball Museum Collections and Inaugural Exhibition

was produced for the
Skirball Cultural Center
by Perpetua Press, Los Angeles
Editor: Letitia Burns O'Connor
Designer: Dana Levy

Printed in Hong Kong
through Mandarin Offset